'Violence i

A History of Football Re

By

Michael Layton QPM

Dedication

To my wife Andry, my extended family in Cyprus, and all of the decent people on the island who deserve to live in peace and safety, and to enjoy the *'beautiful game'* which so many of them cherish.

Original edition published in Kindle by MILO in May 2015.

Revised version completed in May 2016.

Updated paperback edition August 2017 by Bostin Books

Contents

Introduction

On Sunday the 16 February 2003 I became the Divisional Commander (West) of the Akrotiri Division of the Sovereign Bases Police in Cyprus, and was sworn in as a Chief Superintendent, by the then Chief Constable Eric Vallance, at an official ceremony at SBA Police Headquarters on the 21 February 2003.

Under First Schedule Part 1, Oath of Allegiance (Section 14 (1) I took the oath as follows: *'I Michael Layton of the Sovereign Base Areas Police of Akrotiri and Dhekelia, do swear that I will be faithful and bear true allegiance to Our Sovereign Lady The Queen , Her Heirs and Successors, while performing the functions of an officer in the Sovereign Base Areas Police Force, without favour or affection, malice or ill will, and that I will cause the peace to be kept and preserved by preventing to the utmost of my power all offences against the same and that, whilst I continue to perform the functions of an officer in the said Force, I will, to the best of my skill and knowledge, discharge all the duties of such an officer faithfully according to the law. So help me God'.*

Having served for more than three decades in the Police Service in the UK, rising to the rank of Chief Superintendent in the West Midlands Police, and receiving the Queens Police Medal in the 2003 New Year's Honours List, this was the start of a 'dream posting' in a place referred to as 'paradise' by many. I had flown into RAF Akrotiri, from RAF Brize Norton, on Sunday 16 February 2003 full of anticipation and with more than a degree of excitement.

Apart from my last six years' service I had been something of a 'career detective' and whilst I was trained to perform the role of Silver Commander in public order situations, and firearms incidents, my core skills lay in criminal investigation, and intelligence related matters.

I was relishing the opportunity of working with my officers, the British Military, and the Republic of Cyprus Police, as well as getting to know the Cypriot community who were well-known for their warmth and openness.

At the age of fifty-years I believed that I still had plenty to offer policing and, having received a very warm welcome from staff, I was focused on improving the community policing model which was one of the cornerstones of the SBA Police strategy.

My vision of living and working in Cyprus was that of long sandy beaches, blue skies, and equally blue seas, sleepy villages, cold beers, and good food, with good company. I did not expect crime levels to be anywhere near what I had been used to, and certainly had no expectation that violent crime would be a problem.

This was an opportunity to do something unique in a beautiful Country, and I had of course sworn an oath to do this.

Over the last two decades the accuracy of that vision has been tested on a number of occasions and whilst Cyprus is in truth a beautiful place, where the vast majority of Cypriots focus on giving their children, and families, the best opportunities that they can offer, it also has another significant minority who tarnish that image with mindless acts of violence.

They are called football hooligans and this book seeks to chronicle the history and causes of some of the problems, caused by the perpetrators of violence in the name of a sport, in the Republic of Cyprus.

The book focuses predominantly on the period between 2003 and 2014, and highlights more than ninety-seven football games, during that period, and sixteen basketball and volleyball games, where violence has occurred. With the exception of just four of these one hundred and thirteen games, one of the so-called *'Big Five'* Clubs were one, or both of the teams playing.

It does not seek to glorify any aspects of the crimes which have taken place, or seek to find excuses for the behaviour of individuals who should know better, as they threaten the very fabric of a complex society where sport, politics, and inter-city rivalry create a highly toxic cocktail of violence and anti-social behaviour.

Whilst on a visit to see family in Cyprus in April 2014, I observed the reaction to yet another football supporter receiving life-changing injuries, with the loss of an eye, as he was struck by a missile during violent clashes. It made no more sense to me than the many other incidents I had read about over the years but it struck me that a powerful message could be created, by showing the totality of the problem, as opposed to focusing on individual incidents. It seemed to me that whilst there was clear evidence of the outrage felt when violence occurred it tended to be short lived, and 'selective memory' was a routine practice.

I wanted this book to show the whole picture, and all its dismal repetition, in the hope that in some small way it might contribute to change. The issue of football violence is a 'game-changer' for Cyprus and one that must be tackled for the sake of the majority of decent people. Some say that the problem in Cyprus has existed for more than twenty years, during which time there have been numerous occasions for talking – now was a time for decisive action, not just words alone.

Whilst I cannot possibly have captured every single incident of violence that has occurred, the book nevertheless reveals the following statistics within it, which, given that they can only be viewed as being minimum figures, make for stark and depressing reading.

The incidents researched after 2003 revealed that at least two hundred and sixty-nine police officers were assaulted, some seriously, and one police officer died as a result of a heart attack during disturbances. Police officers have been stabbed, burnt, suffered broken noses, fractures, and routinely hit with rocks, missiles and flares, on at least sixty-two occasions during the decade referred to specifically in this book.

More than one hundred and sixty six members of the public have been attacked, or suffered injuries during disturbances, ranging from burns, head injuries, loss of fingers, loss of eyesight, and other injuries, many of which required hospital treatment. The youngest victim, who received extensive bruising to the body after being kicked by a group of hooligans, was just twelve years of age. An even younger child witnessed his father being savagely beaten.

More than five hundred and eighty two arrests were made, during the games referred to, as five successive Republic of Cyprus Police Chiefs battled with the problem, against a routine backcloth of blame and counter-blame.

Damage estimated at 20,282 Cyprus Pounds was caused, in just four incidents alone, pre 2008, and after that, in yet another seven incidents alone, damage estimated at 76,700 euro was caused.

5

Over two hundred and twenty four cars were damaged, which included at least fifty-two police vehicles, five fire vehicles, and more than one hundred and sixty- seven private vehicles.

Political interventions occurred on more than forty-five occasions as efforts were made to try to find a solution involving three Presidents of Cyprus, five Justice Ministers, and other politicians, as well as the House of Legal Affairs Committee, who convened on the subject on more than two hundred occasions.

There have been at least two bomb attacks, one aimed at a referee's vehicle, and one targeting the premises of a Football Chairman, as well as the placing of incendiary devices at fan clubhouses in Nicosia – and all of this in the name of sport.

Prologue

On Thursday 20 March 2003 the Iraq war started and RAF Akrotiri became an extremely busy place to both live and work in.

On Sunday 30 March 2003 I stood in full public-order uniform at the gates of RAF Akrotiri, the only dispensation to the heat being that I was not required to wear the standard blue 'Nato' style woollen jumper common in the UK to resist fire. It didn't make a lot of difference to how I felt in the piercing heat with the full overalls, the body padding, gloves and helmet with full-face visor, and heavy boots adding to my discomfort.

As the Silver Commander for the day's operation I was issued with a round shield to provide a degree of protection from missiles. Was I really going to need it – this was after all Cyprus!

This Sunday was to be an extremely busy day for all of us in the Western Sovereign Base Area. Up to 5,000 people attended what was billed as a peaceful demonstration organised by the Social Forum to protest against the US-led war on Iraq, and the use of the

British Bases in Cyprus to support that Operation. It was a well-organised demonstration with stewards from the AKEL political party, wearing red armbands and white caps, arriving early to ensure that arrangements in the rally area near to the main gate of RAF Akrotiri were safe.

Initially there was something of a carnival atmosphere and there was no hint of trouble with speeches from the then Republic of Cyprus House President, and AKEL leader, Demetris Christofias, as well as activists, who stood on a podium to address the crowd.

The message was very much *'Drop Bush Not Bombs'*, and effigies of US President George W Bush and British Prime Minister Tony Blair were burnt as anti- coalition slogans were chanted. Mr Christofias said *'The war on Iraq was taking place with no other aim but to control the country's oil-wealth'*, and he accused the US of wanting to extend their worldwide rule saying, *'The bombs that are falling on Iraq are aimed at any free conscience, at world security, and at the autonomous presence of Europe. First it was Yugoslavia, then Afghanistan, now it's Iraq and tomorrow, who knows? We cannot accept the logic behind what the coalition call a 'pre-emptive strike'.*

Many members of the crowd had marched more than four miles, in the burning heat, from where they had parked their vehicles, but there was a great deal of what I would come to define as 'Cypriot passion', and after an hour and a half, as many of the crowd dispersed to return to their vehicles, the mood changed dramatically and turned violent.

Up to that point I had SBA police officers in normal uniform deployed within the crowd and, although wearing British Police uniforms, they were in fact predominantly fellow Greek-Cypriots who spoke English as their second-language, and in many cases knew their fellow countrymen on a personal basis.

A small group of known 'anarchists' supported by a group of Iraqis and Palestinians, who were resident on the island, as well as part of the crowd, started throwing missiles at the perimeter fencing, and front gate, and slowly demolished the *'RAF Akrotiri'* sign which was set on a concrete pillar bearing the British Crown.

By the end of the onslaught the only thing left on it was the eagle and crown remaining defiantly untouched. They set light to banners and sprayed all of the signs in the area with red paint, as well as the road itself.

I withdrew the community police officers, under the command of Superintendent Pantehis, and deployed a full PSU, (Police Support Unit), Public Order Unit, with long shields, within a sterile area, outside the main gates, which had been constructed by the military at my request. The AKEL stewards tried, but failed, to keep order and gave up their efforts to contain the troublemakers for fear of violence towards themselves. The SBA officers bravely withstood a barrage of bricks, eggs, and lengths of wood until I withdrew them in an orderly manner behind the perimeter wire so that we could reform prior to advancing again.

Whilst giving instructions to officers I raised my helmet visor at one point so that I could hear myself above the noise. Suddenly one of my officers slammed my visor down as a missile bounced off the heavy duty plastic. It had been a close call and someone had clearly targeted me on the other side of the fence. It was time to take the initiative back.

We deployed through the main gate leaving The Drums

Platoon, part of Chindit Company 1KORBR, a military public order unit, to maintain a presence at the main gate whilst we slowly but surely advanced on the remaining demonstrators and dispersed them with firm but measured policing. Some tried to stage a sit down demonstration in the road, but we refused to allow them to settle and eventually the heat, and our persistence paid off, and they retreated.

This was my first experience of violence in Cyprus, and after being in post for just a matter of weeks I was somewhat shocked by what I had seen. Had I been struck in the face I would undoubtedly have suffered a serious injury and, having previously been assaulted just once throughout the whole of my police career, the irony of the situation was not lost on me.

This was essentially a political demonstration where the vast majority of those attending were united in their common cause, and had no inclination to act violently in order to get their message home. The media photographs and headline, *'Violence Mars Anti-War Protest at RAF Akrotiri'*, told a different story. The mindless minority had had their day and it all had a familiar ring to it.

In the days that followed I oversaw a post-incident

investigation into the activities of some of those who had committed wanton criminal damage, and carried out violent acts. It was difficult to progress, because of the complexities of jurisdiction and law within Cyprus, but not impossible, and a number of individuals later faced court proceedings. My maxim in life was quite simple in that criminals needed to know that 'their actions would lead to consequences'. There had to be sanctions and penalties for criminals, otherwise anarchy truly would reign and whether such criminal acts were in the name of sport, or politics, or in fact both, it mattered not to me.

It was however, to be some time before I realised that violence was in fact as much a part of society in Cyprus, as it was in the UK and elsewhere, and that football hooliganism, known as the, *'English Disease',* was in fact alive and well in paradise.

Some will say that when you are born in Cyprus, for the majority three things are pre-determined, namely, your religion, your politics, and your football club. The second invariably leads to the third, and this book seeks to explain how deeply they are entwined and how critical they are in shaping the way in which the sport of football operates in Cyprus.

Chapter One

Club History – The Big Five

Britain is widely acknowledged as having introduced the game of football to Cyprus in the twentieth century. Those with a true love of the game sometimes refer to it as the 'beautiful game'.

Turkish teams were involved in the founding of the Cyprus Football Association in 1934, but broke away from the islands unified league in 1955, after disputes between the Greek and Turkish communities worsened.

When the island was granted independence from the British in 1960, the Greek Cypriot sides that were members of the CFA were recognised as members of UEFA and FIFA, and since then Turkish Cypriot sides have been excluded from international matches.

The post war period in Cyprus saw the growth of political parties, where support was generally polarised, on either the right or the left of the political spectrum, with allegiances routinely being handed down from father to son.

The newly formed AKEL party succeeded the old Communist Party, and people started to challenge the established norms. It was a complex mix but for reasons that are far from clear, one of which was the impact of the civil war in Greece, football in Cyprus became inextricably linked to politics in 1948 and has remained so ever since.

Premier League teams have been particularly influenced by this phenomenon, and in particular those that are widely considered to be the five top-flight teams within the league, who exercise huge influence amongst their supporters, and by the very nature of the league, which has fourteen teams, play each other frequently.

Their individual positions in the league at any one time, added to the level of tension between fans, which escalates towards the end of each season when the outcome of cup and league finals become clearer, is invariably crucial, as at least one of these clubs are likely to be in the final every year.

To verify the accuracy of this view, and the sheer power of their influence, one has only to look at the outcome of which clubs have been crowned as 'champions' in the Cyprus First Division since the turn of the century:

2001/2 Cyprus First Division season commenced with Omonia as the defending Champions.

2002/3 Cyprus First Division season commenced with APOEL as the defending Champions.

2003/4 Cyprus First Division season commenced with Omonia as the defending Champions.

2004/5 Cyprus First Division season commenced with APOEL as the defending Champions.

2005/6 Cyprus First Division season commenced with Anorthosis as defending Champions.

2006/7 Cyprus First Division season commenced with Apollon as the defending Champions.

2007/8 Cyprus First Division season commenced with APOEL as the defending Champions.

2008/9 Cyprus First Division season commenced with

Anorthosis as defending Champions.

2009/10 Cyprus First Division season commenced with APOEL as the defending Champions.

2010/11 Cyprus First Division season commenced with Omonia as the defending Champions.

2011/12 Cyprus First Division season commenced with APOEL as the defending Champions.

2012/13 Cyprus First Division season commenced with AEL as the defending Champions.

2013/14 Cyprus First Division season commenced with APOEL as the defending Champions - a title that they subsequently retained after much controversy at the end of that season.

***

Sports reporting in Cyprus is to some extent monopolised by the activities of these five teams, with endless TV coverage throughout the week, and highlights played over and again.

At weekends it is estimated that more than 40% of the male

population watch football on television in homes, bars, or 'coffee shops', the latter of which are normally linked to particular political parties. Absent husbands often test the patience of long-suffering wives in this regard, and there are suggestions that the outcome of games was often reflected in the mood of households afterwards.

For many this is indeed a serious business which occupies the minds of individuals for much more than the ninety-minutes of any particular game.

It is quite clear that a substantial proportion of the male population in Cyprus see the game of football as being very important in society.

In any one season in the Championship these top-flight teams will invariably play each other at least four times, whilst in the Cup they will also play smaller clubs. A new football season normally starts in late August of each year and finishes the following May with so-called 'friendly games' being played in July.

***

A brief history of each of these five clubs is outlined as follows:

APOEL FC - Athletikos Podosferikos Omilos Ellinon Lefkosias(Athletic Football Club of Greeks Nicosia) In 1922 a Greek came to Cyprus to run a tobacco company and got involved in the internal problems which existed in football at that time. He was disappointed at the way in which team selections were made so in 1926 he decided to set his own club up thus on the 8 November 1926 APOEL was born.

The club nickname is Thylos (The Legend) and APOEL fans are sometimes referred to as the *'Orange fans'* or *'Portokali'*. They generally wear team colours in yellow and blue, or orange, and are widely recognised as being affiliated to the right of politics in Cyprus, and in particular the DISY party.

APOEL are based in Nicosia and play at the GSP Stadium in Nicosia, which was built in 1999, and is owned and managed by GSP (Track and Field Club PAGKIPRIA) a non-profit company. The ground has a four star grading from UEFA and unlike most grounds in Cyprus has at least forty-six analogue CCTV cameras installed which are linked to the Police Control Room.

APOEL are arguably the most popular and successful club in

Cyprus, due to the number of trophies they have won, and have done well in UEFA where in 2011/12 they reached the quarter-finals. It is a multi-sport club with a number of other sports playing under the club name. In December 2009 more than 6,000 APOEL fans travelled to London to see their team play Chelsea at Stamford Bridge for the last match of the 2009/10 Champions League.

Their support base is predominantly in Nicosia but other offshoots have emerged such as the rather strangely titled, *'Bobby Sands Branch in Latsia Town',* in 2009 which allegedly supported Irish Fighters, Spain's Basques, and Palestinians, and liked Celtic Fans. Labelling themselves, *'Resist to Exist',* it is not clear exactly how serious their focus on football really was!

In a survey published in 2012, by the Centre of Research and Development in Sports Leisure and Tourism, some 22% of Cypriot males, aged between 21-years and 70-years, identified themselves as being APOEL supporters - the second largest grouping.

In 2013 it was reported that APOEL, who had enjoyed two spells in the Champions League in recent years, and were rewarded with almost twenty five million euros, were believed to be looking to reduce their budget by 40%.

According to unofficial estimates, in a three year period between 2010 and 2013, APOEL paid fines, or lost revenues, both in Europe and Cyprus, of around two million euros due mainly to problems relating to hooliganism.

For the start of the 2013/14 season, APOEL faced playing the first three games behind closed doors, although the CFA had actually introduced a system where clubs could 'buy out' their penalty by paying a fine of 40,000 euro.

If you compare these types of sums with the fact that Paralimni, another First Division club, would have had a total budget of 500,000 euro, for the same season, it is not difficult to see the disproportionate impact that the 'Big Five' Clubs have on football in Cyprus.

***

AEL FC - Athlitiki Enosi Lemesou

Set up on the 4 October 1930, and based in Limassol, they generally wear yellow and blue team colours. The original founders wanted to set up a team *'without politics'* but they are generally seen as leaning towards the left of politics.

They play at Tsirion Stadium in Limassol and they are a multi-sport club with men's and women's basketball teams, women's handball, and cricket, operating under the team name AEL. The club has thirteen official football trophies and their basketball team is the only team in Cyprus to have won a European title.

In the cup final of 1985 against EPA Larnaca almost 10,000 AEL fans went to Nicosia, and in the 2009 cup final 9,500 travelled to Nicosia with 7,600 tickets sold in one day alone.

In the survey previously referred to their support base ranked fifth amongst the top five clubs.

***

APOLLON - Limassol FC

This club was founded on the 14 April 1954 and the original fee for fans to become members was ten cents. They generally wear white and blue team colours, the colours of the Greek flag. They use legend names such as *'Kianolefki'* (blue and whites) and *'O Fygas'*

(The Fugitive). They are seen as affiliated to the right of politics (DISY Party) and are based in Limassol.

They have a history of strong support and in the 2001 Cup Final they took no less than 12,000 fans from Limassol to Nicosia. They play at Tsirion Stadium in Limassol and in the 1992 Cup Final, at the stadium, more than 20,000 attended the game. They also host basketball and volleyball teams and have won the Championship three times, the Cup seven times, and the Super Cup once.

In the survey referred to they were ranked fourth, amongst the top five clubs, in terms of numbers of fans.

***

OMONIA FC - Athletic Club Omonia Nicosia –(Which means *'Concord'* in Greek)

Set up on the 4 June1948, their fans are often referred to as *'the Chinese'* because of their numbers. They wear green and white team colours and for years have been seen as the team of the Cyprus 'working class' They are based in Nicosia and are seen as being to the left of politics in Cyprus and influenced by political unrest and the Greek civil war. Many support the AKEL party.

They play at the GSP Stadium in Nicosia. Whilst the club is the only one of the 'Big Five' yet to qualify for a European stage they have won twenty league championships, fourteen Cypriot Cups, and sixteen Super Cups. The club acts as an umbrella for other sports and fields teams in basketball, volleyball, cycling, and futsal.

A poll by the University of Cyprus ranked Omonia as the second most popular team behind APOEL, whilst in another poll 26.8% of those polled said that they supported Omonia. This figure rose slightly in another survey in 2012, which put Omonia as having the largest fan base on the island.

The Omonia Ultras *'Gate 9'* group was set up in 1992, and they occupy the North Stand at home games.

By the end of February 2013 Omonia was struggling to meet UEFA's financial conditions, due in part to the economic downturn. In March 2013 however they managed to pass the criteria due to a fundraising initiative which was launched under the slogan *'I'm with Omonia. I declare present'*. More than 3.5 million euro was raised in less than a month.

For the 2013/14 season it was reported that they would slash their budget by 60% and were even looking at selling two of their star players.

***

ANORTHOSIS FC - Anorthosis Famagusta FC (Short name ANO)

Based in Larnaca, and also known as Famagusta FC from the Occupied Areas, they were founded on the 31 January 1911. They wear blue and white colours and use the nicknames *'The Old Lady'* and *'The Blue and Whites'*. They are affiliated to the right- wing of politics, were inspired by the formulation of the Greek State, and display the Phoenix, which is a symbol of Christianity.

They play at the Antonis Papadopoulos Stadium in Larnaca, which has a seating capacity of 10,230, and also field volleyball and futsal teams under the clubs name. Their original stadium was the Famagusta Gymnastic Club in Evagoras which was abandoned during the invasion in 1974 and is now in poor condition.

They finished sixth in the 2013/14 First Division season. The club has previously won thirteen First Division Titles, ten Cypriot Cups, and seven Super Cups, and Anorthosis is one of three Cypriot clubs never to have played in the second division.

The Ultra group of Anorthosis fans are known as *'MAXHTEC'* (Fighters), the idea being that by fighting they will 'get to the top and return to their beloved town of Famagusta'.

Whilst many of their fans live in Larnaca their general fan base is spread across Cyprus due to the occupation of Famagusta by the Turkish army and dispersal of the local population across Cyprus. There are also supporter's branches in Greece and the UK.

In the 2012 survey they came third, in the top five teams, in terms of the size of their fan base.

In August 2013 the club president Achilleas Nicolaou asked supporters to make small monthly donations to make the club viable and to try to address their debt of 13.5 million euro, of which 5 million euro needed to be serviced. For the 2013/14 season they announced that they would be cutting their budget to 1.5 million euro, having already sold their star striker Laborde for 1.2 million euro to try to make ends meet.

The club has previously claimed to have the third largest fan base in Cyprus with 18% of Cypriots supporting the club.

***

Just to add to the overall dismal picture in terms of finance, in April 2013 a report released by the players union, the Pancyprian Football Association (PFA), revealed that, of the then twelve first division teams, only one had no outstanding payments towards its players. Nine teams owed three, or more salaries, with two clubs having not paid their players anything in 2013. Clubs were running with debts of more than 4-5 times their annual turnover.

Using some of the information on support as a very raw indicator the figures would seem to indicate that approximately 50% of fan base support is linked to the three clubs within the top group, who are traditionally seen as leaning towards the right namely, APOEL, Apollon and Anorthosis, whilst 35% leaned towards the two clubs associated with the left namely, Omonia and AEL, with the 15% balance spread across the other smaller clubs.

Chapter Two

The Early Years And A Death

Cyprus signed the European Convention on spectator violence in December 1986, which was ratified in August 1987, and which some might argue at that time demonstrated some form of political will to engage in dealing with the problems of violence in sport.

On the 24 October 1995 the Board of Administration of the Cyprus Sports Association decided to set up the National Committee for Violence with a view to implementing Council of Europe Conventions numbers 1/93 and 1/94 which provided for measures to be taken to suppress violence in sports grounds, and to make sure that events were safe for both spectators, teams, and officials.

The Committee was chaired by the President of the Cyprus Sports Organisation, Savvas Koshiaris, and included representatives from the police, referees, clubs, players associations, coaches, sports editors, and the Cyprus Football Association (CFA).

***

33

In a sign of things to come, on Saturday 17 January 1998, during a basketball match between APOEL and AEL, fans clashed as cars and shops were damaged. Two police officers were injured as well as one member of the public. Five youths of school age were arrested and remanded for six days following a court appearance.

On Sunday 18 January 1998, following a game between Omonia and Apollon, at the Makarios Stadium in Nicosia, two hundred fans clashed after the game as they threw rocks at each other. Five persons were injured, including one police officer, and two arrests were made. As a result the CFA called for an emergency session of the National Committee for Violence, and the Justice Minister Nicos Koshis called for an emergency meeting to discuss the disturbances.

***

On Saturday 9 January 1999 Anorthosis played Omonia at the Antonis Papadopoulos Stadium in Larnaca in a game which ended in a 2-2 draw.There were clashes after the game, the most serious of which left a thirteen-year-old boy with a fractured skull. Anorthosis fans spat at the car of Omonia fan, and National Guardsman,

Constantinos Christoforou, aged eighteen years, who was alleged to have reacted by reversing his car at them, hitting thirteen-year old Nicos Lambrou, who was rushed to Larnaca Hospital.

Christoforou was subsequently charged with reckless driving and released.

Another Omonia fan, Antonis Ermogenous, aged twenty years, from Nicosia, was charged with an attack on an Anorthosis player during the match. Two others, one aged thirty years, was arrested for attacking Anorthosis fans, and one aged twenty-seven years for throwing a plastic bottle onto the pitch.

On Saturday 6 March 1999 a match took place at the Antonis Papadopoulos Stadium in Larnaca between Anorthosis and APOEL, which was attended by 10,000 fans, of which 3,000 supported APOEL.

The game ended in a 1-1 draw but although there was no trouble during the game, tensions started to rise after an APOEL player was given a 'red card' and sent off.

At the final whistle, live TV pictures showed a number of

players, from both teams, tussling with each other, and punches being thrown as they entered the tunnel, whilst police struggled to keep them apart. Several players chased each other around the pitch, whilst officials tried to restrain them in scenes of pandemonium.

This was the signal for both sets of fans to invade the pitch and the one hundred and twenty police on duty at the game were unable to stop the violence.

APOEL fans ripped up seats and started fires in the stands, and outside the ground riot police charged fans who responded by damaging cars and smashing shop windows. Five arrests were made, four of whom came from Nicosia, who were charged with assaulting police officers and fighting. Three police officers were injured, and treated at Larnaca General Hospital, and APOEL goalkeeper Andros Petrides was taken to a private clinic in Nicosia after being hit in the eye by a missile.

In the aftermath, in a response that was to become common practice, the clubs put none of the blame at their own doorstep. Anorthosis blamed APOEL, and said that they encouraged their fans to be hooligans, and APOEL blamed Anorthosis fans for attacking their goalkeeper.

On Sunday 28 November 1999 Paralimni played Omonia at the Parlimni Stadium in a game that finished in a 2-2 draw. Both goals from Paralimni came from a contested penalty, and a suspected offside, whilst Omonia had two goals disallowed for being offside.

At the end of the game four hundred Omonia fans charged onto the pitch, to protest against the refereeing, as violence erupted. Inside the ground a mat was set on fire, which was used for pole vaulting, speakers were destroyed, signs on the east side of the stadium, and the toilets were smashed to bits, some of the pieces of which were used to smash the windows of nearby shops outside.

During the course of the fighting five police officers were injured, with one sergeant being taken to Paralimni District Hospital, together with two firemen who were injured as they tried to put the fire out. The police were accused of not doing enough but Famagusta Police Chief Andreas Christofi defended his officers stating that, despite having sixty officers on duty in uniform, and twenty in plain-clothes, they had been overwhelmed as people that they had tried to arrest had been snatched back by the crowds. In a message that was to be repeated in later years he said, *'We may have to think about withdrawing the police force from football games if the situation continues'.*

As fans returned on buses through the villages of Xylophagou and Frenaros, some stopped and committed further damage, although they would later claim to have been provoked. At least ten cars were damaged, and nine motorcycles, outside the stadium, as estimates of damage were put at more than 30,000 Cyprus Pounds.

On Monday 29 November 1999 a seventeen year-old youth from Peristerona Village in Nicosia was arrested, and pleaded guilty on his first court appearance, to taking part in the pitch invasion. His case was adjourned for sentencing in December.

Police subsequently arrested one of the bus drivers claiming that he had opened the doors for hooligans to get out and smash windows in the village of Xylophagou. He appeared in court on the 31November 1999 but when police asked for a remand in custody for two days, the court directed that he should be released immediately. Four other people arrested in connection with the disturbances also appeared in court on the same date.

On Sunday 12 December 1999 Apollon played APOEL in a Cup match at Tsirion Stadium in Limassol.

At 4pm, as APOEL went three goals up, Apollon fans started throwing stones at the East Stands where the APOEL fans were. They responded in kind.

Outside the stadium MMAD officers charged at up to three hundred fans who smashed the windscreens of a number of vehicles, including two MMAD vans, before scattering. The police made sixteen arrests, ten of whom were released without charge, with the remainder appearing at Limassol District Court the following day.

At the end of 1999 the first signs of problems of hooliganism occurring at basketball games came to the fore when three cases of violent incidents were reported in a twelve-month period.

***

On Saturday 1 April 2000 Apollon played Anorthosis, in Limassol, and as the teams entered the pitch fans launched dozens of flares, one of which hit Apollon physiotherapist George Asprogenous on the leg fracturing his shin. He was rushed to a private clinic for treatment and doctors estimated that it would take six months for him to recover.

The flare came from the area occupied by Apollon fans and the Health Minister, a former Apollon Chairman called for the *'murderer'* to be arrested and club chairman George Papas echoed his comments by saying, *'This action is a stab in the back for the game and I urge the police to find and arrest the guilty person'*.

Apollon beat Anorthosis with a score line of 3-2.

In September 2000 the National Committee for Violence reiterated its role as a co-ordinating body aimed at limiting and isolating hooligan activity in sport by prioritising such measures as the installation of further CCTV systems in grounds, an electronic system for allocating tickets, better segregation and design of stadiums, and forbidding the sale and consumption of alcohol, foodstuff contained in dangerous packaging, and the possession of dangerous objects inside grounds.

Their objectives also highlighted the need to provide stewards for each club who would be trained at the Police Academy and given the status of special police officers in that ground. They were to be paid for by the Cyprus Sports Organisation, but finance was to become a sticking point in progressing an effective steward scheme in later years, and legal issues remained to be resolved with the Supreme Sports Authority, as to the Committees legal status.

During matches in 2000 police made one hundred arrests in connection with seventy-two violent incidents.

In 2000 there were also eleven cases of violence at basketball games.

***

On Sunday 28 January 2001 Omonia played Olympiakos at the GSP Stadium in Nicosia, which ended in a 1-1 draw.

When the final whistle blew, almost a minute before time, according to Omonia fans, violence erupted as fans were furious at perceived bias shown by referee Nicos Savva against their team. Angry fans hurled missiles at Savva, who needed a police escort with riot shields, off the pitch. Others charged towards the North Stand occupied by Olympiakos fans and trouble broke out at five separate points within the ground.

As they eventually left the ground the hooligans smashed everything in sight, reduced the stadium entrance to rubble, and attacked police officers. To add to the misery of the situation a sixty-one-year-old man, Costas Polystipiotis, collapsed and died as he was watching the match.

Ten police officers, and the Olympiakos youth-team goalkeeper, Demetris Stylianou, were injured and taken to hospital for treatment with damage valued at between 15,000 to 20,000 Cyprus Pounds being caused. GSP Stadium Director Fivos Constantinides said that the proceeds of ticket sales for the match, estimated at some forty thousand Cyprus Pounds, would be withheld until Omonia FC paid for the damage caused. The club quickly agreed to do so.

The chairman of the Football Federation (KOP) Marios Lefkaritis said, *'Where was the police. What measures did they take? The police knew there was going to be a lot of people. They saw tension building and I wonder what they did to prevent it'.* He went on, *'those responsible for this are animals. Not human beings. We do not want them in the stadiums. Football and sport in general do not need these people'.* He said that the Federation had tried everything to combat the *'hooligan plague'* but felt it was too weak to control 'the mob'. He went on, *'Maybe we can suspend the league until they fall in line. If the police do not take drastic measures nothing can be done'.*

For their part Olympiakos officials said that the police had simply stood by as Omonia fans beat up their rivals. Superintendent Andreas Paphitis denied the allegations made and pointed towards the ten officers who were injured trying to do their job.

Three arrests were made initially and they were charged and released. Two brothers, one aged seventeen years and a schoolboy, and the second his brother aged nineteen years, a serving soldier, were charged with assault on the Olympiakos youth goalkeeper and smashing his mobile phone. They were subsequently remanded in custody for five days after appearing at Court.

At 11am on Thursday 8 February 2001 Apollon goalkeeper Sofronis Avgousti, a Cypriot International player, was having a coffee in a café in Ayios Zonis Street, in Limassol, when he was confronted by three football hooligans. They told him that he was going to 'get it' for throwing his jersey at Apollon fans after being sent off during a game between Apollon and AEL the day before, which ended in a 1-0 score.

He tried to run off but was caught and punched and kicked to the ground resulting in him receiving hospital treatment for concussion and extensive bruising. Police subsequently arrested two men aged twenty-eight-years, and thirty-six- years in relation to the assault.

On Wednesday 14 February 2001 AEL played APOEL in a basketball game at the Eleftheria Stadium in Nicosia. With eight minutes left on the clock, and with AEL trailing 61-51 in points, AEL fans started throwing water bottles, coins, and lighters at their opponents. One club member kept up a supply of water bottles to the hooligans so that they could continue throwing.

MMAD officers deployed with shields and during the disturbances some forty AEL fans, and sixteen police officers, were injured. Twelve people, aged between sixteen-years to twenty-six years, subsequently appeared in court and were remanded for two days.

AEL basketball team coach Vassilis Frangias, and player George Palalas, were later charged with incitement to violence and released on bail. Frangias resigned and apologised for his behaviour. AEL condemned the violence but also blamed the referee for being biased.

On Saturday 10 March 2001 AEL played Olympiakos of Nicosia in a First Division game held at Tsirion Stadium in Limassol.

AEL lost the game 5-0 which moved them from second place in the Division to fourth, and up to five hundred fans laid siege to the player's dressing rooms, after the game, and threatened to *'lynch'* the players. Police in riot gear took up positions at the doors to the dressing rooms as fans pelted them with rocks, pieces of metal and Molotov Cocktails.

The fans then made their way outside the stadium where several vehicles were attacked. Police deployed teargas as they tried to restore order, during which twelve officers were injured, and an eleven-year-old girl was hit on the head by a piece of metal and required stitches.

Two men aged twenty-nine-years, and forty-seven-years were arrested, plus two juveniles, all of whom came from Limassol.

AEL fans accused the police of using excessive force, and others said that the players had been bribed to lose.

On Wednesday 11 April 2001 Nea Salamina played APOEL in a Cup semi- final at the Ammochostos Stadium in Larnaca.

APOEL fans went on the rampage, after their team was knocked out, and a twenty year-old, and two seventeen year-olds from Nicosia, were arrested for smashing the windscreens of three Nea Salamina club mini-buses. Police cars were also damaged and shop windows smashed.

At the end of 2001 it was reported that there had been thirty-five reported cases of violence at basketball games, in the previous twelve months, and during one game, players were surrounded by hooligans, and play delayed for forty five minutes.

***

In 2002 it was noted that the football industry was facing a major crisis in Cyprus in the form of football hooliganism. There was a real fear that the problem could bring about the collapse of the football industry. It was also felt that there was a lack of competitive balance with 66% of all football income being generated by games between the so called 'Big Five' teams, namely APOEL, AEL, Omonia, Apollon, and Anorthosis.

Other factors of concern within what is essentially a very tight knit community were fears about bias by referees, match fixing, and the effects of betting which for many male Cypriots is a national past-time. During a survey some 42% of all respondents blamed referees for causing crowd violence, whilst only 27% blamed fanaticism and the fans. Rather perversely nearly one in ten blamed either match officials or the police.

On Saturday 26 January 2002 it was reported that the Olympiakos chairman Christoforos Tornaritis had accused linesman Antonis Papapayiotou, a police officer, of routinely fixing matches. This came after Anorthosis beat the club 2-0 in a Cup fixture.

At the same time an Anorthosis official said that their

goalkeeper Nicos Panayiotou had been approached by two people before the first leg of the match and offered bribes. As an investigation was announced a Cypriot, living in the UK, who used to play in the First Division, said that he had evidence against the linesman and that club officials and referees were also involved.

On Tuesday 2 April 2002, during a basketball game between AEL and Keravnos, troublemakers stoned police vehicles and smashed the windscreens.

On the 3 April 2002, during a meeting with the House Education Committee, the chairman of the sports commentators union Panayiotis Felloukas said that politicians should avoid interfering in cases and said, *'Sometimes high ranking officials use their powers to help release someone who has been arrested because the poor kid does not deserve to be in detention just because he got carried away once and threw a few stones at someone'.*

In the same meeting AKEL Deputy Nicos Katsourides partly blamed referees and said, *'They often have an offensive way of sending players off, or towards fans because they think in this way they show who is in charge'.*

On Saturday 27 April 2002 AEL played APOEL at the Tsirion Stadium in Limassol in a game that saw APOEL crowned champions after the game ended in a 1-1 draw.

An APOEL fan, twenty-five-year-old Akis Sophocleos, suffered severe head injuries after being hit by a rock, and beaten up. Initially he was placed on a respirator in the Neurology Department at Nicosia General Hospital, when his condition was initially described as serious. When he finally woke up the first question he asked his father was, *'What was the score?'*

There was just one arrest during the violent incidents inside the ground and the police were blamed for poor policing. Police Chief Andreas Angelides refused to accept the blame and placed it at the door of bus drivers from Nicosia, whom he said had ignored police instructions as to where to drop APOEL fans off for the game. Limassol Police Chief Theodoros Stylianou said one thousand five hundred APOEL fans were dropped off at a roundabout, instead of at the stadium entrances, and became involved in confrontations with AEL fans. A sixty-two year old teacher had his jaw broken by APOEL fans as he tried to calm supporters down.

At 10.30am on Friday 3May 2002, in a clear illustration of just how freely firecrackers, and the like, were available to football supporters in Cyprus, a car was stopped in Yeroskipou, Paphos, by police and found to contain two boxes containing more than seven thousand fire crackers and explosive devices. Two persons were arrested.

On Wednesday 25 September 2002 the Israeli team MACCABI Haifa played the Greek team Olympiacos in a UEFA Champions League game which Haifa won 3- 0 at the GSP Stadium in Nicosia. Seven hundred uniform police officers were on duty, as well as a sizeable contingent operating in plain clothes, amongst the crowd of twenty thousand supporters.

There were no reports of trouble at the ground, but as supporters of the two teams gathered at Larnaca Airport, to return home, there were reports of clashes at 1am and MMAD Units were deployed to keep fans apart until 5am when they finally all departed.

On Saturday 26 October 2002 AEL played Apollon in an evening game at Tsirion Stadium, in Limassol, which ultimately finished in a score line of 3-3. At the same time APOEL supporters were returning in buses from Paphos where their team had played AEP.

At 7.15pm, whilst the AEL v Apollon match was still on, five buses carrying APOEL fans were ambushed outside the stadium, just off the motorway, by up to eighty hooligans hurling rocks. The police said that the fifth bus stopped after being hit by fireworks and stones, following which they all came to a halt. APOEL fans spilled onto the motorway and also started throwing stones resulting in the police deploying teargas. During the course of the disturbances an eighteen-year old National Guardsman Geadis Geadi suffered a serious head injury and was rushed to Limassol Hospital.

On Friday 8 November 2002 arsonists set fire to the offices of MACHI newspaper, in the Engomi area of Nicosia, at about 1.30am in the morning. Windows were smashed but the fire was contained to the outside of the building. A note was left at the scene which said, *'If you make mistakes you have to pay'*. Police accused youngsters, and in particular football hooligans, of causing the damage.

On Friday 13 December 2002, during a volleyball game in

Nicosia, a group of youths aged between seventeen-years to twenty-five-years went on the rampage at the end of the game. Stones were hurled at the police, houses, and cars, resulting in one police officer being injured and eleven arrests being made.

On Saturday 14 December 2002 crowd violence occurred at a football game in Paphos as fans clashed following the final whistle. Five police officers, including a senior officer, and one member of the public were injured. Two police cars were damaged and two youths from Limassol arrested.

On the same date in Limassol a game between AEL and Omonia went smoothly, until the half-time break, when a group of fans tried to enter the stadium without paying. During the ensuing scuffles one police officer was injured. AEL lost 2-3 to Omonia.

On Sunday 15 December 2002 six arrests were made after the end of a basketball game in the Ayios Dhometios suburb in Nicosia.

Somewhat strangely another report published by the Council of the European Union, on the situation relating to football hooliganism in the EU in 2002/2003, raised no issues for Cyprus in relation to hooliganism, and the only data listed for the country was two bans from grounds.

***

In January 2003 a court sentenced a twenty-eight year old man to eight weeks in prison for common assault, which had occurred during a basketball game in Limassol, but such custodial sentences were rare.

On Saturday 8 February 2003 Larnaca police charged a fifteen year old, who allegedly hurled a plastic seat at rival supporters, during an evening game between Omonia and AEK. Earlier a footballer told police that he was attacked, whilst leaving the pitch, at the end of a game between Anorthosis and AEP of Paphos which was played at the Antonis Papadopoulos Stadium in Larnaca. The game was won by Anorthosis with a score line of 2-0.

On Sunday 9 February 2003 APOEL played Olympiakos at Nicosia GSP Stadium resulting in a 1-1 draw. At the end of the game APOEL supporters threw missiles at the referee and then turned on the police. They in turn deployed teargas which in the strong winds blew across the stadium and caused children to have breathing problems.

A total of nine police officers were injured and a police car, a bus, and a car were damaged.

Eleven people were arrested including a fifteen year old, and a sixteen year old who were released subsequently, whilst the remainder remained in custody.

On Saturday 22 February 2003 Apollon played APOEL at Tsirion Stadium in Limassol during which fights occurred between the two sets of supporters. Apollon fans threw stones, and pieces of smashed sinks from the stadiums toilets, damaging four police vehicles, whilst in the East stand APOEL fans waved a swastika banner, and burnt plastic seats. In one case it was alleged that an Apollon fan had been doused in petrol by a group of APOEL fans who threatened to set light to him.

At the end of the game APOEL fans leaving Limassol in five buses spilled out onto the streets, threw stones damaging four cars and smashing shop windows, as well as beating several people up. Three arrests were made on the day of persons aged between fifteen years and twenty-two years, all of whom were charged and released.

Apollon lost the match 0-1 to APOEL.

On Wednesday 5 March 2003 a disciplinary investigation was launched by the police against up to five officers following an incident, some ten days previous, on Sunday 23 February 2003, at the GSP Stadium in Nicosia, during a match between Omonia and Ethnikos Achna which ended in a goalless draw. The game was deemed to be low-risk and as such very few police were on duty inside the stadium.

Just before the final whistle an APOEL fan sitting in the stand, occupied by the handful of Ethnikos fans, started waving a blue and yellow flag. Almost immediately some two hundred Omonia fans moved towards the fan and several started trying to attack him.

A handful of police officers, and two or three Omonia fans, tried to protect him as he received blows from several directions. He was not seriously injured but the police were criticised for not doing enough at the time.

Television cameras recorded the whole incident as some of the Omonia fans took it in turns to try to hit him. One was actually caught on camera hitting him with an umbrella which broke into pieces with the force of the blow.

At the end of March 2003 the Justice Minister Doros Theodorou announced that the government would be granting permission for Israeli security officers to carry firearms in a forthcoming Euro 2004 qualifier between Cyprus and Israel to be held at Tsirion Stadium. The police had objected but had been overruled.

On Saturday 12 April 2003 eight youths were arrested at a match between Anorthosis and APOEL in Larnaca for stone throwing, possession of flares, and possession of controlled drugs. A twenty year old from Nicosia was arrested on suspicion of possessing counterfeit tickets.

On Sunday 13 April 2003 four people were arrested at Nicosia's GSP Stadium before the start of the game between Omonia and Dighenis. Two aged fifteen years, and seventeen years, who were in possession of flares, one sixteen year old in possession of a screwdriver, and a forty-three year old who went onto the pitch at half time.

Omonia beat Dighenis 1-0.

On Sunday 11 May 2003 six people were arrested, and two police officers injured, after fighting in Eleftheria Square in Nicosia, following Omonia's Championship winning game against Apollon which ended with a score line of 5-0.

Three hundred Omonia fans, who had gathered in the square, threw bottles, stones, and flares and destroyed a set of traffic lights. They claimed that they were attacked by the police first.

In Limassol Avenue two Apollon fans were arrested for throwing stones and flares at Omonia fans.

On Wednesday 21 May 2003 Nicosia Mayor Michalakis Zampelas, and his Turkish counterpart Kutlay Erk, agreed to organise a bi-communal fair, and football matches between amateur teams from both sides of the Green Line.

On Friday 13 June 2003 Justice Ministry Secretary Lazaros Savvides announced that the government were looking at adopting a system used in Australia whereby known troublemakers in sporting events would be banned from stadiums and required to stay in police supervision for up to two days whilst their team played. They were also re-considering the use of community service orders and he pointed out that, whilst a law had been passed in 1996 to give courts the right to sentence young offenders to community service, it had never been put into effect because of the lack of supervising adults. It had now been decided to appoint four people who could supervise work in municipalities or hospitals.

On Tuesday 5 August 2003 a 'friendly' game took place between APOEL and Anorthosis which was brought to a halt twenty five minutes before the end due to a pitch invasion by hundreds of fans. An earlier pitch invasion in the first-half had also delayed play and the police and clubs blamed each other for the disorder.

On Sunday 28 September 2003 twenty people, including twelve police officers, were injured as a result of a match between APOEL and Apollon at Tsirion Stadium, which ended in a score line of 1-0. MMAD Rapid Reaction Units were deployed and eighteen people detained as thousands of pounds worth of damage was caused.

On Monday 29 September 2003 the District Court refused a

request by the police for eight of those detained to be remanded in custody for four days.

On Wednesday 15 October 2003 a fight broke out outside Lefkotheo Stadium in Nicosia involving Omonia fans attending a volleyball game between Omonia and APOEL. The game was abandoned as cars were damaged. Three police officers were injured, as well as two fans, and an eighteen-year old was arrested.

On the same date the APOEL football club President Dinos Fysentzides attacked a group of neo-Nazis called the *'Pirates'* who had attached themselves to the club. The group was founded in 2000 by three individuals and by 2003 was boasting seventy-five members on its website. They wore black T-shirts, and gave Hitler salutes, and espoused support for Adolf Hitler, General George Grivas, and Greek Dictator Ioannis Metaxas, and warned communists and anyone with Turkish blood in them to enter grounds at their own risk. Their motto was, *'Where the law is unjust violence is a duty'*. APOEL made it clear that the group were banned from their games.

Graffiti displaying swastikas could be seen on walls in the Nicosia area, but it is difficult to see how the 'far right' could actually aspire to Hitler's definition of what the swastika represents which was described by Hitler as, *'The mission for the struggle for the victory of Aryan man'*, in his autobiography, *'Mein Kampf'*.

On Sunday 2 November 2003 a political row erupted following a game between Apollon and Omonia at the GSP Stadium in Nicosia. During the course of the game MMAD officers had occasion to speak to the Apollon trainer Antonis Kezos, who they accused of goading Omonia fans from the team's bench. It was alleged that he was abusive to them, as a result of which he was forcibly arrested in front of the 20,000 fans present. Several Apollon players went to his aid, and one of them was arrested at the time, and another subsequently at half time, being then charged and freed immediately.

DISY political party leader Nicos Anastasiades, who was in the VIP section of the crowd, was reported to have spoken to police officers, who later freed the trainer, and the first player arrested.

Justice Minister Doros Theodorou defended the actions of the police, suspended the police officer who had released the prisoners, and criticised Anastasiades for what he saw as blatant political interference in policing matters.

Politicians from all parties then waded in, either supporting the police for doing their job, and denouncing the behaviour of fans and the clubs, or criticising the police for using excessive force.

Before the game a group of Apollon fans attacked two police officers when they tried to stop them taking firecrackers into the stadium, with one suffering a broken nose.

Nine further arrests took place of people aged between fourteen years, to fifty- two years, and a paper recycling factory next to the stadium was broken into, and fifty plastic containers set on fire, causing damage valued at 1,500 Cyprus pounds.

The following day three people were remanded in police custody at Nicosia District Court in connection with the violence.

In the same week a parliamentary committee debated using video evidence as primary evidence in securing convictions, and to increase the penalties for drunkenness and obstruction inside stadiums. Up to that point under Cyprus law videotape evidence was considered to be 'hearsay' and normally ruled to be inadmissible.

61

The Justice Minister said, *'We are probably the only country in the world where football is politicised',* as he called for further measures in relation to CCTV and segregation.

On Thursday 6 November 2003, for the first time in Cyprus, a Nicosia District Court banned Haris Iakovou, aged twenty-one years, from all sporting arenas for twelve months, and fined him 1,200 Cyprus pounds, after he was convicted of being involved in a disturbance at a football match. The case had taken three years to be finalised.

On Friday 5 December 2003 a thirty-year old ex-player from AEL, Luciano de Souza, was detained as he was about to leave the country after terminating his contract. He was accused of breaking the nose of a fan, after becoming involved in heated exchanges about the performance of the team, when confronted in a kiosk on October 19 2003. The fan in turn said that he did not want to press charges and had already received 4,000 Cyprus pounds in compensation from the player.

***

In 2004 Cyprus joined the European Union, and Cypriot teams took advantage of the *'Bosman'* rule to bring in foreign players. The end result was that young Cypriot players became less common in the Cypriot First Division.

On Saturday 7 February 2004 AEL played APOEL in Limassol.

Allegations were made prior to the game that the referee was biased towards APOEL and tension rose between the two sets of fans. A recent agreement between clubs meant that the Referees Commission were able to appoint officials for specific games rather than them being drawn by means of a lottery process.

In the second-half a series of decisions by the referee angered both sets of fans and as the game finished as a 1-1 draw AEL fans rushed onto the pitch and tried to attack the referee and linesmen. Police escorted them to the tunnel to safety, whilst outside the ground police officers were attacked with firecrackers and stones. A sergeant suffered minor burns after being hit by a firecracker, and a constable suffered cuts from being hit by stones.

Six cars were damaged, three of which were police vehicles, and nine people, aged between thirteen years and seventeen years, were arrested at the time and four more subsequently. A fourteen year old was injured when a firecracker exploded in his hands.

On Thursday 12 February 2004 the Legal Affairs Committee discussed a Bill aimed at reducing the violence, with the emphasis on CCTV and better fencing inside grounds, including the provision of protective nets behind goals. At the same time the police called for tougher penalties and stewards. The Football Federation asked for CCTV to be extended to areas outside the ground.

On Wednesday 17 March 2004 the Police Chief Tassos Panayiotou attacked the rise in assaults in general on police officers, and called for Judges to apply stricter sentencing. He went on to say, *'When someone attacks a police officer he is attacking the State and its authority'.*

According to police statistics three hundred and eighty five officers had been attacked in the previous two years, fifty-five of whom had suffered grievous bodily harm. In countering allegations that officers often used excessive force he stressed that officers were trained to exercise patience but said, *'But when you have to stand there and get your teeth smashed in by stones and glass bottles, or your eye taken out by objects thrown at you by people, then what do you do?'*

On Saturday 25 September 2004 Alki and Apollon played in Larnaca, at the GSZ Stadium, and a mob of supporters attacked police in the stands. TV coverage showed three police officers isolated, and trying to retreat, as they were attacked and beaten, whilst other supporters set fire to seats as Apollon were beaten 6-1.

Two police officers were treated for injuries in Larnaca Hospital and an arrest warrant was issued for a person living in Limassol. Neophytos Demetriou, aged twenty-one years, from Ypsonas, was subsequently charged with assaulting police officers and when he appeared in court was remanded in custody for six days, after making a written confession.

During a game between Omonia and Anorthosis, in Nicosia, a twenty-three year old suffered superficial burns to his stomach as a flare thrown by Omonia fans hit him. Anorthosis went on to win the game with a score line of 4-2.

Also on Saturday 25 September 2004 Nea Salamis played APOEL in Larnaca and before the end of the game fist fights broke out amongst fans.

At the end of the game, which APOEL won with a score line of 2-1, a thirty-one year old APOEL fan was attacked by a group of people and stabbed. Bleeding heavily, he was conveyed to Nicosia General Hospital and detained in the Intensive Treatment Unit where his condition was described as 'very serious'.

Justice Minister Doros Theodorou said, *'we have a zero tolerance policy for these thugs and you can rest assured that, if found guilty, they will be prosecuted to the full extent of the law'*.

When asked if 'these phenomena' would continue ad infinitum he blamed poor co-ordination between the various parties and said that various pledges to install CCTV and improve fencing had not been honoured.

***

On Saturday 9 April 2005 football in Cyprus went into crisis mode when the CFA ordered the suspension of all fixtures following a decision by the Cyprus Sports Association to cut the state subsidy to football clubs from one million Cyprus pounds to 800,000 pounds in response to criticism from UEFA that clubs in Cyprus were failing to manage their finances.

It was alleged that collectively clubs had debts of more than twenty-two million pounds and yet were still spending large amounts of money on bringing in new players. The clubs in turn asked the government to give them a share of the tax from betting in Cyprus which was estimated to be in the region of twenty-five million pounds annually. After much 'hand wringing' the dispute was settled by way of a revised government spending formula.

On Wednesday 4 May 2005 APOEL played Dighenis Morphou in the football cup semi-final at the GSP Stadium in Nicosia, a ground with a capacity of 22,859, which finished in a 0-0 draw.

At 8.20pm, shortly after the half-time interval, twenty-three year old Christos Theofanous, from Maroni, was reported to be attempting to throw a firecracker onto the pitch, from the South Stand, which was packed with APOEL fans. The firecracker went off in his left hand and he received serious injuries.

The referee stopped the match for five minutes when he

heard a loud bang coming from the terraces and medics rushed into the crowd to treat Theofanous, and five other people aged between thirteen years to seventeen years, who were experiencing hearing difficulties.

The match was being played live on LUMIERE and the commentator Thomas Franzis was heard telling the Producer to keep the cameras away from the incident as he could see that Theofanous was covered in blood.

The injured man was rushed to a private clinic in Nicosia but he subsequently lost four fingers from his left hand.

APOEL fans started breaking up plastic seating and at one stage a fire was started with damage estimated at in excess of 10,000 Cyprus pounds being caused. Video footage identified the individual who started the fire and an arrest warrant was issued, and fifteen other people were identified as taking part in the disturbances.

When the twenty-two year old arson suspect was finally arrested he was asked to surrender the clothing that he had worn on the day of the match, but offered the police a pair of black trousers and orange T-shirt, when he was clearly shown on the footage wearing khaki trousers.

Police defended their search procedures stressing that as well as personal searches they also swept the grounds before matches and often found firecrackers inside the perimeter walls which had been thrown over by fans.

In response to this latest incident a lengthy meeting took place at the Presidential Palace, on the evening of Friday 6 May 2005, after which the Justice Minister Doros Theodorou called on all those involved to note that the President Tassos Papadopoulas had spoken out about it and that they now needed to show that they were taking the matter more seriously. He added that new procedures would allow for the searching of buses and that in future players entering the grounds would also be searched following allegations that they were also carrying firecrackers into grounds.

The President of the Cyprus Sports Organisation (KOA) said that the government would seek to cut subsidies to any club found guilty of failing to stop dangerous objects being taken into grounds, and that breaches could lead to spectator bans and games being played behind closed doors.

Police subsequently announced that for the 2004/2005 season, ending in May, that a total of thirty-six arrests had been made at grounds including fifteen arrests at Nicosia's GSP Stadium which had hosted fifty-four games and 271,811 visitors, nine arrests at Larnaca's GSZ and AntonisPapadopoulos Stadiums who had hosted fifty- two games and 110,000 fans, and just three arrests at Tsirion Stadium in Limassol where forty-seven games had been played in front of 100,000 fans. Given the sheer scale of the problems that were occurring these figures seemed to be remarkably low.

Arresting people at the time of large-scale public-order incidents can be very problematic, but the challenge is to make sure that post-incident investigations take place routinely as well as expeditiously.

On Wednesday 3 August 2005 street celebrations took place when Cyprus Football Champions Anorthosis got through their second qualifying tie for the European Champions League by beating the Turkish side Trabzonspor in two legs.

The fact that Anorthosis originally came from the occupied

area in Famagusta was not lost on the population, or the media.

In a frenzy more in keeping with the build-up to a war, two headlines read, *'The victory of Anorthosis is also seen as proof that little Cyprus has the capacity to stand up and be counted with proper preparation and strategy'* and *'Through unity we can achieve everything.......We have the right to hope that with planning, faith, self-confidence, and patience we can kick out from our island the Grey Wolves, the Attilas and the Settlers'*.

Pre-season there were problems at a Super Cup game between Champions Anorthosis and Cup winners Omonia when crowd trouble occurred. Anorthosis were subsequently fined three hundred Cyprus pounds by the CFA.

On Saturday 27 August 2005, at the opening game between APEP Pitsilias and AEL, which was held at the Neon THOI Lakatamia Stadium, on the very first day of the new season, there was a further outbreak of violence. APEP subsequently lost the game 1-2 to AEL.

Before the game a supporter was arrested for attempting to smuggle fireworks into the Stadium, when he was spotted trying to secrete twenty-six fireworks into the bag of one of the players, which had been left temporarily unattended prior to being taken inside.

In front of a capacity crowd of 4,000 people, the game was suspended after a flare gun was fired from the AEL stands minutes before the final whistle. The flare whistled across half of the pitch, narrowly missing the son of the APEP caretaker, Demetris Krikon, who was standing behind one of the goals, before it finished up embedded in an advertising hoarding. Krikon finished the day with his son in hospital suffering from shock.

The referee Costas Kapitanis stopped the game and went to the dressing room, with the two assistant referees, before resuming fifteen minutes later. At the final whistle APEP fans attempted to attack AEL fans and once again the police found themselves in the middle.

A fourteen-year old was subsequently arrested after the game, for damaging a car outside the Stadium, amid rumours that a number of fans had gained access to the stadium using forged tickets.

The AEL chairman Akis Agapiou said that he, and the rest of

his Board, would resign if any such incident was ever repeated. Whilst the finger of blame was pointed at the Limassol based AEL fans they denied any involvement and claimed that as they were winning 2-1 it was not in their interests to disrupt the game.

On Friday 2 September 2005 a thirty-two year-old man from Limassol was arrested and held on remand in connection with firing the flare. An examination of a flare gun recovered showed that it would take just forty-five seconds for a flare fired into the air to reach the ground, leaving very little time for people to move out of the way. In reality someone could easily have been killed.

On Tuesday 22 November 2005 a Cyprus referee Costas Theodotou handed in his resignation stating that he feared for his life after someone telephoned him and threatened to kill him. A week before Theodotou had been accused of making racist comments to a foreign player from the APEP Pitsilias team.

On Thursday 24 November 2005 Akis Agapiou was in the limelight again when he threatened legal action against the Chair of the Referees Union, Costas Constantinou, after being accused of using his status in football for political and personal gain ahead of elections, where Agapiou was standing for the AKEL party. This was prompted by comments from Agapiou who had said that he no longer trusted referees in Cyprus, after a number of disappointing decisions, and called for an independent committee to be set up to investigate.

On Saturday 26 November 2005 AEL played APOEL at Tsirion Stadium in Limassol in a game that was to end in tragedy with the loss of the life of a police officer.

Before the game the social networks went into overdrive with AEL fans being 'called to arms' with messages such as, '*You orange sons of whores*'. (Referring to the *'Portokali'* Orange of APOEL) '*You will die. Death to the last orange supporter. We want your passports should you dare to come you cowards. Calling everyone to Tsirion on Saturday. We must make them feel what yellow hell is all about. Their only exit is the sea*'. Club officials were also accused of making inflammatory remarks.

In a search in the vicinity of the ground by police beforehand they recovered one hundred and three Molotov cocktails, and eighteen smoke grenades.

During the match APOEL fans set fire to seats and damaged toilets and a canteen. It was also alleged that they attacked a kiosk owner and stole all of his stock, as well as attacking a fire engine that was sent to put out flames. In all damage was estimated at 1,182 Cyprus pounds within the ground, and electronic equipment, including computers, valued at a further 4,000 Cyprus pounds were stolen.

There was no reported trouble on the pitch and the game finished with a score line of 1-1.

As part of the policing plan, announcements were made at the end of the game for AEL fans to remain behind whilst APOEL fans left to avoid confrontations. AEL fans responded by breaching police containment lines, some twenty minutes after the final whistle was blown, and stormed out of the stadium where rocks and rubble were thrown at the police, the availability of which was increased by the presence of construction work in the immediate vicinity. The windows of nearby houses were smashed and cars set alight.

During the confrontations a forty-three year old MMAD (Rapid Reaction Unit) Sergeant Marios Malekkou was in the process of carrying an injured colleague, who had been hit in the face with a rock, to an ambulance, when he himself collapsed and suffered a fatal heart attack.

A married man, with three children, Sergeant Malekkou was taken to Limassol General Hospital where he died. The State Coroner Nicos Charalambous subsequently said that he had died from stress and fatigue during violent scenes and had a history of heart problems.

Police responded with truncheons, and teargas, and during the course of the disturbances six arrests were made, and twenty-seven people injured, namely eleven fans, and sixteen MMAD officers.

AEL chair Akis Agapiou put the blame for the violence squarely at the doorstep of the police pointing out that the police had overacted by attacking AEL fans when a small fire broke out and saying, *'It was provocative for the police to sport riot gear at the match'.* as he asked for an Ombudsman enquiry.

Police Chief Tasos Panayiotou said, *'Didn't he* (Agapiou) *see the television of the football with AEL fans breaking down walls, and hurling large pieces of concrete towards police officers guarding the changing rooms. How can people be expecting around 300 to 400 police officers perfectly to control 20,000 people? This cannot be achieved unless other parties get involved. We want action from everyone and it should not just be the police battling hooliganism at football grounds'.*

As the CFA called for authority for some games to be played behind closed doors, the Justice Minister Doros Theodorou said that the situation had reached 'breaking point' and that football violence had clearly unveiled a social problem that needed to be dealt with. A government spokesman Kypros Chrystostomides added,

'Hooliganism has reached its final limit'.

AKEL leader Demetris Christofias dismissed claims that political parties were fuelling the problem of football violence, on the island, and said amongst other things, *'The cure to the problem is how we are going to go about raising our next generation'.*

Other politicians highlighted the apparent divisions between the Cyprus Football Association (CFA) and the Cyprus Sports Federation (CSF) who seemed to be constantly working against each other. Yet others pointed towards the fact that several politicians had served as football club presidents and were often seen on television debating on football issues.

On Monday 28 November 2005 a thirty-six year old man from Limassol, who had been viewed on television footage as being involved in the disturbances, was arrested.

The following day the Justice Minister Doros Theodorou had the last word when he said, *'It's high time we all assumed our responsibilities........if we do not I fear that Marios Malekkou's death will not be the last. It is time we all understand it is a fine line between becoming a parent, an arsonist, or a fireman'*.

On the same day Police Chief Tassos Panayiotou transferred fourteen police officers from Limassol to stations some distance away, in Polis and Paralimni, after it was alleged that they failed to carry out a direct command from a supervising officer, to arrest four people who were illegally on the playing field during the AEL v APOEL match. It was stressed that this action had nothing to do with the death of Sergeant Malekkou.

In another intervention AKEL Deputy Yiannakis Thoma

asked the Ombudswoman Eliana Nicholaou to investigate the action, as families complained about the excessive distances that officers would have to travel to get from their homes to work. He also called for events leading up to the death of the officer to be looked at.

In the same week a high-profile sub-committee meeting, involving all of the key stakeholders in football, was held to discuss introducing modified legislation. Whilst there was a consensus that more needed to be done there was no consensus as to what that should be. Clubs and the CFA were vocal about any intention to play games behind closed doors due to a loss of ticket revenue, and questions were raised about the viability of a Section 23, which referred to the fact that bus drivers conveying fans should have lists of passengers and ID card details before transporting them. Further meetings were planned with a view to trying to progress matters.

In a survey in 2005/ 2006, which was conducted on behalf of the Cyprus Football Association, by the Centre of Leisure, Tourism and Sports Research Development, it was revealed that 77% of men aged between 21 years to 70 years, supported a football club and that 20%, who did not support a particular club, still followed football and were well informed about league results. A total of 16,000 children were registered to play football in academies all over the Island.

All this was a clear indication of how high the political stakes were, with every supporter of a particular club representing a potential vote for a particular party, in a country of less than a million people. In a survey completed three years earlier 16% of respondents said that politics had a part to play in football on the island.

At the beginning of December 2005 the British High Commissioner in Cyprus, Peter Millet, initiated a meeting with the Cypriot Justice Ministry Permanent Secretary Andreas Tryfonides to offer British help in trying to come up with solutions to the problems.

On Wednesday 21 December 2005 it was reported that intruders had broken into a laboratory run by the Cyprus Sports Organisation and that eleven samples taken from seven football players, two basketball players, and two tennis players, for drugs testing, had been destroyed.

Midway through another season, but another year ending, as the talking continued.

Chapter Three

2006/2007

Diverse Years For Hooligans

In January 2006 a team of sport and government officials flew to England, to obtain training from football and stadium experts, but on their return they merely indicated that they would be forwarding some thoughts and suggestions to Cabinet.

The British High Commission, who had supported the visit, were asked why there appeared to be no firm outcomes from the trip and a spokesperson said some three months later, *'The offer for British assistance remains open but we are waiting for a more concrete plan from the Government. Nothing has happened yet but our assistance remains open'.*

Justice Minister Sofocles Sofocleous asserted that the England trip was not just a sightseeing trip for the delegation, adding that the police were actively engaged in learning lessons from other countries including England.

On Sunday 15 January 2006 APEP Pitsilias played Anorthosis at the Lakatamia Stadium as APEP's own ground in Kyperounda was not deemed fit to host First Division games.

During the course of the game a seventeen-year old youth from Lakatamia, who was still at school, repeatedly threw stones onto the pitch, and at the end of the game assaulted the referee Petros Panayides after Anorthosis won 1-0.

The youth was arrested the following day, and appeared at Court on the 16 January 2006, before Judge Lemonia Kaotzari, when he pleaded not guilty to two charges and was allowed bail with strict conditions to stand trial on the 18 April 2006.

On Wednesday 26 April 2006 another high-level delegation, including the Police Chief, and a Justice Ministry Permanent Secretary, went to London to hold meetings with the Metropolitan Police, the FA, The Football Fans Union and an Anti- Racism Group. They looked at pre-match procedures, public order roles and the use of technology, and visited Highbury Stadium, the home of Arsenal. A government spokesman said on their return, *'We have identified the need to develop a strategic plan'.*

On Saturday 29 April 2006 a football match took place, between Anorthosis and APOEL, at the Antonis Papadopoulos Stadium during which TV cameras captured a group of nine APOEL fans attacking, and seriously injuring, fifty-six year old Angelos Mina, who was with his eight year-old son at the time. They were shown beating and kicking Mina unconscious whilst his son looked on screaming and pleading with them to stop.

They were targeted simply because the boy was wearing a sweater bearing the photograph of the Anorthosis Coach Timour Ketsbaia. The fifty-six year old suffered head injuries, extensive bruising and two abrasions to his left eye leaving him with a sight problem.

The attack took place outside the stadium after a 2-2 draw which effectively ended APOEL's chances of winning the championship. During the match both sets of fans hurled objects at each other and set fire to an adjoining field.

Using the television footage, police arrested twenty-seven year old Yiannis Pipis, a temporary worker at the Interior Ministry, who subsequently pleaded guilty at Larnaca District Court and was sentenced to four months in prison, and ordered to pay the victim ten thousand pounds in compensation.

The evidence against Pipis was damning and he was clearly shown on the TV footage hurling a stone at the head of Mr Mina. After seeing his image on national TV he went to Larnaca CID and gave himself up saying, *'what can I say? I admit to the crime and I apologise'*. He was a family man with no previous convictions and said that he had done it in the heat of the moment. Whilst the prison sentence was welcomed the reality was that the law provided for a maximum sentence of two years, and an additional year in respect of a charge of unlawful assembly, so it could hardly be considered as being draconian in the circumstances.

In this case there were actually two victims, the father who suffered physical injuries, and his son who would live with the memory of this barbaric attack for the rest of his life, with all of the psychological effects that came with that.

A second person Marios Papayiannis, a salesman aged twenty-three years, from Nicosia, was found guilty of causing grievous bodily harm and was the first person to be sentenced under new legislation to eighteen consecutive weekends of detention, whereby he was required to report to the Central Prisons in Nicosia every Friday at 8pm and released at 5am on a Monday. Failure to turn up for eighteen consecutive weekends would activate a full four-month jail sentence.

This was surely a step in the right direction but its value was dependent on support for the judiciary in implementing a sentencing policy which had a clear deterrent factor to it.

Also on Saturday 29 April 2006 violence erupted at the game between Apollon and AEL in Limassol. AEL fans burnt 168 plastic seats as their team lost 4-1 to the league leaders, and the referee blew the whistle for full time early because of the level of violence. Four police officers were injured, one of whom needed stitches to a leg injury, as a fire was started in the stand occupied by AEL and damage estimated at more than four thousand Cyprus pounds was caused.

On Monday 1 May 2006 six people aged 15 years, 15 years, 16 years, 17 years, 18 years and 20 years, appeared in Court in Limassol charged with throwing objects onto the pitch. They were identified from CCTV footage and five were still in school. As a result of further enquiries a further eleven arrests were subsequently made.

On Sunday 7 May 2006, celebrating Apollon fans clashed with AEL fans and hundreds of youths hurled firebombs, stones, beer bottles and chairs at each other. Shop windows were smashed and ten cars damaged. Five people aged 38 years, 32 years, 18 years, 19 years, and 25 years appeared in court the following day and eventually a total of fifteen people were arrested.

In the same period politicians exchanged verbal blows over youth and political influence in football with AKEL leader Demetris Christofias saying, *'DISY is fermenting nationalism and bigotry amongst its own youths'* and DISY responding *'Leave APOEL alone and not implicate DISY and its officials in their devious scheming. DISY has never been involved in football – at least not in the way they are suggesting'.*

On Tuesday 9 May 2006 Police Chief Charalambos Koulentis pointed the finger at certain individuals for using football problems for political gain and warned officials connected to the game that he would not hesitate to pull police officers out of football games in future.

During a radio interview he reminded listeners that they were in the middle of an election campaign and said, *'I publicly state right now that I will not allow policing at games and I have absolutely no problems taking this stance regardless of what this does to me personally or professionally.....I honestly feel like we have been left twisting in the wind',* as he complained of a lack of support.

DISY Leader Nicos Anastasiades said, *'If the situation is indeed how the police chief says it is then it is purely the state that is to blame'.*

The following day President Tassos Papadopoulos threatened to reduce state funding to football clubs unless they got more involved in trying to solve the problems.

On the 13 May 2006, at the end of the season, former APOEL football player Leonidas Leonidou commented, *'the simple fact is that most fans here don't like to lose. They don't know how to lose and so they end up going berserk'.* He accused the top tier of the CFA of having vested interests in APOEL, Anorthosis, Omonia and

Apollon and said that they were not capable of solving the problems.

Police said that they had made more than fifty arrests during the 2005/6 season.

In June 2006 'dms007' posted on the Cyprus Forum during a debate about the violence, *'I think that the families are to blame. If children are brought up in a good way, then society is also good. Whilst the violence is far more than a 'one issue problem'.* It was an interesting addition to the discussions and a useful reminder that behaviour is fashioned from many different sources.

On Thursday 10 August 2006 APOEL played Turkish side Trabzonspor in a UEFA Cup 2nd Qualifying Round clash at the GSP Stadium. Four hundred police officers were posted to the match to keep the peace between 16,000 APOEL fans and 2,000 supporters of the Turkish side, which ended in a 1-1 draw.

On Sunday 13 August 2006 APOEL played Omonia at the GSP Stadium, a game which APOEL won 2-1. At 6pm as an APOEL bus approached the stadium, a group of people stoned the vehicle causing damage estimated at 600 Cyprus pounds. Meanwhile a truck, bearing no number plates, with four APOEL fans on board was spotted throwing stones at vehicles on the Nicosia to Limassol highway, and the twenty-one year old driver was arrested a short time later.

Almost immediately afterwards more than a hundred fans tried to force their way through to the North Stand, without being searched, and a police sergeant received an eye injury.

As the game got underway a seventeen-year old was arrested for throwing a flag onto the pitch, and nine people, three of whom were women, were injured as rival supporters threw missiles at each other, and received first aid. A club official's car was damaged.

After the game a fifty-five year old man reported being attacked in his vehicle at the top of Makarios Avenue as he stopped at traffic lights next to APOEL's club house, by up to twenty people who threw stones and bottles and caused damage valued at two hundred Cyprus pounds.

A CFA spokesman said after the game, *'It appears that we will be entering yet another season of football violence'*.

On Wednesday 16 August 2006 a Nicosia Judge refused a

request by the prosecution for more serious charges to be laid against six men involved in Sundays clashes because they did not take place in the area of the stadium.

Legal experts gave differing opinions over what was, and was not, covered by the legislation as three men appeared in court charged with causing damage to two separate vehicles, and three appeared for possessing and throwing dangerous objects. When asked by Judge David why the Prosecutor in the first three cases was insisting on strict bail conditions she said it was because they were rival football fans. Judge David said, *'would the charge have been different if they had just come back from a wedding. There is nothing to show that these incidents are football violence. We are talking about isolated offences'.*

A different Judge hearing the other matters took an entirely different view and applied stringent bail conditions.

On Wednesday 23 August 2006 a Nicosia taxi driver, Marios Demosthenous, aged thirty-three years, was remanded in custody at court after being charged with throwing objects at Omonia fans in connection with the same match. He was recognised from a picture published in the press and it transpired that he had not only been convicted in 2003 for similar matters, but he also had football related charges pending from the previous season during a clash with Anorthosis fans.

On Thursday 24 August 2006 one of those arrested for throwing stones during the game, was fined five hundred Cyprus pounds and banned from attending sports events for one year. Father of two Vasilis Demetriou, aged twenty-six years, said in court, *'I acted in sheer anger after rocks from the Omonia stand hit me, as well as a young boy standing in front of me who was around the same age as my daughter'.*

In all a total of twenty people were questioned by police in relation to disturbances at that game.

At the beginning of September 2006 allegations of match fixing in some of Achna's European games were made, in French and Israeli newspapers, and UEFA said that they were going to consider mounting an investigation.

By the end of September 2006 the CFA had already issued a number of fines for violence, namely Apollon fined one thousand five hundred Cyprus pounds for trouble with AEL, an Olympiakos Nicosia player fined two hundred Cyprus pounds for assaulting another player, and an Enosis Paphos player banned for one game for kicking an opponent.

Enosis Neon Paralimni was fined two hundred and ten Cyprus pounds after fans threw stones, Omonia was fined seven hundred and fifty Cyprus pounds for serious disorder, and AEL fined one thousand two hundred Cyprus pounds.

Prior to the game with APOEL and AEL in Nicosia on Sunday 29 October 2006 the CFA held a press conference and appealed for calm. In an effort to reduce potential violence it was decided to try and record details of the 2,000 travelling AEL fans, and to place ID card details on tickets.

During the press conference an AEL spokesman said, *'It is time for a new beginning and starting this Sunday we will show our new standards'*.

APOEL former player Takis Antoniou said, *'both sides are great historic clubs that have set an example for the coming game. I hope that the fans of both clubs will also follow suit'*.

On the day APOEL beat AEL with a score line of 2-1.

On Saturday the 16 December 2006 Omonia were controversially disallowed an injury time winner against APOEL whilst the game was drawn at 2-2. The offside decision by the linesman sparked vociferous protests from the players, and supporters of the club.

The game was suspended for twenty minutes, before play resumed, as match officials locked themselves in a room, whilst the 20,000 crowd waited. Flares were set off in the stands, and one Omonia fan set fire to an APOEL scarf, as some fans used loud hailers to spur on the crowds. In contrast a number of Omonia fans played steel drums at the front of the stand they were occupying, to create a carnival atmosphere.

On Tuesday 19 December 2006 residents in the Nicosia suburb of Anthoupolis woke up to find the whole of their main street covered in graffiti. Only three days previously local authority workers had undertaken an extensive clean-up operation, and painted out much of the old graffiti. Unfortunately they unwittingly just provided a blank canvas for those intent on causing damage to spray shops, bakeries, and children's centres with swastikas, political, and football slogans. The nearby refugee estate was covered in black, green, red and blue graffiti and the police were accused of doing nothing.

On Saturday 30 December 2006 a basketball match, between APOEL and Omonia, was televised live at Nicosias Eleftheria Stadium. Violent clashes took place between fans and an APOEL fan was attacked and injured by a gang of youths after the game had finished.

Police initially arrested three men, two aged twenty-one years, and one aged twenty years in connection with the violence, and more specifically throwing objects in a sports arena, possession of dangerous weapons, causing a disturbance, and causing grievous bodily harm to the APOEL fan. They also issued warrants for the arrest of a further three men aged 19 years, 20 years, and 27 years, and were seeking to identify a further fifteen people who were seen committing violent behaviour on television footage.

***

On Thursday 4 January 2007, in something of a landmark hearing, the three accused appeared before Judge Angelos David in Nicosia for a remand hearing where the police were applying for a remand in custody for four days for further enquiries to take place.

During exchanges between the police investigator Andreas Chrysanthou, and a defence lawyer Chris Triantafyllides, about whether or not one of the accused was actually on the television footage committing acts of violence or not, the Judge took the very unusual step of allowing the television pictures to be shown in court after he had initially declined a request.

Whilst in principle this should have been a positive step forward, the proceedings stalled when the case was adjourned for a short while so that the police officer could go to the police station to collect the visual evidence. Matters became more complicated when he returned with a CD saying that he did not have any still pictures of the accused and there was no computer on which to play the CD in Court.

The Judge was less than impressed and, rather than the four day remand, a two day remand was agreed between the defence and the State Prosecutor Anna Yiallourou.

The use of visual evidence remains to this day entwined within the debate about civil liberties in Cyprus and its full use is still yet to be maximised in Cypriot Courts. The use of such evidence has proved to be a key success factor in combating hooliganism and clearly the police still had some way to go in terms of being able to use it to best effect.

On Friday 5 January 2007 Omonia's Romanian coach, Ioan Andone, resigned saying, *'the main factor behind this decision is unfortunately the refereeing which, with its decisions, is ruling the results of games and is making its own course with regards to the championship, the champion, and which teams will be relegated.....No measures are being taken to improve the situation'.*

On Saturday 6 January 2007 there was crowd trouble at Tsirion Stadium in Limassol before a match between APOEL and Apollon, which Apollon went on to win 2-1. APOEL supporters threw Molotov cocktails and burnt seats causing damage valued at 800 Cyprus pounds. Police and the Fire Service were deployed to the North stand after one Molotov cocktail caused a small fire.

Before the kick-off a twenty-four year old Apollon supporter was arrested for using abusive language after being subjected to a search. After the game two APOEL supporters were injured at the Ayios Athanasios roundabout when the bus that they were travelling on was stoned by Apollon fans.

On Friday 12 January 2007 a high-level meeting took place, attended by Justice Minister Sophocles Sophocleous, Justice Minister permanent secretary Andreas Tryfonides, Police Chief Charalambos Koulentis, House Legal Committee Chairman Ionas Nicolaou, and representatives from the Cyprus Sports Association, Cyprus Football Association and National Committee Against Violence.

The Justice Minister announced that they had two goals, namely to implement the specific law that they were drawing up, and to follow it stringently and decisively, and the second was to see their efforts bear fruit soon.

Their stated aim was to have the new legislation in place before the start of the next season, and to introduce CCTV at stadiums, together with Stadium Inspectors, and a commitment from the police to play a more pro-active role. This all sounded vaguely familiar.

On Tuesday 27 February 2007 referees were blamed for destroying Cyprus football during a meeting of the House Education Committee chaired by Nicos Tornaritis of DISY who said, *'One of the main reasons for violence and hooliganism in the football grounds is the behaviour of referees'*.

The week before, the entire Cyprus Football Associations Referee Committee resigned amid accusations by a number of club chairmen that referees were receiving payments to fix matches. The club chairmen from Omonia, APOEL, Anorthosis, and Apollon all alleged that there were a number of corrupt referees in the Cyprus Championship.

On Friday 9 March 2007 hooligans again switched their focus from football to volleyball as Anorthosis Famagusta volleyball team played Paphiakos in Paphos and lost, by three sets to one, to the home team.

After the game a convoy of four buses carrying fans from the Anorthosis team, who were being escorted by police, were subjected to an attack from a bridge, overlooking the Paphos to Limassol highway, when a hail of rocks were thrown. One rock went through the windscreen of one bus and struck the driver Andreas Constantinou, aged thirty-eight years, who suffered serious head injuries.

Passengers rushed to the front of the bus where one of them managed to grab the steering wheel and bring the bus to a stop on the highway. Had it not been for his quick-witted actions the bus might well have crashed causing further injuries or even fatalities. A hundred or so angry Anorthosis fans then proceeded to block the highway for one hour. Anorthosis Chairman Andreas Pantelis said, *'we utterly condemn actions like these and they have absolutely no place in our society'*.

A second bus and a police patrol car were also damaged.

The driver was taken in an unconscious state to the Intensive Care Unit at Nicosia General Hospital where his condition was described as 'severe but stable and not life threatening'.

On Saturday 10 March 2007 the police arrested two eighteen-year old youths, from the Paphos area, in connection with the incident and remanded them in custody. The following day a third person aged twenty-five years was also arrested.

Justice Minister Sophocles Sophecleous condemned them as *'brainless'* and said that, *'people should not behave like that in our society',* whilst the police said that they were looking at measures to prevent this type of incident from happening again. To some it looked like the somewhat traditional round of condemnation involving three key parties; the police, the sporting officials, and the Government, but many desperately wanted words translated into actions.

On Sunday 11 March 2007 AEL played Omonia in a cup game at Tsirion Stadium in Limassol, and AEL lost 1-0.

Shortly before the game ended two hundred youths, believed to be AEL fans, created a disturbance outside the ground with rocks, sticks, and Molotov cocktails being thrown at the police who responded with tear gas.

Limassol Police Chief Tassos Oikonomides described them as very organised with evidence that many had stashed weapons outside the ground before the game started. Small fires were also lit at nearby shops which were put out by the Fire Service. Residents adjacent to the stadium were yet again obliged to lock themselves, and their children, in their homes in a ritual that was all too common.

Omonia fans were kept inside the ground, for half an hour, at the end of the game, for their own safety, and three police officers were injured, and three cars damaged.

Police made three arrests of youths, all under eighteen-years of age, who were released pending further enquiries and the police promised to hold a meeting to discuss further security measures.

This was the third time, in the current season, that violence had occurred outside Tsirion Stadium and yet again calls were made for the House Legal Affairs Committee in Cyprus to expedite the movement of a Bill through parliament dealing with hooliganism so that it could be in place for the beginning of the next season.

The committee chairman Ionas Nicolaou said that there had been some disagreements with the Cyprus Football Association in the past over the Bill but that he was hopeful that it could be approved, just before the summer, so that it could be implemented for next season.

The CFA President Costakis Koutsokoumnis was less enthusiastic and said that the police needed to do more and that the Bill, which needed lots of changes and revisions in general, was not the answer to everything. He added, *'there is a perception that the clubs are in control of the masses but this might be a false perception'*. It seemed that the debate and the rhetoric was set to continue in tandem with the violence.

Leonidas Leonidou a former Cyprus and APOEL player said, *'the really effective decisions in my opinion will displease a lot of individuals involved in football and that is the basic reason why we are getting nowhere with the problem. In England where the problem of football violence reached unbelievable proportions at one stage a lot of money and a lot of sacrifices were made to tackle the problem. The big question is – are we capable of making the same sort of decisions?'*.

Police Chief Charalambos Koulentis said that he was fed up with the police being blamed for everything whilst clubs continued to receive high income from ticket sales and television rights and said, *'personally I don't think that the associations and clubs do enough. There is definitely a legal platform that is missing and that is one of the biggest problems we have in fighting hooliganism. The simple thing is that the only thing the sports clubs do is collect income from the games. We also need to see stricter sentencing in the courts'.*

At the end of March 2007 one of my old Forces, the Sovereign Bases Police, held a schools congress meeting at Trachoni Gymnasium to deliver a strong anti- violence message to a group of some two hundred and fifty, 14 and 15 year-old, students, many of them involved in either playing or watching sport.

Acting Divisional Commander Theodoros Tsiarlis, and the Deputy Chief Constable David Turner, were in attendance and stressed the need for education and a multi-agency approach in trying to solve the problem. Whilst the principles of education, prevention, and enforcement are well documented in strategic terms, the over reliance of one element over the other two made failure a more likely outcome in an environment where the police simply did not want to upset the local community with robust enforcement policies.

Justice Minister Sophocles Sophocleous also stressed the importance of public discussions on such an important issue.

I know the village of Trachoni well and even today there are little in the way of community facilities to alleviate the boredom of young people with a view to diverting them away from anti-social behaviour and the dangers of drugs.

It was, and still is, a fertile recruiting ground for people who are trying desperately to find some form of social identity. The social challenges are enormous in a place which has been unfairly christened *'The Wild West'* by Cypriots themselves.

A Bases spokesman, Captain Crispin Coates, said of the meeting that was attended by parents, teachers and other agencies, *'this is a way of introducing people to the concept of violence, not just at sporting events, but also in the home and workplace'.*

Whilst this was a laudable aim it was one which would not be achieved in one meeting where the so called 'hard to reach' were very unlikely to even be in attendance anyway as they pondered their future prospects, in coffee shops elsewhere, or raced round the streets in cars, sticking one finger up to society.

On Thursday 29 March 2007, in a country regarded as the 'motherland' by many Greek Cypriots, there was a stark reminder of the ultimate price that individuals could pay, when caught up in violence associated with sport, when a twenty-five year old man was murdered in Greece.

The Greek government suspended all team sports matches until Friday 13 April 2007 after the twenty-five year old was stabbed and then run over by a car after Panthinaikos and Olympiakos fans clashed before a women's volleyball game.

The two sets of fans, who had a violent history of clashes spanning decades, came to blows in Peania an eastern suburb of Athens ahead of the volleyball match. The police seem to have been caught unawares as fans gathered and during the twenty-minute battle six other people were injured, one critically, including a number of minor league players who were on their way to training, and were wearing similar team colours to Panathinaikos, and a vehicle was set alight.

Police made thirteen arrests and subsequently raided fifteen clubhouses used by both sets of supporters where dozens of makeshift weapons were seized. Using familiar language Superleague chief Petros Kokalis said, '*it is time that all of us in soccer come together and once and for all eradicate violence from sports*'.

Ministers indicated that convictions for causing trouble would lead to prison sentences rather than suspended sentences.

Olympiakos Pireos FC in Greece has a significant following by fans in Cyprus.

Sergeant Michalis Erodotou, in charge of the National Football Intelligence Unit at that time in April 2007, highlighted the severity of the problem in Cyprus and confirmed that more needed to be done. Having attended international conferences on the subject, and matches abroad, as well as taking advice from countries like England and Germany, he was clear about what needed to be done.

He confirmed that only two stadiums in Cyprus had CCTV systems, namely GSP, and Antonis Papadopoulos, and that a new ticketing system was required to regulate attendances. His ambition was to start training specialised stewards to free up police resources who were currently doing everything. He wanted two hundred stewards for every crowd of 20,000 spectators.*

There was talk of banning hooligans from stadiums, making them report to police stations during match times, and the use of ID Cards. There was absolutely no shortage of constructive ideas but all of them would fail if there was no political will to implement them.

On Monday 2 April 2007, a volleyball match was held at Themistocleous Athletic Centre in Limassol between Omonia and Anorthosis. At about 9.30pm seventy fans started throwing missiles, and a forty-five year old police officer later required nine stitches to a wound at Limassol General Hospital. Four people aged 16 years, 18 years, 21 years, and 23 years were arrested and later remanded in police custody for three days.

On Wednesday 11 April 2007 Omonia played APOEL in a Cup game which ended in a 1-1 score draw. As if to emphasise the political nature of football, at the highest point of the stand, occupied by APOEL fans, a huge banner was placed saying, *'Cyprus is Greek'.*

In the same month, as if to highlight the dilemma facing the authorities, when trying to change the mind-set of people directly involved in the game, one media commentator flagged up the fact that an Omonia team official had said on a radio interview that, *'we can't control what crowds chant',* whilst at the same time the player who scored a winning goal against APOEL had turned on his opposing fans, some of whom wore swastikas at matches, mimicking machine-gun fire.

All this was in stark contrast to several countries where such behaviour was banned both on and off the pitch.

At the same time the Republic of Cyprus Police published their annual report for 2006, which showed that serious crime was up ten per cent on the previous year.

The media highlighted the problems of violent crime by citing the case of a man who was under police guard after being attacked on the 6 April 2007 by three men wielding knives and baseball bats. The crime figures also revealed that there had been thirty-six bomb explosions in 2006, which at first sight might appear somewhat unusual but is actually a favoured tactic within the Cypriot criminal fraternity, where cars and premises are often targeted in revenge attacks.

***

Footnote: *Some five years later on Wednesday 18 April 2012 I sat in the Aperitivo Restaurant in Nicosia with my wife Andry, and the very same Michalis Erodotou. Having had extensive experience of the problems surrounding football violence, throughout my police career, I was keen to offer such assistance as I could. Michalis still retained a passion for his chosen specialism but many of the issues remained the same, and in a country with a local population of less than one million people it seemed unbelievable after all those years that the violence was still taking place, and in some ways was actually escalating.*

***

On Wednesday 25 April 2007 Omonia played APOEL in Nicosia, and once again violent scenes were witnessed as APOEL lost with a score line of 1-2. A woman was injured after the game when her car was attacked in Kallipoleos Street by APOEL fans. Two days later three people from Nicosia aged 33 years, 18 years, and 19 years were arrested for assault and threatening behaviour in connection with the trouble.

On Thursday 3 May 2007 hooligans again diversified their activities when AEL Limassol played APOEL Nicosia in a basketball match at Kition Stadium in Larnaca. The match was initially delayed for half an hour due to clashes between police officers and AEL fans who objected to the presence of twenty APOEL fans in their section of the stadium. They were eventually moved to another section for their own safety.

After the game ended, violent incidents continued in Larnaca and a number of fires were lit outside the stadium as well as on the highway between Kofinou and Ayios Theodoros, the Dromolaxia Industrial estate, and the river bridge, leaving the Fire Service struggling to keep up. A National Guard soldier was taken to Larnaca General Hospital suffering from the effects of smoke inhalation as a result of one of the fires.

Larnaca Police Chief Soteris Hadjichristofis, and three other officers, were slightly injured in the disturbances. In what was to become something of a recurring theme he said, '*after this we are debating very seriously the participation of the police in such matches. I believe this does not honour Cyprus. The police leadership will think about policing such matches in the future where there are fanatical fans. We have told the police leadership that it must respect the rights and positions of our officers who go to stadiums and are mercilessly assaulted by fanatical fans'.*

On Saturday 5 May 2007 Dighenis Morphou played Olympiakos Nicosia at the Makarios Athletic Centre in a crucial relegation decider. A sixteen-year old was arrested by police as he tried to enter the ground whilst in possession of a concealed knife. He appeared in court on Tuesday 8 May 2007, flanked by his father and grandfather, when he pleaded guilty and the case was adjourned. He seemed not to be overwhelmed by the proceedings and even managed to chat and smile to the police investigator.

On Thursday 10 May 2007, new Police Chief Iacovos Papacostas outlined his vision, and strategic plan for 2007 to 2011, which included proposals to improve the Force's relationship with the public. He outlined twenty-four basic pillars, upon which the strategic plan would be based, one of which was 'clamping down on hooliganism'.

He said, *'as of today, Cyprus's police will stop standing*

opposite citizens and instead take a place by their side'. Whilst this was indeed an admirable objective, to aspire to, the reality was that it would take time to achieve, as at that time in Cyprus the police, in general, saw themselves as very much in a job working within the public sector.

On Thursday 17 May 2007, a meeting took place at the Justice Ministry involving the Justice Minister Sophocles Sophocleous, and representatives from the Police, the Cyprus Football Association, and Cyprus Sports Association.

The police had twice threatened to stop policing sporting events claiming that those involved in sport were not doing enough to keep their own house in order.

At the meeting a decision was however reached to regulate policing, and other security issues, ahead of high-risk games, with a three-member committee from the Police, the CFA and the CSA.

The Chairman of the CFA Costakis Koutsokoumnis welcomed the move which he said would assist in identifying the need for extra police resources, as well as segregation issues and games which might need to be played behind 'closed doors'. He made particular reference to the challenges faced with high-risk encounters such as the matches played between APEL and Omonia where more than 20,000 supporters might attend.

On the 21 May 2007, the police in Greece offered a potentially new tactic to people wrestling with the problem of football violence when they announced that they would fire paintball pellets containing different colours to identify any rioting fans during the forthcoming Champions League final between Liverpool and AC Milan at the Olympic Stadium. A police spokesman said that they would be deployed in open spaces, rather than inside the stadium itself, and that as well as marking troublemakers who could be arrested retrospectively they were also quite painful.

In July 2007 the English League Division One side Luton Town cancelled a planned friendly game, in the occupied part of Cyprus, against the 2007 Turkish Cypriot champions Cetinkaya, after protests were made to the British FA.

On Thursday 23 August 2007, a so-called 'friendly' game was played between Apollon and Omonia at Tsirion Stadium in Limassol on the day that the new CCTV system was switched on.

During the 55th minute of the game, both sets of supporters started throwing stones at each other, both inside and outside of the ground. Trouble started after Omonia fans held up a banner which showed Cyprus split in two with a message, *'Look what you have done',* emblazoned on it.

For their part, Apollon fans were accused of constantly chanting *'EOKA'* at the opposition, a reference to the so-called 'terrorist' organisation which fought against the British colonial power prior to Cyprus being granted independence. There were very few police officers on duty, and police from all over Limassol, and MMAD Units, were drafted in urgently to assist.

The actual game was stopped five minutes before the end as cars, motorbikes, and the Omonia bus were damaged, as well the stadium itself. Police expressed surprise at the violence given the 'friendly' status of the match, and said that they would be reviewing the CCTV coverage to identify offenders. Given the history of violence between the two sets of supporters this seemed to be rather a strange viewpoint to have.

The Cypriot First Division for the 2007/8 season started on

the 1 September 2007 with APOEL as the defending Champions.

Their fans always had the very highest expectations of the team, and indeed on one occasion, whilst playing Nea Salamina in a fifth-round championship match, they had decided not to sing and chant for players as a sign of discontent at their performance.

On Monday 22 October 2007 the car of Apollon Chairman Frixos Savvides, who took over in 2006, was attacked sometime before 9pm whilst he was talking on a TV chat show in Limassol. He was a guest on Limassol TV's sports show when his car windscreen and bonnet were damaged with rocks.

The previous day, a game between APOEL and Apollon was called off at half- time at the GSP stadium in Nicosia, with a score line of 2-0, after Apollon fans threw rocks, a flagpole, flares, plastic pipes, and even a Swiss Army knife at APOEL goalkeeper Jane Nikoloski who was positioned in front of the designated Apollon stand.

After the match the air was filled with the sound of police sirens, and smoke from flares, as fans gathered outside the stadium in numbers, chanting and behaving in an intimidating manner.

The CFA subsequently awarded the game to APOEL with the existing score line.

Savvides accused the fans of, *'trying to destroy everything the club was trying to build'*. He also however blamed the referee for abandoning the match. Trouble had begun after APOEL's Helio Pinto, a former Apollon player, scored an opening goal after thirty minutes. Shortly afterwards another player, Nicos Machlas, scored a second goal for APOEL, after which Apollon fans started pelting the APOEL goalkeeper. The Police Chief Iacovos Papacostas said, *'we warned that games would be interrupted if violence broke out'*.

On Saturday 8 December 2007, APOEL beat Omonia 1-0 in a game at the GSP Stadium in Nicosia, before a crowd of 17,446 supporters. Two days later the APOEL Ultras posted the following on a social networking site after claiming that 11,000 APOEL fans were singing throughout the game, *'what a feeling...humiliating the green rabbit, giving it the kiss of death, playing the last game of the coffin. Things can't get much better than this....God have mercy for these fools, it's about time they realise that it is AKEL that decides their future and no one else'*.

On Sunday 9 December 2007 another volleyball game took place between Anorthosis and Omonia at the Themistokleio Stadium in Limassol. Whilst the game was still underway fans started fighting outside, resulting in two persons being injured and six cars damaged. A nineteen year old from Limassol suffered a head injury, and a police officer suffered leg wounds. There were no arrests.

At the end of the match, which Anorthosis won three sets to two, the Omonia players confronted the referee complaining that his decisions were not fair.

On Saturday 15 December 2007, AEL played APOEL in an evening game at Tsirion Stadium, and in an effort to reduce the potential for confrontation, police closed off Stelios Kyriakides Street to all traffic, and tried to designate specific parking areas for both sets of fans. The game was attended by 5,645 supporters and ended in a 1-1 draw.

In 2007 the Cyprus Police reported twenty-eight cases relating to football.

Chapter Four

2008/2009

On Saturday 26 January 2008 APOEL played Nea Salamis in a game which they won with a score line of 3-1. In a comment on social media posted by *'Apoel Ultras'* for once there was no venom against the opposition as it read, *'Apart from the excellent appearance of our team the orange fans also made a strong presence on the away stand and throughout the forty five minutes they never stopped singing, pushing all APOEL fans creating thus an unprecedented atmosphere'.*

On Saturday 2 February 2008, Apollon played APOEL at Tsirion Stadium, and 5,676 supporters attended.

A minute before the end of extra time the referee Marios Stamatis was attacked by a number of Apollon players, following a number of controversial decisions. A number of Apollon fans also charged onto the pitch to join in the attack.

In the melee that followed, two police officers were injured, whilst a Sigma and Plus TV cameraman Demetris Papademetriou was attacked and his camera valued at 3,700 euros was destroyed. Further damage estimated at 4,500 euro was caused within the ground as toilets were smashed, and seventy-four plastic seats burnt. Rubbish bins were set on fire and a fire was started at the adjacent Olympian Indoor Court.

The referee's car was also damaged and police later confirmed that they had made five arrests and were seeking five more people involved in the disturbances.

The referee later spent three hours at Paphos Gate Police Station giving a statement to police which included details of the attack by Apollon players, five of whom were officially sent-off for assaulting him.

Justice Minister Sophocles Sophocleous said, *'day after day our football is being strangled. This event is not an exception and fanatical supporters and party control of the teams is to blame'.* Although he acknowledged that there might be issues relating to refereeing and policing he also added, *'inflammatory statements are often made before games by team spokesmen, presidents and the like which create a war atmosphere'.*

In contrast the chairman of the House Legal Affairs Committee Ionas Nicolaou lay responsibility on the State and highlighted the length of time it was taking to try to get a draft Bill passed through the House.

Elsewhere, political parties declined to accept that there was any political control.

Because of the attack by Apollon players APOEL expected to get the three points for the match awarded to them by default by the CFA, although they did make a statement deploring the actions of a minority of APOEL fans who set fire to seats.

They were in fact subsequently awarded the game on a 2-0 win.

In contrast, on Sunday 3 February 2008, Apollon FC issued a statement condemning the referee, claiming that he was biased. They also blamed the Referee Association, the Cyprus Football Association for doing nothing about hostile refereeing towards the team, and the Limassol Police Chief for not calling off the game when the trouble started.

They said nothing about the conduct of their players fighting on the pitch, or the fans, and instead said thank you to their supporters who, *'despite the blatant and provocative injustice against their club showed great restraint'*. The team coach said simply, *'the match was fixed'*.

Finally the public had their say in the media when they complained about the indiscriminate use of teargas by the police and one woman in a lengthy interview said, *'it was a desperate situation, as if we were in the middle of a TV war scene. We couldn't breathe, people around me kept spitting, some throwing up. After the game was stopped Apollon fans left Tsirion Stadium and a group set fire to a bin outside a field. Police approached them and stones were thrown. The police lined up ten metres away from fans and at least fifteen shots were fired into fans who included women and children'*.

On Sunday 24 February 2008, the results of the presidential victory of left- wing candidate Demetris Christofias sparked violence as hooded youths emerged on the streets of Limassol, and Nicosia, attacking moving cars and setting fires.

Just after 7pm, following the defeat of right-wing candidate Ioannis Kasoulides, the fire service was kept busy as fires were started in several districts of Nicosia. Half an hour earlier a twenty year old student was driving his car in Ayios Antoniou Street, behind the APOEL Football Fan Club, when he was forced to stop and his car was attacked by twenty hooded men, wearing APOEL scarves, and wielding iron bars, who caused 3,000 euro damage.

In Limassol, Apollon fans also came out onto the streets and at about 9pm a thirty-nine year old man driving in Anexartisias Street was attacked by hooded youths wielding bats and clubs. Half an hour later a twenty year old man in his vehicle was attacked on the same street by hooded youths wearing Apollon T-shirts and waving Greek flags. Damage valued at 2,500 euro was caused.

A police car was called at 11pm to investigate a report that hooded youths were throwing stones at passing cars in Pasteur Street and on arrival the police car was attacked and windscreen smashed. Finally at the same time a twenty-seven year old, driving his car in Gladstone Street, was stopped by Apollon fans who punched and kicked the bodywork of the vehicle. No arrests were made.

On Wednesday 27 February 2008, police were on full alert for a match between Anorthosis and Omonia, after a fortnight's break for the presidential elections, amid fears that the game would be polarised by the politics of the right and left.

The ground was packed with fans, as flares erupted from sections of the stands, in a clearly orchestrated manner, and Anorthosis went on to win the game with a score line of 2-0.

At the end of the month the CFA announced a new initiative to try to combat allegations of biased behaviour by referees. They decided to bring two referees in from Greece for 'crunch' matches on an exchange programme whereby two Cypriot referees would officiate at games in Greece.

CFA chairman Giorgos Papastavrou said, *'we are happy that with this plan we will change the all too common preconception that our referees are to blame for the outcomes of games. As a nation we are always quick to say that it is the referees' fault, but now people will understand that it is not them who are to blame'.*

On Thursday 13 March 2008, the Chairman of the House Legal Affairs Committee Ionas Nicolaou, announced that the new

Bill that they had been working on, for over a year, was close to completion, and submission to the House for approval.

The Bill listed measures which included a requirement for fans to produce their ID card when purchasing tickets, which would then be allocated to specific seats. It also called for increases in the use of banning orders, and the length of sentences.

On Saturday 15 March 2008, Apollon fans set fire to plastic seats in Tsirion stadium during a game, which was won by relegation strugglers Aris with a score line of 3-1, as they chanted, *'Sold Out'*, at their players.

Later that evening Omonia played APOEL, in Nicosia, and a sixteen year old was arrested for possession of a flare, and another sixteen year old for entering the pitch. Fans threw missiles, including coins, at each other whilst it was alleged that the police stood by, and a twenty-six year-old year old woman from Nicosia was injured by a missile and received first aid.

After the game the Turkish Cypriot press reported that APOEL fans had attacked a vehicle containing Turkish Cypriot Omonia fans, and smashed a window, but that the incident had not been reported to the police.

Omonia won the match with a score line of 2-1 before a packed crowd. At the beginning of the game APOEL fans choreographed a large picture scene on the stands, before the carnival atmosphere changed.

On the same day violence erupted during a game between CyTa and A.D in the Second Division of the Nicosia Amateur Championship. During a scuffle between a forty-two year old player, and an opposing player, a small number of fans rushed onto the field, and began to beat the middle-aged player, who later received hospital treatment.

On Sunday 23 March 2008 three people were injured during, and after, a game between Apollon and Omonia, at Tsirion Stadium in Limassol, which ended in a 3-3 draw.

One fifteen year old boy suffered facial injuries, whilst watching the game from his seat, when a firecracker hit him. Two fifteen year olds were arrested during the game for throwing firecrackers and found to be in possession of six more. The red smoke of flares being ignited was evident all around the ground, and two police officers were injured when they were bombarded with stones after the game by Apollon fans.

Justice Minister Kypros Chrysostomides, on a visit to Larnaca Police Headquarters, pledged to tackle the problems and called it a *'plague against the spirit of sport'*.

On Thursday 27 March 2008 Ionas Nicolaou had to appeal for 'self-control' amongst members of the House of Legal Affairs Committee, who were debating the proposed new Bill on football violence.

Rikkos Erotokritou, from EVROKO the European Party, asked, *'why is AKEL the only party that is strongly opposed to my proposal for the addition of a provision that would strongly prohibit insults of our national memory in sporting areas through banners and chants'*. By way of an example he referred to a banner used by Omonia fans which read *'ISTANBUL 1453'* a reference to the year that Constantinople was taken over by Turkey, and the use of which was seen as a provocation by APOEL fans.

AKEL Deputy Aristophanis Georgiou responded by saying that his Party had been supporting the process of trying to find a solution to the problems of violence for the last three years, during which time they had attended more than two hundred sessions on the subject, as opposed to the three or four attended by Erotokritou.

AKEL maintained that there was no place for religious or political symbols in sport.

DIKO Deputy Nicolas Papadopoulos called for calm and said that his party had suggested that the clubs should have a list of what was acceptable to put on banners and that any breaches should lead to fans being penalised.

Early on Sunday 20 April 2008 a gang of more than twenty masked youths armed with bats, pick axe handles, and rocks attacked three men outside APOEL's clubhouse in Nicosia. The three were parked in a vehicle near to the club and the assumption was made that they were APOEL supporters. One of them, Michalis Michael, suffered a serious eye injury and potential loss of sight, as the attackers also tried to set fire to the clubhouse and caused damage.

One person was arrested at the time, and two others subsequently, but the attack caused an outcry, and led to a request by police for the forthcoming semi-final game between APOEL and

Omonia on the 23 April 2008 to be postponed.

After a meeting with the Cyprus Football Association this request was agreed to and the match was postponed until the 30 April 2008. It was to take more than three years for the court case to be concluded and for some form of justice to be seen to be done.

The President of Cyprus, Demetris Christofias also announced that he would chair a meeting on Tuesday 22 April 2008 with the Justice Minister, the Attorney General, and the Chief of Police, to discuss the problem of hooliganism.

After the meeting, which lasted ninety minutes, Government spokesman Stephanos Stephanou said that he thought that the reason that the problem would not go away was because of, *'the global crisis in values which inevitably effects our country as well'.*

There was talk about forming a social alliance against youth violence and hooligan behavior, and EDEK leader Yiannakis Omirou suggested twelve new measures to prevent a situation that, *'could only provoke shame in our society',* and said that it was high time the State took action. He added, *'it is a country which is occupied by a foreign nation, we cannot stand idly by and watch part of our younger generation squander itself on hooliganism. It is time everyone assumed our responsibilities'.*

On the 25 April 2008, *'Apoel Ultra'* posted on social media, *'Omonia fans are the disgrace of all Cypriot fans, they are pro-Turk and rabbits, they always run, their second name is green rabbits'*. It was the classic approach of de-personalising the opposition to make them look like an entity rather than a group of fellow human beings with families and feelings.

On Wednesday 30 April 2008 the delayed game between Omonia and APOEL took place at the GSP Stadium in Nicosia before a crowd of 11,920 supporters.

Omonia won the match with a score line of 2-1.

In May 2008 during a game between Omonia and APOEL, an Omonia fan was thrown down a flight of stairs on the terracing at the GSP Stadium. Fortunately the man was not seriously injured.

Anorthosis were crowned Champions at the end of the season with three games in hand, and without losing a single match.

On Wednesday 9 July 2008 the Apollon team was training in

their field next to Tsirion Stadium, whilst being watched by a number of supporters.

At about 6pm about thirty fans broke away from this group and went towards AEL's training field nearby. They set fire to bushes, defaced walls and tried to burn a number of wooden benches. It was not unusual for fans to turn up for their teams training sessions and up to 2,000 AEL fans had actually gathered for their teams opening session that season, with 3,000 Apollon fans attending their teams first training session, and 700 AEK fans in Larnaca.

As the police and fire service turned up they were attacked and two officers injured. One twenty-two year old fan broke the window of a police vehicle and threw a burning torch inside. An officer managed to retrieve it but burnt his hand in the process. All three of the officers were treated at Limassol Hospital and a warrant was issued for the arrest of the arsonist.

On the 1 August 2008 a meeting took place at the Ministry of Justice to discuss new legislation which had been passed as law on the 1 July 2008. Justice Minister Kypros Chrysostomides said that a special brochure would be produced to make people aware of the new provisions which, amongst other things, forbade the carrying of dangerous items inside stadiums.

He said that notices would be put outside grounds to list all such items and that the penalties for committing such an offence would range from a one to two year prison sentence, or fines of up to 2,000 euro. The display of banners containing provocative content would also be banned, as well as inflammatory statements by sports agents. The Justice Minister said, *'I hope that this year we will see a football season without violence, something which would correspond to our sport and culture civilisation'.*

Ionas Nicolaou added that the law would allow for a 'grace period' of three years for the implementation of ticketing systems, CCTV, and the training of supervisors in grounds.

The Cyprus Sports Federation (KOA) welcomed the new law and confirmed that it had around five million euro available for 2009/10 in order to start installing systems at stadiums, and that the first monitoring system would be put into the GSP stadium on a 'pilot' basis.

On Tuesday 19August 2008 the ground at Anorthosis FC at Kato Polemedia in Limassol was attacked for the third time when, during the early hours of the morning, windows were smashed and considerable damage caused. The club criticised the police for their lack of response and claimed that 'drunken young boys from opposing clubs' were probably to blame.

The Justice Minister held a further meeting during August 2008 to stress the need for all parties to work together but as if to highlight the *'mountains that needed to be climbed'* one Anorthosis supporter made the following comments after attending a cup game between APOEL and Anorthosis at the GSP Stadium in Nicosia on Saturday 23 August 2008, *'we got there forty-five minutes before the 6pm kick-off and APOEL were already shouting insulting political chants at us. These included 'You didn't fight to save Famagusta' and the insults continued throughout the match which we lost 1-0. This was doing my head in and if you hear this rubbish long enough it really winds you up and I wanted to cross over and fight those idiots'.*

On Wednesday 27 August 2008 Anorthosis played

Olympiakos Piraeus in Athens in the Champions League in a game which finished with a score line of 0-1. Hooligans from Olympiakos rained stones down on Anorthosis fans as they arrived at the stadium wearing Greek flags. In a moment of sheer irony, police with shields had to protect them in violent scenes that appeared on Cypriot TV.

Anorthosis officials condemned the violence and the fact that the Greek side had offered no apology. They also pointed out that the club chairman had been assaulted by a security guard as the team had turned up for training the day before, and that the Greek press had inflamed the situation.

On Thursday 28 August 2008 Omonia beat AEK Athens on aggregate in the UEFA Cup, whilst APOEL beat Crvena Zvezda in the same competition. President Demetris Christofias, and the rest of the political parties, rushed to praise the teams and Archbishop Chrysostomos expressed his warm congratulations saying, *'without doubt this great success of yours as well as the victories of our islands two other football teams honour our small island. We hope that God strengthens and supports you'.*

One TV presenter went further saying, *'we Cypriots have*

this. We are a people that have stubbornness. We have this obstinacy. We do not give up. We know how to fight. We keep going and we win'.

It was interesting to note the extent to which the team players in the three games actually came from Cyprus, with Anorthosis fielding just one Cypriot player in the starting line-up, and with three more on the bench.

Omonia had three Cypriot players starting with a further three substitutes, and APOEL had three Cypriot players starting with two others on the bench.

Of the forty-one players who actually made it onto the pitch, from the three teams, twenty-nine came from Brazil, Argentina, Albania, Croatia, Serbia, and Poland and played for three quarters of the games, whilst the remaining twelve Cypriot players played for the remaining quarter. To cap it all the coaches from all three teams were from foreign countries.

In the early hours of the following morning, between 1am and 2am, more than one hundred and fifty hooded APOEL fans came out onto the streets of Nicosia and started attacking vehicles bearing Omonia scarves, as well as cafes in the area of Makariou Avenue. Nicosia Police Chief Kypros Michalides said, *'wearing hoods and helmets and carrying iron bars they flooded Makarios Avenue and caused damage to cars and a particular café. These people chose to blacken their team victory'*.

Due to the sheer amount of vehicle traffic in the area, because of the celebrations, police vehicles were unable to get through to deal with incidents which also spread to Limassol Avenue, where APOEL fans outside their clubhouse threw stones at passing vehicles.

Four people were injured, including two women seated outside a café, who were hit by rocks, and needed hospital treatment, and seven cars were reported damaged, with three of the occupants being attacked inside.

On the morning of Friday 29 August 2008 sixteen back-packs loaded with teargas, flares and smoke bombs were found by police during a pre-match search of Tsirion Stadium, with Apollon due to play AEL next day. The backpacks were found in one of six store rooms, all of which had padlocks forced.

On Saturday 30 August 2008 a group of youths, obviously unaware of the discovery, went to the stadium and broke into a maintenance room. Two young men were arrested and remanded in custody by Limassol District Court, whilst an arrest warrant was issued for a third person.

The game itself finished with a win for AEL with a score line of 3-1.

The Cypriot First Division 2008/9 was the seventy-first season of top tier football in Cyprus and started on Saturday 30 August 2008. The defending champions were Anorthosis.

The season started off on a further bad note when a game in the First Division between Peyiaside APOP Kiniras and AEK Larnaca was abandoned after twelve minutes when police said that they could no longer guarantee the safety of the spectators.

Fans were throwing flares, smoke grenades, and firecrackers into the stands, and onto the pitch, and the stadium manager warned, by tannoy, that the match would be called off if they did not stop. His call went unheeded and as one flare hit the netting of one of the goals it was game over, as the police instructed the referee to abandon the match with the score standing at 1-1.

As rival fans left Peyia Municipal Stadium they began throwing stones at each and set off confetti cannons, one of which interfered with an 11kv overhead line near the stadium, and caused a power cut to all of Peyia village at 8.09pm, which was restored by the Electricity Authority (EAC) at 8.38pm.

Afterwards police, who blamed AEK fans for causing the trouble, found stadium seats sprayed with offensive graffiti.

No arrests were made, and the CFA announced that it would decide whether to replay the match or award points accordingly.

It was all very familiar with one genuine APOP Kirinas fan commenting, *'I was horrified to see the disgusting behaviour of some of the away supporters...I hope that the police make some arrests and the culprits are publicly named and shamed ....These thugs don't love football, they use the game as a 'reason' to behave badly. They're violent aggressive bullies, and should be made an example of '.*

Paphos Police Chief Costas Soteriou said, *'officers are*

currently studying CCTV footage and film from our own cameras to identify offenders. Make no mistake they will be identified in Larnaca and arrested. There are these types of hooligans all over the world and now we also have them in Cyprus football. It's a big shame and very sad for the players and teams'.

On Monday 1 September 2008, Justice Minister Kypros Chrysostomides said that the Government was determined to enforce the new law in relation to football violence in full.

On the same date the Head of Police in Nicosia Kypros Michaelides stressed that the police would only make three warnings to unruly crowds, and that a zero-tolerance approach would be taken.

On Saturday 20 September 2008 it was announced by the UEFA Treasurer Marios Lefkaritis that Turkish Cypriots had turned down a proposal by FIFA and UEFA that their 'federation' should join the Cyprus Football Association.

On Monday 22 September 2008 Apollon played Omonia at Tsirion Stadium. Prior to the match starting a twenty-four year old Apollon fan, from Limassol, was arrested and remanded in custody after trying to enter the ground whilst in possession of 1.5 grams of cannabis, and two firecrackers. A search of his home address revealed another half a gram of cannabis.

During the first-half opposing fans chanted obscenities at each other and threw flares. In the second half, with Apollon losing 2-0, fans began to set fire to stands and fired flares onto the pitch as the final whistle approached. The police officer in charge called for the game to be abandoned, as he could no longer guarantee safety, as seats were set on fire and rocks hurled.

Outside the stadium in Stelios Kyriakides Street, fans hurled rocks and as a result four police officers were taken to Limassol Hospital with minor injuries. At this stage the Justice Minister supported police action, as did the Police Chief Iacovos Papacostas. Four persons were arrested aged between sixteen-years to nineteen-years.

This was now the second game at the start of the new season where police had called a halt to the match.

At a meeting on Friday 26 September 2008, chaired by the Justice Minister, it was determined that the referee would have the final say as to whether or not a football match would be interrupted, and that the police would have to comply with this decision. The parties present included the CFA, Cyprus Sports Association, Attorney General, Referees Association and representatives of the First Division Clubs as well as the Police who argued that they should be responsible for what took place off the pitch.

It was eventually decided by the Justice Minister that the police could offer advice to the referee depending on what was going on in the stands, but that the final decision to abandon a game rested entirely with the referee. The Justice Minister made it clear that whilst the police could ask for reinforcements under no circumstances would they depart from a match and that they must stay and protect supporters and the referee. This decision seemed to 'fly in the face' of the comments made on the 1 September 2008.

On the 2 October 2008 the 14th European Fair Play Congress entitled, *'Violence and Racism, a Challenge to the Sporting Community'*, was held in Nicosia, sponsored by the European Fair Play Movement and the Cyprus Sports Organisation.

During the two-day seminar, speeches and lectures were heard from delegates from forty countries, and addressing the congress on behalf of the President Demetris Christofias, Undersecretary Titos Christofides said, *'violence and racism are social phenomena developing outside sports venues and with variable ways are being transferred to sports. It should not be neglected that sport as such does not promote violence or racism'*.

On Monday 27 October 2008 Anorthosis lost to Omonia 4-0 in Nicosia, and after the match Anorthosis fans boarded three buses to take them back to Larnaca. During the course of the trip back several fans started throwing stones at passing vehicles, and as they got to Rizoelia roundabout, at the entrance to Larnaca, one of the buses was brought to a halt. Several fans alighted and again started pelting passing vehicles.

As the police arrived many of the fans fled on foot and the three buses were then escorted to Aradippou Police Station. As a result of this disturbance nineteen vehicles were damaged and two men slightly injured who were treated at Larnaca General Hospital and discharged.

On Saturday 8 November 2008 AEK played AEL at Larnaca's GSZ Stadium but the match was stopped, with a score line of 2-0, as AEL fans burnt down the Physiotherapy Room and assaulted police officers.

The police subsequently released CCTV pictures of suspects and six arrests were made initially. After a further press release four others were arrested and charged, all of whom admitted their part in the disturbances. Two gave themselves up, one was found by the police, and another was picked out by an anonymous informant. Local police said at the time that they were still looking for a fifth person who had hit a police officer with a fire extinguisher. The officer received severe bruises to his head and face but was undoubtedly saved from serious injury by the fact that he was wearing a helmet.

The Police Chief Iacovos Papacostas expressed his grief at the public's apathy in trying to identify offenders from the pictures released.

On the same date APOEL played AEL in a basketball game at the Lefkotheo Athletic Centre in Nicosia. Violence broke out as up to two hundred APOEL fans threw stones and a police officer sustained a wound to his right arm. An AEL coach, a trainer, and a player were all injured and the team had to be escorted from the premises in police vehicles. One other person was also injured as twenty windows were smashed and two fire extinguishers stolen. The damage was estimated to be somewhere in the region of 3,000 euro.

On Friday 28 November 2008 it was reported that UEFA's Control and Disciplinary Board had fined APOEL 30,000 euro after finding its fans guilty of engaging in racist behaviour during a game with Red Star Belgrade in late August 2008.

The fine related to a home-tie with the former European Champions, who APOEL went on to beat on the away goals rule in the return leg in Belgrade. Andis Polydorou the APOEL club vice-chairman and lawyer, who handled the case, said that it indicated that UEFA had a zero-tolerance attitude towards racism, whether it be chants or symbols worn, and that it could have been much worse had it not been their first offence.

On the same day Police Chief Iacovos Papacostas announced an investigation by his Headquarters CID into alleged financial irregularities at Anorthosis FC following complaints made by seven members of the Board against the club president Andreas Panteli who said he was 'disappointed and shocked' at the stance of his colleagues, and the rumours circulating.

Anorthosis fans took to the streets in Larnaca to demonstrate over the issue which was alleged to involve the theft of 500,00 euro in cash, and one million euro in cheques. The team-coach Temuri Ketsbaia announced that he was standing by his president's side.

The following day it was highlighted in the press by local councillor Linda Leblanc that one third of the annual budget of Peyia municipality was being spent on the local football team APOP Kinyras Peyia, in the same week that there had been claims of positive dope testing against two of their players.

She highlighted the fact that, from an annual budget of six million euro, two million euro had been spent on the club. This was at a time when it was widely acknowledged that Peyia did not have enough medical facilities to support the community, many of whom were British ex Pats.

In 2007 everyone who was a member of the local council had been offered a free season-pass to the club, an offer which

Councillor Leblanc had declined.

In December 2008 speculation started to rise that Turkish Cypriot clubs would re-join the Cyprus Football Association.

On Friday 5 December 2008, during a game between APOEL and Anorthosis at the GSP Stadium in Larnaca, attended by 11,566 supporters, stones were hurled at the police, resulting in one officer suffering head injuries. The game was won by APOEL with a score line of 1-0.

During the early hours of Sunday 7 December 2008 someone placed six camping gas canisters outside Omonia FC and set them alight at about 2.30am. Police arrived and put the fire out.

Also on Sunday 7 December 2008 Apollon played Doxas in a match in Limassol which was stopped in the 51st minute of play by the referee, when a man wearing a balaclava went onto the pitch and attacked a linesman. The masked man hit the official in his back causing him to lose his balance and fall to the ground.

At the time there were only five police officers on the pitch itself for some unexplained reason, which became the subject of an internal investigation. As they tried to arrest the offender they were pelted with missiles, by fans in the Western stand, and he made good his escape. The linesman was taken to Limassol General Hospital for treatment and the game abandoned.

At this point fans destroyed seats and a room in the West Stand. Others tried to storm the pitch but were prevented from doing so by the police. Four police vehicles were subsequently damaged, as well as the vehicle belonging to Tsirion Stadium's Technical Director.

The following day the Justice Minister backed the idea of posting photographs of banned hooligans at the gates of stadiums as a means of *'naming and shaming'* them.

On Tuesday 9 December 2008 APOEL FC was attacked and glass panes shattered causing damage valued at 3,000 euro. During the course of 2008 Law number 4/2008 was enacted to deal with the prevention and suppression of acts of violence at sports grounds which was to be amended in 2012 to introduce rules on stewarding.

At the end of 2008 the Cyprus Police recorded thirty-eight cases relating to football.

***

On Saturday 17 January 2009 Omonia played APOEL at Nicosia's GSP Stadium in a game which APOEL won 1- 0. Violent incidents occurred between Omonia and APOEL fans as an Omonia player was sent off in stoppage time of the first-half.

Omonia fans burst through a security barrier, separating the two sets of fans, and hurled stones at their opponents. MMAD officers were deployed, and used tear gas to disperse the fans, and one officer received a serious foot injury that required surgery. Twenty fans were treated in the ground for respiratory problems.

The violence led to fourteen supporters, and nineteen police officers, being treated at Nicosia General Hospital. Police officers were subsequently accused of using 'excessive violence' finding themselves once again in a 'no win' situation. One MMAD officer was suspended from duty.

En route to the game, masked youths targeted cars with Turkish number plates, and in one incident smashed the windscreen and windows of a vehicle which was stationary at traffic lights.

The Turkish-Cypriot occupants, which included a child, were unhurt and they were assisted by Greek-Cypriots passing by.

Although this had the potential for 'political fallout', all parties recognised that such attacks were rare, following the opening of the crossing points six years previously, and that it was the work of 'football fanatics' rather than 'extremists'.

In a separate incident, a bus loaded with Omonia fans was stoned, and as they disembarked to respond to their attackers two Traffic police officers were injured.

A total of five people were arrested during the disturbances.

In the aftermath, Omonia blamed the police for getting their own back, as the AKEL government was seen to be cracking down on the police force, following the arrest of two Drug Squad officers. Omonia maintained that their political affiliation to AKEL made them a target.

Nicosia police Superintendent Kypros Michaelides denied the allegations and said that the police were merely trying to do their job. He pointed out that in one incident alone, two police officers had been trapped against a wall by one hundred fans, who were hurling stones at them.

On Sunday 25 January 2009 a large-scale disturbance took place at the Antonis Papadopoulos Stadium in Larnaca when Omonia fans caused damage valued at 34,000 euros. The game ended in a win for Omonia against Anorthosis, with a score line of 2-1 and a crowd attendance of 8,000 supporters.One of those involved in the trouble, a twenty-three year old, was later sentenced to seven months imprisonment. He was shown on CCTV wielding an iron bar, which he used to smash stadium furniture, whilst Omonia fans 'egged him on' to cries of *'Ole'* every time he made a strike.

During that season Omonia FC paid out 150,000 euro in fines to the football association for trouble caused by its supporters.

On this particular date, clashes broke out in Larnaca, on the stadium car park, as supporters pelted each other with rocks. Thirty-four police officers, and two supporters, suffered minor injuries and were treated at Larnaca General Hospital. Twelve vehicles were also damaged and the situation was reported to have been out of control for some forty-five minutes before police finally restored order. No arrests were made.

The windscreen of a police patrol car escorting buses back to Nicosia was smashed when fans hurled a bottle at it. On arrival in Nicosia other Omonia fans attacked the same police vehicle with rocks, at which point the officers withdrew.

On Tuesday 27 January 2009 politicians once again condemned the violence, saying, *'hooliganism and fanaticism have taken on epidemic proportions'*. The Justice Minister Loucas Louca indicated that he was considering changing the times of games, so that the police could operate more effectively during daylight hours, and also banning fans from some games.

At the end of January 2009 during a House Legal Affairs Committee meeting to discuss the previous weekend's violence the Police Chief Iacovos Papacostas said that, *'the police were scared'*, although he did not elaborate on what he meant by this astonishing statement.

Following discussions, where fifteen new measures were also debated, it was decided to send a directive to all District Court Judges that they should try to deal with all football related cases within fifteen days.

Committee Chairman Ionas Nicolaou said afterwards, *'we are observing hooliganism being turned against the police to the point where policemen themselves are starting to get frightened'.*

DIKO Deputy Nicolas Papadopoulos said, *'We should be ashamed as a state when the police are saying that they are too scared to monitor high risk games'.*

The Committee were asked to review the legislation passed in 2008 as there was a view that very little of it had actually been put into practice.

All this was against a backcloth of club websites often referring to, *'hate them for 90 minutes',* in the run up to high profile games.

On Sunday 15 February 2009 Apollon played APOEL at Tsirion Stadium in Limassol.

There were no incidents during the course of the game, which was heavily policed by three hundred Officers, including MMAD units.

APOEL won the game 1-0, and the end of the match was the signal for violence, from elements within the crowd of 8,936 supporters.

Outside the stadium, two groups of opposing fans, numbering up to one hundred and fifty in each group, confronted each other, and engaged in 'hand to hand' fist fighting and stone-throwing. A group of seventy APOEL fans then made their way to Ivikou Street, situated to the east of the stadium, and near to the Ayia Phlya roundabout. They then started to attack the residential area, which was unguarded, as police resources were focused elsewhere.

One fan set a car on fire with a Molotov cocktail, oblivious to the fact that it was actually owned by an APOEL supporter. Fourteen vehicles were damaged in total as well as three houses, and two shops, one of which had only just been renovated. Residents who came out of their homes to plead with the group to stop were threatened with violence. One female resident said, *'we felt thoroughly unprotected. We were literally hiding in our houses and they were throwing stones at us through our windows. It was terror'.*

Some of those involved were seen leaving the area in a van

and one of the residents managed to take details of the licence plate which were passed onto the police.

A police patrol car subsequently stopped the vehicle, on the Limassol to Nicosia Highway at the Moni Exit, and the occupants, thirteen people aged between 21 years to 37 years, all from Nicosia, were taken to Limassol Police HQ for questioning.

Some of residents who had been subjected to the attack identified this group as being involved and were able to point out one of them as being the person responsible for throwing the Molotov cocktail. They all appeared at Limassol District Court on Monday 16 February 2009 and were remanded.

Despite all the violence, and the rhetoric spoken afterwards in support of the police, at a meeting held on Thursday 19 February 2009 all parties backed away from imposing any real new measures.

On Sunday 8 March 2009 Anorthosis played APOEL at the Antonis Papadopoulos Stadium in Larnaca with a 4pm kick-off. Police had already stipulated that Anorthosis would occupy the West, North and East stands, whilst APOEL would take the South stands. A total of 9,500 supporters turned up to watch the game which APOEL won with a score line of 2-1.

After the end of the match, whilst fans were leaving the ground, a twenty-year old man attacked a young police officer and pushed him to the ground. Together with a juvenile he then proceeded to kick the officer in various parts of his body, until they were both arrested by officers from MMAD. A third person aged twenty-nine years, who was a relative of the twenty-year old, got involved, and after attacking a MMAD Sergeant, he was also arrested. All three were charged to appear at Larnaca District Court on March 16 2009.

On the same date a basketball game took place between APOEL and AEL, at the Spyros Kyprianou Sporting Centre, in Limassol. Before the game, three hundred APOEL fans were escorted into the centre by police with AEL fans already in situ. APOEL fans were allowed to leave first and AEL fans were requested to remain in their seats to avoid confrontations.

AEL fans then proceeded to attack police at the exits to the centre and after making their way outside confronted APOEL fans, with stones being thrown and MMAD Units deployed. As two young brothers, aged just twelve years and fifteen years, were making their way to their mother's car, who was waiting to pick them up, they were attacked by up to twenty five people who punched and kicked them.

The twelve-year-old suffered extensive bruising whilst the fifteen-year-old suffered a head injury whilst trying to protect his brother. Their father said, *'I heard on the 11 o'clock news that the boys had been injured. At first I didn't believe that it could be my sons, but ten minutes later I found it was my children. If it wasn't for the four or five people who intervened to save my 12-year-old who was being kicked all over as he was on the ground I don't know what would be happening today'.* His wife took the boys to Limassol General Hospital but after apparently waiting for an hour for treatment she took them to a private clinic.

AEL Manager Charis Papadopoulos said, *'if any violent incidents took place outside the stadium of course we condemn them. I am not aware of how it started and to what degree they were. What happens outside the stadium is the responsibility of the police'.*

The police were then blamed by AEL by not complying with

the arrangements for the game which had previously been agreed with the club.

As a result of the disturbances three people were injured, as well as four police officers. Six private vehicles were damaged plus a police car and a police motorbike. One arrest was made after a twenty-eight year old man went to Limassol Police Station to report damage to his car and was recognised by a police officer as having been involved in the disturbances.

On the morning of Tuesday 10 March 2009 a swastika, and the name APOEL, was found spray-painted on the wall of the Soloneion Book Centre in Nicosia.

During the weekend of the 14 and 15 March 2009 further incidents of violence occurred at three games.

On Saturday 14 March 2009 at the end of a game, which took place in Paphos, between APOP Kinyra Peyias and Omonia, that Omonia lost with a score line of 2-0, around two hundred supporters from both teams gathered at the stadium's side- entrance and began to throw stones at players. Two Omonia players were injured, and damage caused to the team bus. The bus then had to be escorted back to Nicosia by the police.

At Larnaca, after a game between AEK and Anorthosis, which was won by Anorthosis with a score line of 3-1, fans threw stones and damaged a vehicle. During a game, between Enosis Neou Paraliminiou and APEP, police confiscated firecrackers, and a firework, and made one arrest.

On Sunday 22March 2009 AEL played APOEL in Limassol, in front of a crowd of 5,690supporters, and whilst the game itself, which APOEL won with a score line of 1-0, was quiet, fighting broke out afterwards, as AEL fans tried to break through police lines to get to APOEL fans, and stones and firebombs were thrown.

After the violence the CFA dismissed any thoughts of banning away fans from high-risk games. At the same time it was highlighted that due to a backlog some cases relating to football violence were taking up to two years to come to trial.

On Friday 24 April 2009 police provided a heavy police presence for a volleyball game between Anorthosis and Omonia, at Larnaca's Kition Athletic Stadium. The Cyprus Volleyball Cup match was attended by 1,000 supporters, in a game which ended in a

3-2 win for Omonia and saw them crowned as 2009 champions.

Before the game, fans entered the stadium and threw stones at each other. MMAD officers intervened and two officers received face and hand injuries, which required hospital treatment, following clashes with Omonia fans. After the game officers were stoned by Anorthosis fans, and a third officer was injured as police vehicles were damaged. A bus waiting to transport Omonia fans back to Nicosia was attacked and the windscreen and windows smashed. Three other people sustained injuries in the fighting.

The following day the police were again present in numbers at the Antonis Papadopoulos Stadium for a game between Anorthosis and APOEL, with 2,500 tickets being allocated to APOEL fans, and the same number given to Anorthosis.

On Sunday 10May 2009 APOEL played Omonia at Nicosia GSP Stadium with APOEL already technically the champions. A total of 6,250 fans turned up to watch the game. Even before the referees whistle blew at the start of the match a group of fans stormed through gates of the northern tier, which was reserved for Omonia fans, looking for a fight.

After Omonia scored the first goal both sets of fans hurled smoke-bombs and firecrackers onto the pitch. Referee Panicos Andronikon, and his assistants, went to the centre of the pitch, to wait for things to quieten down, but as the Omonia goalkeeper was struck by a firecracker he made his way to the tunnel with his assistants, and had to be persuaded to return by club officials.

After the game re-started, Omonia scored a second goal and at this point a loud firecracker was set off in the intersection of two of the stands, seconds after the fourth Assistant had held up a board showing that twenty three minutes of extra time had been added on due to the interruptions in play. At this point the referee decided that enough was enough and abandoned the game.

Departing fans clashed with police in the parking lot outside, and as police deployed teargas, shrubs were set on fire. Some APOEL fans went back inside the ground and attacked a group of six girls on the North Stand who had remained behind. For a short period Limassol Avenue in Nicosia was closed by police as disturbances continued.

Nine people were injured, one of whom was treated at

Nicosia Hospital for head injuries, and six people were arrested, two of whom, a nineteen year old, and a twenty year old, were charged.

Neither team coach turned up for the post match press conferences and APOEL Club Chairman Fivos Erotokritou said, *'under these circumstances it's not worth being in football'.*

The CFA decided that the match would not be counted in the table of results but would be considered as being played.

On the 10 May 2009 the season finished with APOEL winning the championship three match weeks before the end of the season. Sadly, statistics in relation to points allocated by the CFA, rather than being based on the full time score, followed a familiar trend:

- **a)** APOP Kinyras versus AEK – awarded to APOP with a score of 2-0 after being abandoned due to crowd violence.

- **b)** Omonia versus Apollon – awarded to Omonia with a score of 2-0 after being abandoned due to crowd violence.

- **c)** AEK Larnaca versus AEL – awarded to AEK with a score of 2-0 after being abandoned due to crowd violence.

d) Doxa Katokopias versus Apollon – awarded to Doxa with a score of 2-0 after being abandoned due to crowd violence.

***

On Thursday 14 May 2009 a media report highlighted the plight of one resident living near to one of the official AEL clubhouses in Limassol who said, *'People are there day and night, every day drinking, shouting, chanting, setting off firecrackers in the street and blocking traffic'.* When he took his concerns to a senior police officer in Limassol it was alleged that he was told that there was nothing they could do. A police spokesman later said, *'we're not God Almighty. We can't sort everything out to everybody's satisfaction but we do all we can to uphold law and order'.*

He also confirmed that AEL fans had attacked the Apollon clubhouse in Limassol a few days before, and that police were monitoring the area.

During the early hours of Thursday 6 August 2009 violence again came to the streets of Nicosia. Disturbances broke out after APOEL succeeded in progressing to the final UEFA Champions League qualifying round. They were defeated 1-0 away to Partizan

Belgrade but secured a place in the next round on a 2-1 aggregate win.

At around 11.40pm, the previous evening, around two hundred APOEL fans gathered outside their club in Nicosia, whilst at the same time a police patrol car was sent as a precautionary measure to patrol the area around the Omonia clubhouse in Pallouriotissa.

At 12.30am a group of up to twenty people left the Omonia club house and started moving towards Makarios Avenue where they then caused damage to cars by throwing stones. Upon the arrival of police however, they dispersed and went back to their own clubhouse.

At 1.30am a group of fifty APOEL fans went on foot to the Omonia club- house, where there was a confrontation between the two rival factions and stones were thrown, during which three passing vehicles were damaged.

Police intervened and arrested a twenty-three year old student at the scene on suspicion of assault, public assault, affray, and resist arrest. Officers said that he had been bare-chested and wearing a black T-shirt to hide his face whilst he pelted Omonia fans with stones and all the time was shouting obscenities. He had allegedly been standing to one side of the main group, which had made it easier to arrest him, and despite trying to run off he was tackled to the floor and handcuffed by two officers.

He duly appeared in Court, on the same day, when a police officer from the Minor Crimes Unit (MCU) asked for a remand in custody for six days, on the basis that he needed to take up to thirty statements from family members to try to see if he could establish the prior intent of the accused, and to speak to people at the two fan clubs. He also said that ten local residents had reported damage to their property and that these reports needed to be investigated.

For his part, despite being advised by his Solicitor to say nothing, the accused told the court that he wanted to make a formal complaint against the police, whom he alleged had assaulted him when arrested. Standing in the court wearing jeans, and a T- shirt, he had red marks on his chin and lips, and scrape-marks on both arms. He was seen to smirk as the circumstances of his arrest were detailed to the court.

District Judge Stavros Stavrou took a different view to the remand request and said that the damage caused to neighbour's properties had nothing to do with the case and couldn't understand why the police would want to speak to anyone at the two fan clubs. He insisted that the officer had 'highly exaggerated' the need for a six day remand, bearing in mind that the main evidence for the case would come from the arresting officers, and remanded the accused in custody for just twenty-four hours.

On Friday 7 August 2009 a seventeen year old schoolboy appeared at Nicosia District Court, in connection with the same disturbances, charged with public assault (swearing in public) and causing a disturbance and a commotion.

Police applied for a remand in custody for four days, which Judge Olga Loizou rejected, on the basis that he had already admitted his part in the offences. She pointed out that the first charge carried a maximum penalty of one month in prison and/or a fine of 128 euro and was therefore not a charge to warrant depriving an individual of their freedom. She went on, *'despite the alarming rise in hooliganism the remand process cannot be used as a deterrent.*

Clamping down on this phenomenom is done through the courts, and by way of sentencing, and not by remanding a suspect'.

A second seventeen-year old schoolboy, a friend of the other seventeen year old, appeared on the same date before another Judge Tasos Katsikides, who heard similar evidence, but determined that the individual could be remanded for two days in custody.

Both sets of parents expressed their dissatisfaction with the way in which the police had handled the case. They alleged that they first came to notice when the first youth attended hospital, with a head injury received during the fighting, and was asked to visit the police station during the day to discuss how he had come about his injury. He duly did so and admitted his part as well as naming his friend as also being present. The second youth attended the station and made a 'willing statement' but parents claimed that this had all been done without their knowledge or the presence of a solicitor.

On Tuesday 18 August 2009 a 'friendly' game took place between AEL and Anorthosis at the Antonis Papadopoulos Stadium, in Larnaca, which ended in a 0-0 draw. At the end of the game up to five hundred fans, from both sets of supporters, threw stones at each other during clashes which lasted for forty minutes and turned the area around Papanikoli Avenue into a battlefield.

During the trouble the windscreens of five police vehicles were smashed, and damage was caused to four private vehicles. Damage valued at ten thousand euros was also caused to the reception area of the ground, and one police officer was slightly injured, and received hospital treatment.

A twenty-one year old from Limassol was arrested in connection with the trouble and remanded in custody for two days, when he appeared in court on the 19 August, charged with common assault and public profanity.

After the game the Cyprus Police Association condemned the violence and a spokesman said, *'unfortunately hooliganism in Cyprus continues to be on the rise while in other countries it has been wiped out'*. They said that they were looking at measures to put forward to the government to protect their members.

At the beginning of September 2009 police announced that they would not allow any matches to take place at four stadiums from the 11 September 2009 unless they complied with the recommendations of a review, which had been carried out on nine grounds in June 2009, by the Fire Service Safety Department.

Justice Minister Loucas Louca made it clear that the four stadiums at Makario in Nicosia, Tsirion in Limassol, Pafiako in Paphos, and the new GSZ in Larnaca, would have to deal with issues relating to crowd exit points and poor access for the fire service.

The Cyprus Sports Association (KOA), who owned two of the stadiums, undertook to pay for the work that they needed to complete, but KOA president Nicos Kartakoullis criticised clubs, and the CFA, for being happy to take hundreds of thousands of euros each year from ticket sales whilst failing to spend one cent on safety shortcomings.

On the 6 November 2009 the House Legal Affairs Committee highlighted the fact that the majority of basketball stadiums were unsuitable to host games, with the only one in Cyprus classified as fit for purpose being Tasos Papadopoulos Eleftheria in Nicosia. Police had made inspections and recommendations that had largely been ignored.

The chairman of the Basketball Federation Giorgos

Chrysostomou said, *'unfortunately these arenas cannot host supporters of both teams – but even if they did the mentality and behaviour of fans do not allow co-existence'.* Some of the stadiums did not have seats or even segregated toilet facilities.

Police subsequently announced that in the 2008/9 season, a total of eighty- three people were arrested for football related offences, many of which were for assault.

It was however noted that very few trials had been completed and Deputies complained that many investigations were not even completed. Chair of the House Legal Affairs Committee Ionas Nicolaou complained about, *'the tolerance shown all these years towards unruly fans'.*

The 2009/10, seventy-second season, of the Cyprus First Division started on the 29 August 2009 with APOEL as the defending Champions.

In September 2009 APOEL played Chelsea FC in the first leg of the Champions League in a game in Nicosia which they lost 1-0. During the course of the game 'nationalist chants' were heard from one section of the ground which the club chairman, Fivos

Erotocritou, described as *'disgusting and mindless'*. Three months later APOEL was fined 40,000 euro for racist behaviour by UEFA.

On Sunday 25 October 2009 AEL played APOP Kiniros Peyias in Peyia in a game which AEL lost 1-0.

Before the game some fans made their way to the ground setting off a continuous air-siren, and started five fires in Spyros Kyprianou Street, as well as littering the road with beer bottles. Graffiti was sprayed onto the front gates of houses and windows were smashed as the police and fire service raced to the scene.

An eighteen year old from Limassol, who was part of a group who set fire to dry scrubland, was arrested as two cars and a fire truck were damaged. A nineteen-year old National Guardsman, also from Limassol, was also arrested for swearing at a police officer.

On Sunday 15 November 2009 a confrontation took place at the Nuevo Campo futsal ground where APOEL fans on their way to Larnaca attacked Omonia fans, who were organising a five-a-side football tournament.

One twenty-year old APOEL fan was beaten with hockey

sticks, and almost lost his life with head trauma. He was placed on a ventilator in Nicosia General Hospital. The attack had nothing to do with the weekend's football fixtures but was just part of the ongoing vendetta between the two sets of fans.

The Cyprus Mail reminded the public that just eighteen months previously another APOEL fan was blinded, and yet another doused in petrol, and told that he would be set alight. Fortunately he was not, but who knows what would have gone through that person's mind in those immediate seconds after being threatened.

As usual there was more than one version of events.

On their official website APOEL fans said that they had been travelling to Larnaca when they were ambushed on the motorway by stone-throwing Omonia fans, who were attending a youth tournament, at a futsal ground nearby. They claimed that to protect their vehicles, and themselves, APOEL fans then chased Omonia fans to the futsal ground where they were confronted by up to one hundred Omonia fans armed with hockey sticks, iron bars, stones and sticks.

A photograph in the daily *'POLITIS'* showed three Omonia

fans using hockey sticks to beat a man on the ground who was wearing an orange T-shirt - the colours of APOEL.

On the official website of Omonia fans it was claimed that APOEL fans had come out of their vehicles, wearing hoods and crash-helmets, and attacked people, including children attending the tournament. They claimed to have video which clearly showed that APOEL fans were the attackers and that they had hurled flares and stones.

One witness claimed to have seen APOEL fans on the motorway taunting and throwing stones before the fighting started.

On YouTube there is a video produced by *'ApOelaRa1979'* showing scenes from the attack. In 2015 it recorded 24,595 views, with 68 likes, and 113 dislikes, and compares the attack on the APOEL fan with the attack in 1996 on a Greek Cypriot by Turkish police. At one point still pictures of both attacks are shown, side-by-side, in a heavily politicised script.

'OmoniaSupporters92' uploaded their own version of events onto YouTube, which in 2015 had received 82,651 views with 272 likes, 69 dislikes, and a staggering 311 comments. Nothing is left to

the imagination in terms of its portrayal of brutality and a sense of 'triumph over the opposition' with victory music and chants of *'Gate 9 Anti Fascists'* and *'They shall not pass'*.

One comment from *'Apoel le le kai tre lelele'* said, *'I'm not fascist and I do not like the swastikas nor Golden Dawn or Hitler as you believe. I support APOEL and I just love my nation. I don't follow this bullshit. But you seriously need to open up your mind'*.

Later in the day the game between Nea Salamina and APOEL was cut short in Larnaca due to violence. The game was interrupted twice before, in the 75th minute, the referee abandoned the game as fans threw stones at each other, and at the assistant referee, and police struggled on the terraces to keep order.

Seven police officers were injured after the game, when more stones were thrown, after which the police suggested to the CFA that away supporters should be banned for high-risk games.

It was subsequently confirmed that the police had been at the scene of the incident at Nuevo Campo earlier but had left when it had been assumed that all of the APOEL fans going to the match had passed through the area.

CFA chairman Nicos Kartakoulis said, *'this is not an issue of sport anymore. There are political implications, social implications and economic implications. It is out of control. We are one stop before disaster'*.

Justice Minister Loucas Louca said, *'the critical injury was the tip of the iceberg and the use of force is the only option'*.

On the 16 November 2009 Antenna Channel said it would change the format of its radio sports show 'Kerkida' by refusing to take calls from ordinary fans, and in future only taking calls from sports officials and club representatives.

Replay Television said that for one month they would stop showing a ticker at the bottom of the screen that featured SMS messages sent by fans and would no longer host press releases from clubs which were regarded as having 'incendiary' content.

In a twist to the story, on Thursday 19 November 2009 the Police Chief launched an internal administrative investigation after it was disclosed that the police had received a tip-off about the possibility of pre-planned trouble at Nuevo Campo, and there was pressure to establish how the information had been assessed and acted upon.

The Justice Minister was initially somewhat 'put out' because he only learnt about this from a third party, but he later supported the police in saying that they received lots of tip-offs and that the disturbance could have taken place 'in any one of fifty places'.

Three people were later arrested and charged with causing grievous bodily harm, which carried a maximum life sentence in the Assizes Court. Two of the three were already facing football related charges in respect of other matters.

Two others were charged with rioting and released, and the injured APOEL fan also faced a charge of rioting. In the following days two further arrests of a twenty year old, and twenty-six year old took place.

This incident once again raised the level of debate, with some people pointing towards ever increasing violence in schools, and a lack of discipline brought about by the Ministry of Education introducing charters on *respect for children's rights'*.

The Chairman of the House Education Committee however said, '...*we need a comprehensive national strategy and the forging of a unified line'*.

Some people highlighted the way in which many countries, including the UK, clamped down hard on trouble-makers, with mass arrests and zero-tolerance, but it was pointed out that such an approach would not be popular in Cyprus where Deputies, Journalists and the Human Rights Commissioner would treat it as an affront to the principles of democracy itself in Cyprus.

Professor Andros Kapardis, a leading criminologist at the University of Cyprus said, *'it's time we stopped talking about hooliganism and started doing something about it'*.

He suggested that a task-force be set up dedicated to constraining sports related violence and wanted matches to be seen as 'celebrations' as opposed to 'battles'. He went on, *'without doubt it's related to violence in the schools and in the family. Many of these guys commit offences outside sports grounds'*. *

On Friday 20 November 2009 the Cyprus Footballers Association held a press conference themselves where their chairman Spyros Neofytides announced that they would walk onto the pitch that weekend wearing black T-shirts printed with *'No Violence'* and hold red cards in their hands.

APOEL midfielder Marinos Satsias said, *'football clubs are not enemies but rivals. The only thing that separates us is the ninety minutes on the field'.*

***

Footnote.* *In 1987 I ran an undercover police operation targeting Birmingham City FC's hooligan element who were known as the Zulu Warriors. The operation was known as Operation Red Card. It resulted in sixty-seven arrests and did severe damage to their ability to mount organized attacks – the majority of which were conducted outside football grounds.*

***

At 2.30am on Saturday 21 November 2009 a bomb blast occurred at the offices of Minerva Insurance Company, owned by the CFA Chairman Costas Koutsokoumnis, in Omirou Street in Limassol. The Limassol Police Chief Yiannikis Georgiou confirmed that an improvised explosive device was used which shattered windows.

Koutsokoumnis said that he had received a threatening phone call, the previous day, from someone purporting to be an AEL fan who warned him that a bomb would be planted at his offices due the fact that Leontios Trattos had been appointed as referee for a game between ARIS Limassol and Omonia.

AEL fans blamed Trattos for losing the Cup the previous season. Koutsokoumnis said he had told friends, but not the police, because he received so many threats but said later on state radio, *'It is clearly a terrorist act exclusively covering football matters'*. Police however urged people not to 'jump to conclusions'.

A thirty-six year old man from Nicosia was subsequently arrested in connection with the bombing.

On Thursday 3 December 2009 the Cyprus Mail reported on the remand of a twenty-six year old from Limassol district for twenty-four hours on suspicion of making a threatening phone call. The suspect was a coach at the football academy of a local team and he was arrested in relation to a telephone call which was made on the 24 November 2009, three days after the bomb attack, to the offices of the CFA Chairman, where threats were made against Costas Koutsokoumnis.

The call was traced to the suspect's phone. In court he admitted that he was the owner of the phone, but denied making the call in question.

On Friday 4 December 2009 another person aged twenty-two-years was arrested in connection with the attack at Nuevo Campo.

On Tuesday 8 December 2009 APOEL played Chelsea at Stamford Bridge, in the UK, in a Champions League fixture which ended in a 2-2 draw.

Ferzi Hussein, the chairman of a Turkish Cypriot organization called *'Embargoed'* claimed in the North Cyprus Free Press to have worked closely with the Metropolitan Police on 'spotting patrols' to ensure that there was no racist action by the 3,000 visiting Greek Cypriot fans.

He was shown posing in a photograph standing next to a police sergeant and a banner left in Fulham Road which read,

'Chelsea fans support a free and united Cyprus'. In any event the area was a virtual sea of Greek flags and no issues were reported.

Takis Antoniou, a Board member from APOEL, dismissed the report as a fabrication and that no concerns had been raised during meetings with Chelsea and UEFA.

On Sunday 13 December 2009 Omonia played APOEL in Nicosia at the GSP Stadium in a game which ended in a 1-1 draw.

Amid fears of reprisals, relating to the Nuevo Campo attack, three hundred and thirty police officers were deployed in and around the stadium, two sections of which were left empty to segregate the fans. Protective nets were placed behind each goal to prevent objects being thrown at the goalkeepers from the crowd of 16,500 supporters.

Two people, who were on a list of nine known troublemakers, were stopped from entering the ground. One of them was arrested after it was deemed that he had deliberately tried to breach the order, and the second, who had not previously known about the ban, was escorted home by police.

The previous day the Chairmen of both clubs held a joint press conference denouncing violence, and Omonia even congratulated APOEL on their performance in the Champions League. In any event the game passed off peacefully and a police spokesman commented, *'this proves that whenever people are willing and determined the outcome can only be a positive one'*.

As if to deny the authorities time to savour a welcome success story, at 11pm on Monday 14 December 2009, arsonists tried to set fire to a shop owned by APOEL FC in Demofontos Street, in Nicosia City Centre, which caused damage to the windows.

A camping gas canister was detonated, which was attached to a container of flammable liquid, but fortunately failed to ignite. Police forensic officers collected cigarette ends at the scene in an effort to find DNA, and APOEL described it as a 'criminal act'.

At the end of December 2009 the Pan Cyprian Footballers Association (PFA) threatened strike action in a dispute with the CFA over guarantees to play a normal length season, in the B and D teams, as this affected their ability to be paid enough to support their families.

At the same time the Cyprus Police recorded forty-eight cases relating to football, a year on year increase over the last three years.

Chapter Five

A Mad Month In May 2010

On Thursday 18 February 2010 AEL played APEP in a 7pm kick off at Tsirion Stadium. During the second half about forty supporters, from one team, attacked the opposition. The referee stopped the game and the police made eight arrests. A police sergeant was injured during the disturbance and was taken by ambulance to Limassol General Hospital.

AEL won the game 2-0.

On Saturday 20 February 2010 APOEL played Nea Salamina at the GSP Stadium in Nicosia, in another evening game, which ended in a 0-0 draw in front of a crowd of 7,657.

At about 7pm, what were later described by police as seventy 'brainless APOEL fans' approached the tiered section of the stands, occupied by Nea Salamina fans, in a threatening manner. Orders were given to close the gates to the Nea Salamina tier and ten police officers formed something of a 'human shield' in front of those gates.

They were subjected to a sustained barrage of missiles from the APOEL fans, and all ten officers were injured, one of them seriously.

At 7.25pm police deployed tear gas to disperse the troublemakers, and a further twenty officers were sent to the car park at the stadium, where more fans were gathering.

By 7.40pm police had restored some form of order at which point they escorted the Nea Salamina fans safely to their cars. No arrests were made.

On Sunday 7 March 2010 APOEL played AEL, in a league fixture, at the GSP Stadium and following the final-whistle trouble broke out when police tried to implement their post-match plan which was to allow APOEL fans to leave first, whilst AEL fans were requested to remain behind in their seats to avoid confrontations.

Whilst most complied, a group of twenty AEL fans started pushing and banging on one of the doors on the northern terrace which they eventually broke down. Two hundred AEL fans then poured outside to confront APOEL fans.

MMAD riot teams once again found themselves caught in the middle of opposing fans as sticks and stones were thrown. Teargas was deployed and four police officers were injured, one of whom received an arm injury. After the game the Police Association said, *'This situation will no longer be tolerated'* and accused clubs of trying to shift the blame on to the police. They predicted a rise in violence as the season came to a close.

On Sunday 14 March 2010 Apollon played APOEL at Tsirion Stadium, in a game which ended in a 2-0 win for Apollon, in front of a crowd of 9,104.

Before the game, a bus taking APOEL fans to the stadium stopped on the highway and youths got out and started throwing stones at oncoming cars. Another group attacked a house, and a shop, next to the stadium.

Minutes before kick-off three hundred APOEL fans arrived in one group at the entrance gates and tried to rush officers. Several objected fiercely to police body- searches and in the ensuing melee a number forced their way through carrying flares. Only the day before, following a tip-off, police in Nicosia found eighty flares which they were believed were destined for the match.

Ten minutes before the end of the game violence erupted after Apollon scored a second goal. In the eastern wing of the stadium APOEL fans started ripping up seats and burning them. Fireman who turned up to try to put the flames out were bombarded, with soda cans and water bottles, which had been looted from the canteen in the stadium. Police officers who went onto the terraces to try to clear a path for the fire officers got the same treatment.

Flares were thrown onto the pitch and MMAD riot units deployed teargas in an effort to restore order, although heavily outnumbered. Toilets in the ground were smashed, as was a pane of glass in one of the emergency exits, pieces of which were then thrown at the police and opponents. The track around the pitch was extensively damaged and APOEL subsequently agreed to pay 10,000 euro to cover the damage. One police vehicle was also damaged and eight police officers injured. Two private cars were damaged.

Police made eight arrests of men, aged between 18 years to 25 years, who appeared at a remand hearing on Tuesday 16 March

2010. The court was held in Limassol General Hospital, where one of the accused was receiving treatment for extensive bruising. Four others were examined by a State doctor after they accused the police of mistreating them. They were all ordered to be held over-night pending a court decision.

Police spokesman Michalis Katsounotos said that the clubs were still currently only introducing 'half measures' and the debate turned towards the issue of CCTV in grounds. It had been assessed that it would cost one million euros per stadium to equip them fully with CCTV and it was disclosed that an FA official had visited the island some two months previously and produced a report with recommendations which however was still 'being considered'.

On Wednesday 17 March 2010 a charity futsal tournament took place which was aimed at 'highlighting the beautiful game' under the slogan, *'Scoring Against Violence'.*

The mini tournament took place at 'Daluz' futsal grounds in Nicosia and kits for First Division Clubs were put on sale, the proceeds of which would go to the *'Make a Wish'* cancer association.

Those attending included government officials, the police, the fire service, National Guard, and journalists, who were expected to play against each other in an effort to focus on the positive elements of the game.

On Tuesday 23 March 2010 members of the government started calls for renewal work to be carried out at Tsirion Stadium in Limassol. Although recent reports had not highlighted safety fears it was nevertheless pointed out that it had been some twenty years since work had taken place, particularly in relation to shelters and the stands, and with three clubs regularly using the facility it was felt that it was in need of an urgent upgrade in terms of facilities.

On Sunday 28 March 2010 Omonia played APOEL at the GSP Stadium in Nicosia, in front of a crowd of 16,178 supporters, which Omonia won with a score line of 1-0.

As two Turkish Cypriots left the ground, in a vehicle with Turkish Cypriot number plates, they were surrounded by APOEL fans wearing scarves over their faces. Speaking to the Turkish Cypriot daily newspaper *'Kibris'* afterwards one of them said, *'Two youths came alongside the car and pointed to the number plate on the car. Another guy then got off his motorbike and started shouting in Greek. All I could understand was the word 'Turko' (Turk). In around ten seconds about two hundred APOEL fans encircled the car. Immediately we closed the windows and locked the doors as the group began to make threatening gestures'.*

The group began trying to open the doors of the car, and then started punching and kicking it, at which point four other APOEL supporters stepped in and stood either side of the vehicle to protect the occupants until the police arrived.

The two Turkish Cypriots made a complaint to the police and said of their rescuers, *'we owe our lives to these guys. If they hadn't intervened we might have been killed or seriously injured'.*

The owner of the car, Tekin Birinci, was a regular attender of Cyprus League football matches, and also a registered football coach. In a gesture of support the CFA offered to pay for the damage to the car, and the Turkish Cypriots said that they were trying to track their rescuers down on Facebook so that they could express their thanks.

On Sunday 11 April 2010 Apollon played APOEL at Tsirion

Stadium Limassol in a game which Apollon lost 1-2, and saw them drop to fourth place in the League, in front of a crowd of just 3,362.

In a familiar tactic, just before the kick-off two hundred Apollon fans rushed police at the turnstiles and managed to get inside without body checks. During the melee three police officers were slightly injured. During the match, as the game turned against the home team, a crowd wielding crowbars went outside and made their way to the VIP section where they started hurling stones at the entrance. A private security guard was injured and two police cars damaged.

After the final whistle another group of sixty Apollon fans went back to the VIP Section and threw stones at the police. One police officer was injured after being struck by a firecracker.

Despite being the winners, APOEL protested to the CFA about the appointment of the Bulgarian referee Anton Genov who they said was biased towards them during the game, making blatant errors, and a late sending-off of a midfielder.

They accused the CFA of not making proper checks when it was revealed that Genov was banned from officiating at European fixtures pending an investigation into 'obvious irregular betting patterns' during a game between Macedonia and Canada in November 2009. During that game Genov awarded four penalties, and betting officials were alerted by a number of bets placed on at least three goals being scored, and the number of penalties awarded.

On Sunday 25 April 2010 an Israeli referee, who was due to oversee a game between Omonia and Apollon, was questioned by police two hours before the match was due to be played, after a complaint was made that he might have been 'influenced'.

The substance of the complaint was that an Omonia fan had seen the referee in a hotel lobby talking to a Cypriot, and watching an old match between APOEL and Omonia. The fan reported it to the clubs Board who in turn told him to report it to the police.

The general consensus was that the police had overstepped the mark with the CFA chairman threatening to sue police spokesman Michalis Katsounotos for insinuating that he had tried to obstruct the police from talking to the referee and DISY MP Ionas Nicolaou saying, *'It is with great surprise that I was informed on the zeal shown by Cyprus police in investigating a claim by a fan that efforts were made supposedly to influence the referee'.*

On Wednesday 28 April 2010 Apollon played AEL at Tsirion Stadium in a cup semi-final match which was won 1-0 by Apollon.

Briefly before the game fans threw stones at each other, and flares were thrown onto the pitch, which narrowly missed two children wearing high visibility bibs who were in possession of footballs. At one point the pall of smoke, from the flares, completely obscured the view of the stands from the pitch.

During the match it was relatively quiet, although there was a brief pause in play, whilst a burning plastic emergency exit sign was extinguished, after being set on fire by fans.

Further trouble started after the final whistle, when three hundred Apollon fans broke through the crowd safety barriers to get onto the pitch waving huge team flags. They made their way to the stand occupied by AEL fans, and both sets of fans traded insults and firecrackers and flares were thrown.

MMAD Units were deployed to keep them apart as some

AEL fans also made their way onto the pitch. A number of supporters removed their T-shirts and wrapped them around their faces in an effort to hide their identities. Finally, as Apollon fans withdrew, AEL fans threw water bottles, and stones, at the police who fired four teargas canisters into the crowd, Supporters then went on to set fire to bushes and raided the gardens of nearby houses for missiles to throw.

During these clashes another three police officers were injured and three civilians. They all received hospital treatment at Limassol General Hospital and one person was kept in for further treatment.

A number of videos were subsequently posted on YouTube showing some of the events, and in some cases the contorted faces of individuals expressing sheer uncontrollable anger towards their opponents. The pictures also showed police tactics becoming fragmented and officers in insufficient numbers being unable to prevent fans from entering the pitch area. Officers became separated from their colleagues in the ensuing melee, and the use of shields was of limited use in such close proximity to the fans.

Later in the evening stones were thrown at cars driving on Makarios Avenue, near Ayios Nicolaous roundabout, near to the AEL club house. A sixteen-year old female was hospitalised with a head injury.

In a separate incident between seventy to a hundred fans attacked a 'coffee shop' beating the owner, and a customer who was wearing a scarf from the opposition. They were likewise treated in hospital and released.

Police spokesman Yiannis Georgiou said after the game, *'With the dynamic and forceful intervention of police.....fans were driven back'*.

The Justice Minister Loucas Louca however took a somewhat different view and said that in future the police would have to, *'step up and do a better job'*.

He cited a lack of comprehensive police resources to deal with the trouble, and planning oversights which he had raised with the Police Chief.

On Sunday 2 May 2010 a league-deciding match took place

between Omonia FC and APOEL FC at the GSP stadium in Nicosia, before a crowd of 13,644. In their final local derby of the year Omonia beat APOEL to officially win the championship with a score line of 1-0. Police numbers at the match were at an all-time high in an effort to prevent outbreaks of trouble occurring.

During the game the two sets of fans hurled objects at each other, injuring one police officer who was treated at Nicosia General Hospital for minor injuries. At the final whistle a group of APOEL fans made their way to the stadium's western stand where they bombarded Omonia fans with stones. Police officers dispersed them and arrested one seventeen year-old from Nicosia. Although no further injuries were reported the windscreen of a Fire Department vehicle was smashed.

After the game groups of APOEL fans set about ambushing motorists in their cars as they left the stadium. Near Latsia one driver was injured slightly after his car was hit by stones. Later a group of APOEL fans wielding iron bars, and bats, attacked passing cars on Makarios Avenue in Nicosia with further damage reported before four youths were arrested at the scene of the attacks.

In Limassol a twenty-one year old female celebrating the result threw a firecracker into a car near to the Ayios Nicolaos junction injuring the driver. In keeping with most countries the engagement of females in football related violence was however a fairly rare event.

On Friday 7 May 2010 the official shop for APOEL in Nicosia was vandalised with a series of slogans and abusive messages sprayed across the shops windows. The word *'Omonia'* was also sprayed in bold letters.

On Saturday 8 May 2010 Omonia FC played Anorthosis FC in Larnaca in the final league game of the season.

Before the kick-off around fifty Anorthosis fans threw stones at Omonia supporters who were in the north stand. Omonia supporters responded in kind but then things calmed down until champions Omonia, who ultimately won the game 4-2, equalised 2-2 in the second half.

A large number of supporters left the ground and started throwing stones. Teargas used by police to disperse the unruly crowds spread onto the playing field causing play to be suspended for fifteen minutes. Two youths aged eighteen years and nineteen years were arrested, the first for assaulting a police officer, and the second for possessing a metal club.

Police promised more arrests.

By the end of the day twenty-one private cars were reported as damaged, a number with smashed windscreens, as well as sixteen police and fire vehicles. Further damage was caused to the stadium as well as to local homes and businesses. Fourteen police officers were treated in hospital for injuries sustained in the disturbances.

On Sunday 9 May 2010 Omonia fans celebrating the championship threw stones and bottles into the courtyard of the Central Nicosia Police Station but no damage was caused. A group of fans also damaged a fire engine slightly injuring the two firemen who were inside.

At 11.30pm that day Omonia fans celebrating their team's win lit a fire on the pavement outside Lycavitos Police Station on Makarios Avenue. A fire engine called to the scene was attacked by fifty Omonia fans who managed to climb on board the vehicle.

They started removing equipment, causing extensive damage and smashing headlights, side mirrors, and bodywork. They also sprayed graffiti on the vehicle. They then climbed onto the roof of the fire engine and assaulted the two firemen who tried to drive off towards the Hilton Hotel but were again brought to a halt by other fans.

Both firemen were subsequently taken to Nicosia General Hospital for minor injuries and given sick leave.

Two Omonia fans aged thirty-three years, and twenty years, from Nicosia, were subsequently arrested for the attack on the firemen after witnesses had placed them at the scene. Both of them denied any involvement, although the twenty year old admitted being at the scene.

At their initial court appearance police investigators asked for a remand in custody for six days saying that they had taken five statements but needed to take fifty more. In any event they were granted a remand for four days.

By the end of the season the CFA had again intervened twice to award points following the disruption of matches:

a) Nea Salamis Famagusta versus APOEL was awarded to APOEL, when whilst winning 3-0 in the 76th minute, there was a pitch invasion by Salamis fans, leading to the game being abandoned.

b) Ethnikos Achna versus APEP was awarded to Ethnikos when whilst winning 3-0 APEP's players walked off the pitch in protest at the officiating.

***

On Saturday 15 May 2010 Apollon FC played APOEL FC in the Cup Final in Larnaca, which was eventually won by Apollon, with a score line of 2-1, following which players celebrated lifting the cup with an official tickertape and firework event in front of a huge 'Coca Cola' sign on the pitch.

At Larnaca's GSZ stadium, the venue of the Cup Final, police fired smoke- bombs to disperse fans after the game, and four youths were later treated at Larnaca General Hospital for respiratory problems.

A few hours before the game started, acting on a tip-off, Larnaca police found a stash of weapons intended for use by the hooligans in a vehicle which was on false plates. They included fifteen Molotov cocktails, thirty wooden bats, twenty-seven crash helmets, a plastic container filled with flammable liquid, and a large bucket filled with rocks. This all seemed like preparations for a civil war rather than a football match.

The disturbances migrated to Limassol as returning Apollon fans were stoned in their vehicles by what were believed to be AEL FC fans. The previous evening several cars parked in the vicinity of the Apollon fan club had been damaged heightening tension in the area.

Following a celebration and a fireworks display, outside the Apollon fan club headquarters, groups of fans started making their way to the Enaerios area of central Limassol, where AEL fans had their own club, and were massed in some numbers waiting for the violent confrontation that was to come. Hundreds of people gathered in the area of the roundabout at Ayios Nikolaos.

At least three hundred AEL fans were ready to defend their fan club at all costs and were well prepared. Some of them had obtained a medicine from Greece, which negated the causes of teargas, and a group of ten to fifteen people wearing masks were trained to spray the eyes of anyone affected. It was said that within fifteen minutes they would be able to recover.

Republic of Cyprus Police deployed officers in riot gear to the area in an effort to keep the two sides apart. They fired regular volleys of teargas as they came under a crossfire of stones and Molotov cocktails, from both sets of fans, who set fire to a number of rubbish bins and smashed shop windows. Firefighters who attended the scene of the fires also found themselves under attack and some hooligans deployed slingshots to target people.

Fighting continued until the early hours of the Sunday morning before all parties departed from the 'field of battle'. On a social media web-site, *'European Ultras Forum 'Syfael 1989 Gate 3'* posted a video in 2011 of some of the scenes showing petrol bombs being thrown as smoke-filled the night air and said, *'The police could not fight off the AEL Hools and asked for a truce'*.

Eleven police officers were injured during the fighting, two of them seriously. One officer suffered a slashed tendon on his right arm after being struck with a shard of glass, and a second suffered a broken nose when his shield failed to deflect a missile which struck him in the face.

A cache of petrol bombs and incendiary devices were also found on a construction site next to AEL's fan club, and crates of empty 'Carlsberg' beer bottles provided a ready supply of ammunition.

Four people were arrested after seeking hospital treatment for cuts and bruises, and remanded in police custody, although initially denying any involvement. Two further people were being sought by police, with a promise of further action.

On Wednesday 19 May 2010 four more people, aged 28, 29, 32 and 37 years, were remanded in custody for football related violence over that weekend. The hearing was held at Limassol hospital where one was being treated for an alleged health problem. After the hearing one of the suspects lost his temper and lashed out causing damage. A fifth suspect from Limassol aged forty-five years was also remanded in custody in connection with the discovery of the stash of weapons in a vehicle.

Eventually a total of fourteen arrests were made and arrest

warrants issued for another two persons.

Police spokesman Michalis Katsounotos, hinting that they might in future refuse to provide security at football matches said, *'We've hit rock bottom. The question on everyone's minds should be where are we heading as a society?*

Describing officers as *'Heroes',* he said that it was hard to comprehend the level of rage and violence displayed towards the police and that it would be necessary to review policing during the season to try to ensure that they were better prepared for the next.

When pressed by the media as to what that might mean he commented,

'Otherwise there is no choice but shutting up shop.....Thought should be given to whether the league should be suspended until some people get their heads straight'.

In something of a show of disunity the Police Chief Michalis Papageorgiou said subsequently, *'Yes this issue has troubled us...but it is not up to the Chief of Police, or the Force, to decide whether the football league should be suspended or not'.* He made it clear in his remarks that in his view much of the recent violence was premeditated.

Justice Minister Loucas Louca declined to comment on whether the 2010- 2011 championship would be suspended but agreed that they had reached 'a cut-off point' and that they were looking at many alternatives to the problem.

Andreas Santis the alternative deputy chairman of the Cyprus Football Association (CFA) voiced the views of football clubs and politicians in saying that the idea was out of the question. He said, *'You wouldn't prohibit traffic because of a high road death toll would you?'*.

DISY party spokesman Harris Georgiades asked the Government to come clean on the issue and asked, *'these type of comments are very disconcerting. Is this the official position of the government, of the executive, or of the Justice Minister ...that the police are giving up? Are we to become the only European country with no football league?'*.

AKEL MP Yiannos Lamaris pointed out that there was evidence of infiltration of fan clubs by right-wing and neo-fascist groups intent on causing trouble. Whilst there might well have been some truth in this statement it was perhaps not surprising coming from the party of the 'Left' and reinforced yet again how politicised football was in Cyprus.

At that time the State spent 3.2 million euro a year, on policing football fixtures, with costs set to rise still further to 4 million euro in the coming year, and a proposal that the Cyprus Sports Federation (KOA) should add a two euro surcharge to tickets to subsidise costs.

The question remained – exactly what was going to be done to de-escalate the rising tide of violence? The view was that the few measures that had been introduced, such as banning orders, and holding games behind closed doors, had failed to have any impact. It was clear that sports related violence was on the increase but the question was whether a full-blown riot on a Saturday night, in the middle of a major tourist area, would be the catalyst for change.

The media made it clear that constantly blaming the police for the problem was grossly unfair whilst there appeared to be no political will to support their actions. They were either accused of using excessive force or of deploying the wrong security measures so constantly found themselves in a 'no win' situation.

At the same time politicians seemed to be either unwilling, or unable, to introduce measures to combat violence for fear of alienating football clubs, or their supporters, who were of course also voters, in what is a relatively small community where political allegiances pass through generations in the same way that their allegiance to specific football clubs does. The need for promises on reform to be implemented in a speedy fashion and for a tough sentencing regime were highlighted as the public outcry continued.

To add to the debate, at the beginning of May 2010, the Attorney General Petros Clerides withdrew the case against those involved in the Nuevo Campo attack in 2009 from the Assizes Court and filed it with the Nicosia District Court, who could only impose a maximum sentence of five years.

He asserted that no court would impose a sentence of more than five years even if the defendants were found guilty.

In a rare move Omonia FC announced that month that it was suing one of its own supporters, the person arrested in relation to the damage at the Anorthosis ground, in January 2009, for 34,000 euro. Having paid a significant amount of money again in fines for fan behaviour they had decided to strike back. Having been asked to pay for the damage they decided to act against one of the individuals involved by taking out a civil case against him.

A club spokesman Theodoros Kafkarides said, *'Here was proof that a specific fan had caused damage which we were asked to pay. A decision was made that we would not pay for the damage – he would'.*

Michalis Katsounotos the police spokesman said, *'Omonia's act is very positive towards stamping out violence phenomena from sports grounds and if it is adopted by other clubs it will undoubtedly contribute positively'.*

In a news conference shortly after the riot in Limassol, police gave details of football related incidents of violence including injuries and arrests, damage and cases pending before the courts. It was revealed by the police that there had been a 52% increase in football related violence in 2010, compared to the previous year, with a 44.3% increase in arrests. The link was made with the increase in crime committed by youths in the age group 14 years to 18 years, which was up by 113.9%.

In 2009 police recorded 79 instances relating to football related violence and in 2010 a total of 114 cases.

On Sunday 23 May 2010 the Cyprus Mail reported the views of a retired sixty- year old British Police Officer living in Larnaca, after it was announced that British Police experts were going to be consulted about football violence. Using an assumed name he told the paper that he had watched TV footage of police being unable to control the crowds during the rioting the week previous with horror. He said, *'what I saw on TV was police aimlessly running around as individuals, and not as a coordinated unit. It looked like they had not been trained to work together and if they don't do this they will be terribly affected'.*

Responding to the comments police spokesman Michalis Katsounotos said that a review of training and strategy had taken place and it had been realised that there was a need to not only prevent fighting but to make more arrests. He went on, *'to this end the police have hand-picked two hundred and forty policemen to join a newly created riot control unit and the CFA have agreed for the Metropolitan Police to train them. We have also requested advice from Portuguese police based on their experience of hosting the 2004 UEFA Euro Football Championship'.*

The retired officer concluded, *'clearly all of society including parents need to pull together and stamp this disease out. I just don't like to see a police force in a democratic country maligned'.*

On the same date another British resident highlighted the fact that the island had a very successful international rugby team which had won eleven out of twelve games and had never experienced any signs of trouble.

The month of May was a month that would not be forgotten but for all the wrong reasons.

At 3.30pm, on Sunday 8 August 2010, nine police officers went to Omonia's fan club to check the buses that were going to transport Omonia fans to the GSP Stadium in Nicosia to watch a Super Cup match between Omonia and Apollon.

They were also intending to escort the buses to the ground.

Subsequently up to forty fans began abusing and threatening the police, and started throwing water bottles at them. The officers were then punched and kicked and the attacks only stopped following intervention from Omonia's security team. Other fans from Nicosia attacked officers trying to check another bus in the capital a little earlier.

Two police officers were injured and two cars damaged. One officer was taken to a private clinic for treatment, whilst the second was treated in hospital.

As the match was about to start about one hundred Apollon fans attempted to enter the area occupied by Omonia fans, and were held back by police officers, although no further injuries were reported.

The game finished with a full time score line of 1-1, with an attendance of 7,681.

On the 27 August 2010 the 2010/11 seventy-third Cyprus First Division commenced with Omonia as the defending Champions.

In order to combat hooliganism it was announced that the police had been issued with a handbook which provided advice on how to deal with high risk football matches. Police spokesman Michalis Katsounotos said, *'there will be absolutely no concessions on these measures. The force is determined to act decisively and to arrest people misbehaving'*.

The measures announced included the setting up of crisis-centres at District Police HQs to deal with violent behaviour at these games. Drunken fans would not be allowed into stadiums and if missiles were thrown onto the pitch the police would suspend the game, and if such actions were repeated the game would be abandoned.

Police would also ask clubs not to transport fans to games on buses, and indicated that as they could not insist by law that they should do so, they would in any event check buses at departure and arrival points.

In the same week Greek national Alexandros Papadopoulos, who had been involved in tackling football violence in Greece on the part of supporters of the team Panathinaikos, for seven years, announced that he was going to tackle the problem in Cyprus.

He said that he was going to lead a team of one-hundred-and-twenty stewards, who had graduated from a four-year training programme with Global College, which included presentations on sociology, and psychology.

In a statement which was heavy on passion he described how, just over two weeks previously, he had been involved with ten stewards in restoring order in the stand occupied by Omonia fans as to use his words, *'the police were nowhere to be seen'*.

He went on, *'we entered the throng and I will tell you that I even had to use violence at some point when as I saw a father holding his two year old girl in the middle of all the mayhem, both of them crying in fear. When I see young children being attacked of course I will intervene. It is shameful to watch these things and have you seen any arrests? No'*.

He stressed that the police needed to make more arrests and explained how he himself had once been easily led by the 'mob' and got involved in an incident of wanton damage. The shame he had felt when his father had to pick him up from the police station, followed by the one and only beating he had received from him, stopped him from repeating the activity.

Papadopoulos, having been appointed as the Head of Security for GSP Stadium went on, *'I didn't come here to fix this problem in a year. I intend to be here ten, or even twenty years, if that is what it takes. But we will change things. 2010 is the year authorities want it to stop'*.

Recognising that hooliganism was getting steadily worse, it was highlighted that there had been a lack of arrests, and that the Attorney General had been asked to speed up the judicial process. A committee consisting of representatives of the police and CFA would highlight high-risk games and decide on the maximum number of tickets to be sold.

The CFA second deputy president, Andreas Santis, also expressed fears about busloads of fans turning up at games, who could not be controlled, and said that two games at the start of the season would be played without fans, as two teams were being punished for violence in the preceding season.

In commenting on an article in the Cyprus Mail outlining the new measures someone using the pseudonym *'Bish, Biah, biah'* said, *'Yeah, Yeah, Yeah. Heard it all before. Isn't it the same every year? What happened when the specialist came over from England a few years back? Having been on many occasions to Old Trafford to watch Manchester United I felt safer amongst 77,000 fans than 7,000 here!'*

Just before 1am on Tuesday 28 September 2010 around fifteen people in balaclavas surrounded the Anorthosis building in Kato Polemidhia in Limassol. They started smashing windows and causing damage using planks of wood and metal bars. Three men aged 17 years, 19 years and 20 years, who were in the building at the time, came under attack sustaining head injuries as well as extensive cuts and bruising. All three were treated in Limassol General Hospital and discharged. This was the second attack on the premises in recent times.

On Sunday 3 October 2010 APOEL played Omonia FC at the GSP Stadium in Nicosia, with 17,168 supporters in attendance. APOEL fans were displaying a large number of Greek flags but this was apparently not reciprocated among the Omonia fans.

In the previous season Omonia had beaten APOEL on three occasions.

A few minutes into the second-half, with APOEL leading the match 3-0, which was the eventual final score, there was a delay of twenty-one minutes due to a flare being thrown onto the pitch.

A thirty-one year old Omonia fan then took a Greek flag from his pocket and took to burning it, which enraged APOEL fans, who had themselves earlier been chanting nationalistic slogans.

He was arrested for insulting a national symbol but he immediately claimed to be mentally ill and produced medical documentation to prove it. Although he was charged the police said that a successful prosecution was unlikely in the circumstances.

The burning of the flag was viewed as an illegal act because it is seen as a national Cypriot symbol. Many APOEL fans see Greece as their true 'motherland' with Cyprus being an annex of Greece. Extreme right-wing elements exploited these feelings to the full to look for new recruits with the expansion of ELAM (National People's Front) some of whom took to wearing black shirts at APOEL games and wearing swastikas on the terraces.

At the end of the game APOEL's Greek goalkeeper Dionysis Chiotis appeared distressed by the incident and took a Greek flag and, whilst hugging fellow players, took a lap of honour around the pitch.

At a post-match press conference he said, *'we are all Greeks. I am Greek and you are Greek Cypriots. I will not tolerate anyone burning the Greek flag. It is unacceptable for them to swear at your country while they are on Greek ground. I hope that the incident has also bothered the Greeks of Omonia'.*

For their part a spokesman for Omonia, Theodoros Kafkanides, condemned the action and said that the fan involved had managed to offend fourteen thousand Omonia fans.

EDON the youth wing of AKEL said that it was a 'vulgar act' but also criticised APOEL fans for chanting abusive slogans against President Christofias.

They added, *'no APOEL officials found the strength to condemn this fact and almost all of the media only chose to present the unacceptable action of one or two Omonia fans'.*

On Tuesday 5 October 2010 the thirty-one year old, who burnt the flag, appeared at Nicosia District Court and pleaded 'not guilty' to three counts. His case was adjourned until the 13 January 2011. It appeared that the 'wheels of justice' would continue to grind somewhat slowly.

Both teams were referred to the CFA, and APOEL were subsequently fined 5,000 euro for the entry of a fan onto the pitch, and 6,000 euro for abusive chants by fans against President Christofias.

The most severe punishment however was handed out to Omonia who were fined 3,000 euro for fans throwing objects on the field, 1,000 euro for unsportsmanlike conduct by the team, and 2,500 euro for allowing fans to bring dangerous objects into the ground. They were fined 8,000 euro for causing the game to be temporarily stopped, and for burning a Greek flag a further 10,000 euro fine.

With the season only five games old the CFA had already determined fines of 194,840 euro, to clubs and players, of which 55,000 was in connection with AEL's dispute with LTV over television rights.

Anorthosis FC had already been fined more than 6,500 euro and, in an effort to avoid further fines, the club President Kyriacos Kousios said that in future any fans wishing to use the North Stand, where most of the hard-core hooligans gathered, would have to buy tickets from official sources and have their ID card details taken as well as a photograph.

The organised supporters group PAN.SY.FI Anorthosis said, *'we believe that photography is a measure of discrimination against a portion of our fans. It is illegal and we will refuse to comply with it'.*

During this period the media began to raise issues over the award of several government public works contracts to a key individual in one particular club, who had a civil engineering company. The award of the contracts appeared to run parallel to the clubs ability to engage within the players transfer market and whilst they were not saying that anything illegal was taking place there were concerns that politics was playing its part in supporting one club against others.

On Sunday 17 October 2010 Apollon were beaten 5-0 by

APOEL, at Tsirion Stadium in Limassol in front of a crowd of 7,131.

Before the game there was a good atmosphere but five minutes after kick-off Apollon fans threw flares, and chairs were thrown onto the pitch, as they chanted offensive slogans.

Some areas of the stands were set on fire resulting in the referee Vassilis Demetriou suspending the game for twelve minutes in the 82nd minute so that the fire service could extinguish the flames, as smoke enveloped the whole of the pitch and stands. APOEL fans also responded with flares.

An APOEL fan who was present at the game said, *'there was so much smoke in the stadium it looked like an inferno. Someone will lose their life soon. How many more warning signs do the authorities need before they take action?'*

APOEL fans were shepherded away by police at the end of the game as one hundred and fifty Apollon fans starting attacking cars, shops, and houses adjacent to the stadium. They threw rocks, flares, and Molotov cocktails at the police, and two officers were subsequently treated for injuries at Limassol General Hospital. One of the officers was hit by a stone, whilst the second was injured when he was bitten on the hand by a fan. Wheelie bins were torched and fields set alight. The fire engine that turned up to extinguish the flames was stoned.

Seven members of the public were also injured and police had to deploy teargas to contain the violence.

Apollon fans then gathered in Vassilios Constantinou Street with a view to marching on the town-centre but were stopped by police. At this point seven arrests were made, namely a 12 and 14 year-old, who were charged and released into their parent's custody, and two 24 year-olds, two 15 year-olds, and an 18 year-old who were remanded into police custody for three days when they appeared at Limassol District Court the following day.

Limassol Police Chief Andreas Kousioumis said that he believed that the riots were premeditated and praised his officers, who chased some offenders for 1 km, before arresting them.

Police Chief Michalis Papageorgiou took a slightly different approach and called for an internal enquiry to establish how supporters had got into the ground with so many flares.

The Chair of the House Legal Affairs Committee, and DISY Vice-President Ionas Nicholaou, went a step further in publicly criticising the police and said, *'we need to respond immediately before somebody is killed'*. He went on, *'there is a big issue regarding the preventative actions the police should have taken in order to prevent the episodes'*. He said that he had information that the police had not body- searched fans going into the stadium and whilst the police denied this he concluded, *'how were so many Molotov Cocktails prepared under the noses of the police?'*.

Both teams were referred to the Cyprus Football Association for sanctions to be applied.

Commenting at the time on the increase in juvenile crime, much of it connected to football, Professor Andros Kapardis a Criminologist from the Law Department at the University of Cyprus said, *'we have been studying the problem of hooliganism in Cyprus and have made many proposals to the police, and to the teams. The problem is serious. If I was a police officer I would refuse to go to a game'*.

On Saturday 30 October 2010 Apollon played AEL in

Limassol, at Tsirion stadium, and a video posted on YouTube by *'Xaris Xarous'* showed a packed stand of Apollon fans in good voice, amongst them young children. On this occasion AEL fans took the lead in causing trouble, as after the match, upset at losing 3-0, they began causing disturbances outside the stadium.

Riots began in Stelios Kyriakides Street, and in Spyros Kyprianou Avenue, when police had Molotov Cocktails thrown at them and as tensions grew the police also found themselves in a confrontation with local residents.

Plastic bins, grass, shrubs, a telephone pole, and cars were damaged.

A total of fifteen people were arrested, ten of whom were aged between eighteen years and thirty-one years, who were charged with inciting a riot and destruction of property. They were all remanded in custody for five days when they appeared at Limassol District Court the following day.

Five police officers were injured, two of whom were placed on sick leave.

In a separate incident five residents, who lived in Ivykou Street, were arrested after police accused them of attacking officers and preventing them from doing their duties. Four were charged and one was taken to a private clinic for treatment. Two of the group later made official complaints against the police claiming that they had been arrested after asking the police to stop beating a youth. A prominent MMAD officer was later to face court action in connection with this incident.

On Monday 22 November 2010 two masked men hurled a Molotov Cocktail through the rear window of referee Aristides Christou's car, in Limassol, whilst he was having lunch with the Chairman of Association of Referees, George Papoutsis, in a nearby fish-restaurant. The two men smashed a car window before throwing the Molotov Cocktail inside the car which was extensively damaged.

Although considered to be one of the best referees on the island, and someone who had refereed international games, he nevertheless was deemed to have made a controversial decision when he allowed a goal to stand for APOEL, in a game against Anorthosis, amidst claims that it was clearly offside.

On Tuesday 23 November 2010 a fifty-two year old man was arrested in connection with a fire that was started at the Antonis Papadopoulos ground, home to Anorthosis.

The fire started at 7am and the physiotherapy room was damaged and numerous windows were smashed as an explosion erupted in the East Wing of the stadium. Police made the arrest after trawling through CCTV and identified a suspect. In the same week the Chairman of the club Kyriakos Kusios had resigned due to the team's poor performance.

On Tuesday 21 December 2010 APOEL played Turkish side Pinar Karasiyaka in a FIBA Eurochallenge basketball held at the Eleftheria Athletic Centre in Nicosia. The game was attended by 2,000 people, of which some five hundred were APOEL fans.

At some point APOEL fans started throwing lighters and coins at the Turkish team bench, and eventually police had to escort the whole team to a locker-room for their safety where they fended off efforts by fans to storm the room.

Fighting continued outside, and the police deployed teargas, as reinforcements were brought in. Four officers were injured, including one female officer who received an eye injury. Three fifteen year-old fans were arrested and later released.

These disturbances caused a large-scale political row with phone calls taking place in Brussels, Athens, and Nicosia as the Turkish government insisted that the team be moved to the 'occupied areas' in the north of the Island for their own safety.

This was resisted strongly by the Cypriot government who kept the team at a GSP Stadium Sports facility, under police protection, until they were escorted to Larnaca Airport next morning for a flight home via Athens. The Turkish team vowed never again to set foot in Cyprus.

The figures for recorded police cases relating to football had exceeded the previous three-year high.

Chapter Six

2011

A Stabbing And More Violence

On Saturday 22 January 2011 APOEL played Omonia at the GSP Stadium in Nicosia, in front of 16,442 supporters, in a game which APOEL eventually won with a 1-0 score line.

Before the game took place, which saw some three hundred and fifty police officers deployed at a cost of 100,000 euros – the largest yet, several pleas were made for calm.

The then President Demetris Christofias ordered the police to be *'unrelenting and merciless'* in their fight against hooligans, whilst APOEL President Fivos Erotokritou, and Omonia President Miltiades Neophyton eventually appealed for calm following a meeting with Police Chief Michalis Papageorgiou, but all to no avail.

In the days before the game hundreds of green coloured leaflets, purporting to come from Omonia fans, were found scattered in Nicosia.

The contents made brutal reading and read, *'the time of battle is here. This week will feature the tomb of the most hated thing that this planet has given birth to.* (Referring to APOEL fans*) It's time we sent them where they belong...in the sewers. Let's all join together as one fist to turn the graceless GSP Stadium into a blazing hell. We will melt anyone who dares stand in our way. The time is now. Let's fuck them'.*

In turn the APOEL President Fivos Erotokritou said after Wednesday's defeat by Apollon in the Cup, *'we are being pushed to the edge. We got knocked out of the cup by the referee and trust me when I say we have ways to protect ourselves both in the short-term and the long-term. Our fans are a volcano ready to erupt'.*

It was agreed that Omonia fans would occupy the West and North Stands, whilst APOEL would occupy the East and South Stands. This was designed to assist with segregation and traffic flows but no-one could cater for traffic hold-ups around the ground.

The headline that day was the stabbing of a thirty-three year old off-duty police officer an hour before the game at 5pm.

He was in a car with a twenty-year old friend when they got stuck in a traffic jam at Latsia Highway Bridge leading to the GSP Stadium. The officer, who was actually a member of the Presidential Guard, was wearing an Omonia team shirt and scarf and was sat in the front passenger seat of the vehicle.

He was approached in the car by individuals, some wearing balaclavas, at least one of whom was on a moped, and stabbed three times in the left arm and shoulder with a 20cm blade as he tried to protect his face. One of the offenders forced his door open and kicked him whilst the driver's window was smashed. They attacked the vehicle with sticks, and clubs, and caused damage estimated at 1,000 euros.

His attackers made good their escape and the officer was taken to Nicosia General Hospital by his friend where he received forty-stitches to his wounds.

Police made three unrelated arrests on the day for carrying firecrackers and rocks.

Two people were initially arrested by the police, in connection with the attack, and appeared in court when a request was made for a remand in police custody for three days.

Chief Investigator Costas Constantinou said, *'the suspects, a nineteen year-old hairdresser from Nicosia, and a twenty-one-year-old Greek, were arrested after a witness placed them at the crime scene. They faced charges of conspiracy to commit a crime, assault, criminal damage, and carrying a concealed weapon'.*

The victim had placed the nineteen-year-old, who was not wearing a balaclava, running towards his vehicle just prior to the attack, and other witnesses had identified the Greek as riding a moped on which the nineteen-year-old was a passenger.

Although both admitted to being on the flyover at the time of the attack they denied any wrongdoing. Police confirmed that they had already spoken to seventeen people and expected to take fifty more statements. They were still searching for the weapon used.

Police spokesman Michalis Katsounotos in a plea to the public said, *'this was a senseless and unprovoked attack...... Help us put an end to attacks that blacken the name of Cyprus football'.*

On the 31 January 2011 three more men were arrested, two

aged twenty-one- years, and one twenty-seven years from Nicosia, in connection with the attack, and were remanded in police custody for three days.

Witnesses said that one of those in custody had tried to pull an Omonia scarf from the injured officer's neck whilst the other two had been implicated by others already questioned. Two days later a sixth person, a twenty-four-year-old from Nicosia, was also arrested and after appearing before Nicosia District Court was remanded in police custody for four days.

On Wednesday 2 February 2011 the leader of the police union, 'Police Officers Association', Andreas Symeou, appeared to have second thoughts on the issue of non- policing of football matches, and stepped away from recommending a boycott by officers, which he had raised only twenty-four hours previously.

Nevertheless he highlighted a game the week before between AEL and ARIS in Limassol where an officer had been beaten senseless with 'pipes, stones and anything that was available' and said that in recent games thirty police officers had been injured.

Only three days after this latest violence a seminar, organised with the co- operation of the British High Commission in Nicosia, and attended by 'experts', called for an, *'integrated approach by police and football clubs to solve the problem of football hooliganism'*.

Two of the guest speakers were Chris Whalley, Senior Manager of Stadia Safety and Security with the English FA, and Professor Steve Frosdick an expert in crowd control and stewarding.

Amongst those attending was the Limassol Police Chief Andreas Kousiomis.

Both guest speakers also attended two football matches in Cyprus as observers, and afterwards commented that there was a need for the creation of an integrated safety and security plan, using well-trained stewards to take on work currently being done by the police so that they could concentrate on their primary role. They were also concerned about the use of barbed wire fences to segregate fans, describing them as 'medieval', and noted that hard-core fans were just left to their own devices in the stands.

The Justice Minister Loucas Louca again condemned the violence but highlighted the political paralysis which often existed when he quoted an instance where an MP who had been critical of hooligans subsequently took them to lunch because they threatened not to vote for him again.

In defending the police against criticism, for lax searching at the entrances to stadiums, he said that he had even heard of a six-year-old boy having had a firecracker put between two slices of bread in his sandwich instead of cheese.

In the disturbance that took place after a Cyprus Cup game on a Wednesday between AEL and ARIS a number of AEL fans made their way to the teams dressing rooms after watching their side beaten by the second division side.

They were stopped from entering the rooms by police, and sticks and rocks were thrown with the inevitable response from police of teargas. Cars were damaged and the AEL Romanian Coach Mihai Stoichitsa, who was blamed for the team's performance, was led away by police using a separate entrance.

On Sunday 13 February 2011 Apollon beat AEL 3-2 in a Limassol derby game and teargas was deployed by police, as five hundred Apollon fans charged police lines outside the stadium, to avoid body searches. Three officers were injured as a result of missiles being thrown.

MMAD officer Andreas Symeou, the same officer who had spoken out against the violence at the beginning of the month, was hit just below the left eye by pellets fired from a slingshot, and required stitches to the wound. Another off-duty officer was hit on the hand by a flare, fired from a pistol, and a twenty-year-old man was hit by a flare which had been aimed at another officer.

Apollon coach Andreas Michaelides said after the game, *'I would like to congratulate our fans who created a fantastic atmosphere which a derby such as this definitely deserves'.*

It was indeed a game of high tension as fans clashed after the final whistle and threw stones, sticks, marbles, metal screws, firecrackers, and bottles at each other.

On Friday 18 February 2011 three AEL fans appeared before Limassol District Court to answer charges in relation to football violence in 2008 during a game between AEL and AEK, during which a MMAD Sergeant was injured after being hit with a fire extinguisher.

The three were accused of stopping the match from running smoothly, unlawful assembly, and rioting after losing the match, as well as attacking the police, the use of dangerous objects within the stadium, and damage at the stadium when seats were set on fire and the physiotherapy room damaged.

A twenty-five year-old, and a twenty-seven year-old from Limassol, were sentenced to six months in prison and a thirty-three year-old was sentenced to three months in prison. This was the first time that sentences had not been suspended in such circumstances.

On Saturday 19 February 2011 a homemade firecracker exploded at APOEL's fan club in Klirou at 2am in the morning.

On Sunday 20 February 2011 a game between AEL and Apollon was due to be played behind 'closed doors' after violence the previous week where makeshift pipe bombs were thrown as well as rocks and metal screws, and flare guns were fired.

Hundreds of fans had overwhelmed police at turnstiles trying to conduct searches. The CFA subsequently reversed their decision, as the Chief of Police reported new policing measures to the Under Secretary to the President, Titos Christofides, who had been made head of a special committee tasked with dealing with the problem of hooliganism.

On Monday 21 February 2011 Omonia played Enosis Neon Paralimni at the GSP Stadium in Nicosia, a game which ended in a scoreless draw, in front of a crowd of 10,000 fans.

Violence started at about 9pm just before the end of the game when one hundred and fifty Omonia fans gathered outside the entrance to the stadium's underground car park and started chanting against their team's football players and the management. As they were eventually moved on by police a number of hooded youths started throwing stones, and teargas was deployed by police, in what was termed a 'restricted' manner. Two police officers were injured as they escorted the team from the stadium and a van was damaged.

On Sunday 27 February 2011 Anorthosis played Omonia, following which Molotov Cocktails were thrown by fans, and teargas deployed by the police, as bins and car tyres were set on fire. Some five hundred fans had tried to push their way into the Antonis Papadopoulos Stadium in Larnaca but on this occasion the police stood their ground and pushed them back. The game ended in a 0-0 draw in front of a crowd of 8,500.

Thirty-two arrests were made by the police, ages ranging from seventeen years to twenty-seven years. This was the highest number of arrests in one single incident thus far, and all of them remained in police custody overnight to appear at court. They all denied the charges, and were released into the custody of their parents for initial court hearings to be held on the 8 and 9 March 2011.

This was not good headlines for the Marfin Laiki Bank, being the main sponsors of the League, or the Cyprus Football Association, who were trying to promote engagement with fans through the introduction of a new website.

On the same day the police lined the Nicosia to Limassol highway to stop APOEL and Omonia fans coming face to face with Omonia returning from Larnaca, after playing Anorthosis, and APOEL arriving at the GSP Stadium for a game with Paphos team PEYIA.

On Friday 4 March 2011 police announced that they were investigating allegations of attempt bribery of a second division player. The allegation was that the Dhigenis goalkeeper had been offered 8,000 euro by a player from Onisilos to underperform in the forthcoming match between the two teams. Onisilos rejected the allegations and said that they would take legal action to protect themselves.

On Sunday 27 March 2011 the Lefkotheo Arena in Nicosia was the scene of a major disturbance as violence erupted during a first division basketball championship semi-final between Cytavision APOEL and Intercollege ETHA.

APOEL fans started attacking people and a police officer was injured, with damage caused to local shops. Justice Minister Loucas Louca said, *'we have reached breaking point'*.

On Monday 28 March 2011 a group of APOEL fans calling themselves PANSYFI told DISY leader Nicos Anastasiades that he was an 'undesirable' and warned him to stay away from the club's headquarters where he was due to give a speech on the 1 April 2014 commemorating the anniversary of the start of the EOKA campaign against the British.

In a statement, the fan club, which was not officially

recognised by APOEL FC said, *'it was Mr Anastasiades who in 2004 championed the 'yes vote' for the Annan Plan which would have Turkified our Country and turned it into a protectorate of foreign interests. In 2005 he went to Turkey and pardoned the Turks for the pogroms they committed against the Greeks of Constantinople'.*

They went on to hint of a conspiracy to allow Apollon to win the cup trophy, through poor refereeing, in a match the previous week, designed to boost the chances of Andreas Michaelides, the Apollon team coach, who was standing as an MP for DISY in Limassol.

In any event the fans got their way and the event was cancelled.

On Sunday 10 April 2011 three people aged sixteen years, eighteen years and nineteen years, were arrested by police at the game between APOEL and Omonia, after being found in possession of firecrackers.

The match at the GSP Stadium in Nicosia resulted in APOEL becoming league champions, as they won the game with a score line of 2-0, but will be remembered for the injury caused to the Omonia goal keeper Antonis Georgalides when he was hit by a firecracker thrown onto the pitch and injured.

On Saturday 16 April 2011 twenty people aged between sixteen years to thirty-five years were arrested in Limassol outside the Themistoklion Stadium after a women's volleyball game between AEL and Apollon.

Police were pelted with stones, sticks, petrol bombs and fireworks as they struggled to control the crowd, and discharged teargas. They also recovered an improvised explosive device which could have had lethal consequences. It was made up of a petrol bomb containing shards of metal attached to a firecracker.

On Wednesday 4May 2011 Anorthosis played Apollon in the cup semi-final at their home ground, Antonis Papadopoulos Stadium in Larnaca.

Anorthosis lost 2-1 and after the game their fans remained in the vicinity of the ground.

Prior to the match, on a car park outside a huge 'montage'

had been prepared and laid on the floor, prior to being displayed in the ground, which read, *'you are probably wondering where you are? You are in the place you will die. You think it's over but the game has just begun'*. It was filmed and uploaded on YouTube by *'UltrasFamagustaTV'*.

As MMAD Units tried to disperse the fans they came under attack, from missiles thrown within the crowd, and twelve people were arrested, four of whom were under the age of fourteen years, and the eldest being twenty-six years of age. Two of the juveniles were taken to hospital, suffering from abrasions to their faces, and the eight adults were kept in custody overnight for Court next day.

At the beginning of May 2011 the police took to the media to hit back at criticism that they used 'excessive force' in football related public order incidents. They produced a number of photographs of recent violence which they said showed their 'human side'.

On Wednesday 11 May 2011 three people aged seventeen-years, thirty-five years and thirty five-years, were arrested in disturbances at the GSP Stadium following a game between APOEL and Omonia.

Fifty APOEL fans gathered in a parking lot to the North end of the stadium before the game and exchanged stones with Omonia fans, with MMAD teams deploying teargas.

APOEL lost the game 1-0 and police deployed teargas again, as APOEL fans sought to confront Omonia fans at the end of the game, which attracted a crowd of just 2,318.

In a pre-match search police recovered twenty-six firecrackers that were hidden in the stands.

On Wednesday 18 May 2011 Omonia played Apollon in the Cup Final at Larnaca GSZ Stadium which ended with a 1-1 score line, and was then won by Omonia 4-3 on penalties.

As fans celebrated in Nicosia a number of them started paying attention to the Scaraveos Nightclub, situated in a side street off Themistocles Dhervis Avenue.

Just after 10.30pm fans started driving past the premises and on one occasion there were some exchanges with customers outside, who were believed to be APOEL fans. During another pass the

Omonia fans threw a firecracker into the gardens of the club and the owners came out and donned motorcycle helmets to protect themselves and their property.

By this time hundreds of Omonia fans, possibly up to five hundred, and with many wearing masks, had gathered in the street nearby and armed with petrol bombs, shovels, clubs, and even a sickle they attacked the front of the club. The owners retreated inside and locked themselves in as windows were smashed, and motorbikes parked outside damaged. Customers were ushered out of the back of the premises for safety.

The attack was over before the first police car arrived, by which time one of the club's four owners had suffered burns to his legs from a petrol bomb exploding at his feet, another lost a finger which doctors were unable to re-attach, and yet another suffered head injuries. In all five people were hurt in the attack, three of whom were treated in private clinics.

Police spokesman Michalis Katsounotos said, *'this was an organised and unprovoked attack. If police had not been there in time they would have killed them'.*

The violence continued for several hours, with rubbish bins being torched, and nearly every wall in Makarios Avenue was daubed in graffiti, whilst political parties kiosks, and billboards set up for the forthcoming election that coming Sunday were destroyed.

In separate attacks someone tried to torch the offices of the nationalist party ELAM, situated close to Omonia's clubhouse, and a gang of youths attacked Lykaviti Police Station, with five arrests being made and two police officers injured.

Six people were arrested by police as they drove around Nicosia in a stolen vehicle, inside which was found two wooden clubs. Six people were arrested after the game outside the GSZ Stadium, and a twenty-eight-year-old in Limassol was arrested for smashing windows in a shop in Ayios Tychonas.

All in all police made eighteen arrests on the night, as police fought to gain control and teargas was deployed, but at that stage none of them were in relation to the attack on the nightclub.

On Monday 23 May 2011 a twenty-eight-year-old man was arrested, in connection with the attack on the Nicosia nightclub, the week before, as police also studied footage from the club's security cameras.

A twenty-six-year-old, and another twenty-eight-year-old, had already been arrested and police were actively looking for another two known suspects. Police revealed that one of those arrested had already received a suspended prison sentence for football related violence and was also banned from attending sporting events for six months.

APOEL won the Championship four weeks before the end of the season that year.

End of season statistics showed that the CFA were again obliged to award points to Ermis, in relation to a game between Ermis and Anorthosis, on the 28 January 2011. The game, which was played in front of a crowd of 3,500, in Larnaca, was suspended when Ermis were leading 2-1, following the violent conduct of Anorthosis fans, who filled the air with smoke from flares, some of which were thrown onto the pitch.

***

In June 2011 the police revealed a number of statistics

relating to football violence, and gave a comparison of the available statistics for the 2010/2011 season, which ended in May, compared to the previous 2009/2010 season.

Police expenditure was up by 32% on the previous season, reaching 2.58 million euros.

The actual number of police officers deployed at matches was 18,958, which was a 24% increase on the previous season.

Despite the increased police presence there had been a 30% increase in violent incidents.

The cost of damage caused reached more than 200,000 euro, compared to 140,000 euro the previous season.

Forty-one members of the public were injured in the season just gone, and sixty-two police officers, which was a drop on the eighty-four injured in the previous season.

Arrests increased from ninety in the 2009/2010 season, to two hundred and forty nine in 2010/2011. More than one hundred banning orders were issued, but the police pointed out that some court cases took up to three years to conclude, by which time the courts were more prone to giving lighter sentences.

***

On Wednesday 4 July 2011 during a football cup semi-final match between Anorthosis and Apollon a stand-off took place between fans and the police.On Saturday 6 August 2011 police spokesman Michalis Katsounotos appealed for no violence at the Super Cup Game match between APOEL and Omonia to be held on Sunday 7 August 2011 and said, *'this Sunday's game should be a springboard for hailing better things in Cypriot football for the new season'.* He stressed that the game should be played in the *'spirit of morality'* to honour the thirteen dead following the blast at the Mari Naval Base.

The game was eventually won by APOEL with a score line of 1-0 in front of a crowd of 9,838 at the GSP stadium in Nicosia.

On the 27 August 2011 the seventy-fourth season of the 2011/12 Cyprus First Division commenced with APOEL as defending Champions.

On Thursday 15 September 2011 police announced that a football fan, and a club official, who had attacked a referee had been banned from attending their team games for six months and fined.

The twenty-six-year-old fan, and a forty-one-year-old official from Nicosia team Olympiacos, had assaulted the referee, and a police officer, after the end of their team's game with Apollon in Limassol in March 2011 after protesting against the referee's decisions.

The fan was fined 1,200 euro, and the official, 2,500 euro. On the days that their team played the two would have to report to Nicosia Police HQ where they would remain for the duration of the match.

On Monday 19 September 2011 Apollon played AEK in Limassol, in a match that AEK won 3-0.

Three minutes before the end of the game Apollon fans threw three firecrackers onto the pitch injuring a sergeant and a constable who were standing in front of the Apollon stands. They were both taken to a private clinic and treated for perforated eardrums and loss of hearing as a result of the loud blast.

Police Chief Michalis Papageorgiou ordered an immediate

investigation, and on Wednesday 21 September 2011 a sixteen-year-old youth was arrested in connection with the incident.

On Thursday 22 September 2011 the police called for the speedy introduction of stewards to help them and police spokesman Michalis Katsounotos said, *'it would be a mistake to credit the problem of hooliganism and its resurgence on a weakness of the police to tackle it. The state must take brave and immediate decisions'.*

It was pointed out that plans to introduce stewards, numbered seats in stadiums, and CCTV costing nine million euros had been under discussion since 2003 and the Chair of the House Legal Affairs Committee Ionas Nicolaou criticised the government's lack of political will in providing a legal framework to complete the work.

They were arguing for a list of stewards, who would be paid forty euros per game, to be held centrally, but the Cyprus Sports Association (KOA) wanted each club to have their own. Equally the KOA did not want to take responsibility for training and funding the stewards. At the end of the day the Ministry of Education and

Culture under which the KOA operated decided not to reach any decisions, leaving the issue in limbo.

On the same date two petrol bombs were thrown at the building that housed the Cyprus Referees Association, one of which exploded and started a small fire. Abusive slogans were also daubed on the walls.

On Sunday 16 October 2011 Omonia played Anagennisi in a first division game in Paralimni which ended in a 1-1 draw, in front of a crowd of 5,800.

Omonia fans removed plastic seats and threw them, and water bottles, at the referee. They then tried to enter the locker rooms by forcing the entrance door but police forced them back with teargas. Five cars belonging to the Chair and Board members of the opposing team were then damaged.

Police made two arrests, both nineteen-year-olds, one a student from Avgorou, and one a serving soldier, and three police officers were slightly injured.

On Wednesday 26 October 2011 two men aged twenty-five

years, and twenty- six years were sentenced to nine months in prison after being found guilty of causing grievous bodily harm and attempt arson, following the attack on the APOEL clubhouse on the 20 April 2008. They were part of a group of twenty Omonia fans who beat three people, and left one with permanent eye damage.

In rejecting a plea by defence solicitors for the sentences to be suspended District Judge Lefteris Panteli said, *'it has to be understood by everyone.....that lawful societies do not tolerate such behaviour which represents terrorism and barbarity. Dominance and revenge, especially with such serious consequences have no place among us'*.

A third defendant was found not guilty of the above charges, but was fined five hundred euro for possessing an unused pepper spray, which was found at his home following his arrest.

On Wednesday 23 November 2011 fans smashed cars and attacked a rival team's clubhouse in Nicosia as they celebrated APOEL's qualification to the last sixteen of the Champions League.

More than 3,000 APOEL fans gathered on the streets after 9pm after their team's away game against Zenit in St. Petersburg,

Russia, which ended in a draw.

The Fire Service was called out seventeen times to extinguish torched rubbish bins, and two police cars, and a fire engine, were damaged at Makarios Avenue near to APOEL's Club house.

The clubhouse of Omonia was attacked, and windows smashed and nearby cars damaged by youths wielding steel bars, and bats. A seventeen-year-old, and eighteen-year-old were arrested at the scene.

Two further men aged twenty-five years were arrested as they threw flares from a moving vehicle being driven around the streets.

Seven arrests were made in all.

On Friday 25 November 2011 the CFA announced its decision to ban the Omonia Coach Neophytos Larkou, and Club Chairman Miltiades Neophytou, from attending their team's games for six months. This followed an attack on a referee in October 2011 during the game between Omonia and Anagennisi, when it was alleged that the coach pushed the referee by the shoulder, and the chairman hit him in the face whilst shouting obscenities.

Prior to the announcement by the CFA disciplinary committee, Omonia fans issued a statement saying, *'a six month ban would constitute six terrifying months for Cyprus football and any such decision will not be taken lightly by Omonia fans'*.

After the decision was announced one of the disciplinary committee Panayiotis Kyprianou, who was also the Mayor of Latsia, resigned, saying that the decision was not proportionate to the offence. Omonia FC also announced an appeal against the decision.

That same evening someone threw a rock and smashed a window at the referee's home.

On Sunday 27 November 2011 two police officers were slightly injured when fans clashed in Paralimni during a game between APOEL and Enosis. Whilst the game was still underway eighty APOEL fans gathered outside and threw sticks, rocks and metal objects at the police. The two injured officers were treated at Paralimni General Hospital and discharged.

APOEL won the game with a score line of 2-0, in front of a

crowd of just 2,500, at the Tasos Markou stadium.

On Thursday 8 December 2011 a professional women's volleyball championship game was held in Limassol between Apollon and a Turkish team Galatasary as part of the CEV Cup.

Some five hundred home fans packed the Apollon sports area at one end, whilst at the other end fifty visiting Turkish fans faced them.

During the game Apollon fans threw chairs and firecrackers onto the court. They stormed the guest's restrooms and caused damage. Teargas was fired by police, who managed to push the troublemakers outside, where the windscreen of a police vehicle was smashed. One man from Limassol who went onto the court was arrested, although later released.

A Cyprus channel Sigma Live subsequently reported that visiting fans had been provoking the Apollon fans with indecent gestures.

In a similar incident a year earlier, in December 2010, APOEL met another team, Karsiyaka from Turkey, at the Eleftheria

Stadium for a basketball game that ended in similar circumstances. There were no handshakes between the teams at the end of the game, as locals threw stones at visiting players.

Five years earlier a Turkish team from Trabzon hosted Anorthosis for football and this time it was the Turkish fans who attacked the Cypriots.

On Wednesday 21 December 2011 APOEL were fined by the CFA, and fans were banned for one game, following the clashes with Omonia earlier in the month. Up to a hundred fans from both teams fought each other and vandalised buildings outside the Lycavitos Police Station in Nicosia leading to the arrest of eight persons aged between fifteen years to twenty-two years.

To try to combat racism in sport in Cyprus, organisations such as *'Peace Players International'* a locally registered non-profit group have done work with Greek, and Turkish Cypriot youngsters to try to promote mutual respect through the sport of basketball. Several thousand children, including many from the Apollon fan base area, have benefited from attending bi-communal events.

Other individuals like Mario Joseph, a world-class coach and trainer, tried to diversify youngsters into other sports to try to create more local Cypriot role models.

The reality was that the majority of young Cypriots would never make it into top- flight football within Cyprus because of the advent of foreign players and to balance this he gave his support to eight ten-pin bowling academies, with up to thirty teams, operating island wide with over four thousand regular players.

Chapter Seven

2012

Can It Get Any Worse?

On Sunday 8 January 2012 nine people were slightly injured at a basketball game between Omonia and Apollon. Three Apollon basketball players, and three club officials, were injured in scuffles, whilst Omonia claimed that one of their club officials, and two former players, were assaulted during the game at the Tassos Papadopoulos Eleftheria Stadium in Nicosia.

There were only five police officers on duty at the game at the time and they had to call for backup as the dressing rooms were damaged. The match was cancelled at half time with Apollon players being chased off the court by Omonia fans, who were the only set of fans in attendance. This rule had been brought in by the Cyprus Basketball Association in an effort to reduce violence.

Some Omonia fans were armed with weapons, including one allegedly armed with a sword, and teargas was thrown at Apollon players by Omonia fans.

The usual three-way 'blame game' started with Apollon accusing Omonia officials of failing to intervene to stop the violence, whilst Omonia blamed poor refereeing and provocation by former Omonia players, some of whom were wearing APOEL shirts.

Omonia officials claimed that they had provided their own kit to the Apollon team to help them to get away from the stadium safely. The police were blamed for a lack of policing, and in turn they criticised both teams for failing to turn up at an arranged meeting to discuss policing requirements. It was all very familiar territory.

On Monday 9 January 2012 Nicoletta Tyrimou was appointed as the new police spokesperson for the ROC Police following the transfer of Michalis Ksounotos to the position of head of traffic in his hometown Limassol. He had become a familiar figure on the subject of football violence and said, *'I rest easy that I fulfilled to the fullest capacity the duties entrusted in me defending the force based on principles of transparency, honesty, and objectivity'.*

On Monday 16 January 2012 a twenty-seven-year-old man was remanded in custody for two days in connection with an attack against a member of the CFA disciplinary committee, which had occurred in December 2011, after the committee's decision to ban two Omonia officials for six month. That ban was actually cut to four games on appeal.

On the evening of the 2 December 2011 Aristotelis Misos had been attacked by two hooded men, as he left a betting shop, and was hit with a stick as well as being sprayed with teargas. He was treated for head injuries in Larnaca Hospital.

The suspect had been linked to the scene by DNA.

On Sunday 5 February 2012 AEL played APOEL in an evening game at Tsirion Stadium. Two men aged thirty-one years, and twenty-nine years, were arrested for hitting the Limassol Head of CID Yiannikis Georgiou in the face with a bottle whilst he was on duty at the ground. A twenty-two-year-old was also arrested before the game after being observed trying to throw a bag full of firecrackers over a wall into the stadium.

The game, which was watched by a crowd of 8,160

supporters, ended in a 0-0 draw.

On a Wednesday 8 February 2012, at 8pm, following a football match in Larnaca between Nea Salamina FC and Omonia FC, fifty hooded youths went to the nearby Antonis Papadopoulos Stadium, home to Anorthosis FC, and smashed the glass door to the stadium entrance, as well as damaging five cars.

No arrests were made in a match which Omonia won 8-1.

In the same period the Chair of the House Legal Affairs Committee Ionas Nicolaou welcomed a proposal by the European Union to set up an EU-wide database of known football hooligans saying, *'we are at an initial stage when it comes to combating hooliganism'*.

On Friday 24 February 2012 a twenty-eight-year-old former first division player reported to police that he had been beaten, and threatened at gunpoint, to sign papers saying that he would not claim wages owed to him by his old Nicosia Club. The club denied all knowledge of the matter, which was condemned by the CFA.

On Sunday 4 March 2012 five arrests were made, after a

game between Omonia and Ethnikos Achna, at the GSP Stadium in Nicosia, during which stones were hurled at the police and damage was caused. Eleven police officers were injured and one of those arrested, a fifteen-year-old, was found to be in possession of a knife.

The game finished in a 1-1 draw in front of a crowd of 6,172.

On Sunday 18 March 2012 a local derby match was played in the afternoon between AEL and Apollon in Limassol.

AEL won the game 3-1.

Some AEL fans gave a show of strength, driving in convoy on bikes in the streets, and waving flags. None of them were wearing helmets in a flagrant breach of the law, although many of them had the hoods of their yellow jackets up as they sounded their horns, set off flares, and blocked the road, caring less for the traffic stuck behind them.

The game was suspended by the referee Yiannakis Anastasios for ten minutes early in the second half, after objects were thrown onto the pitch, and then suspended during injury time after a goal scored by an AEL player Silas increased their lead to 3-

1 and provoked a shower of objects being thrown onto the pitch again by Apollon fans.

An AEL spokesman said, *'I want to congratulate our fans on not responding to the provocations as that was the right thing to do and by doing so they have protected their loved club'.* MMAD teams needed to deploy twice to try to calm the crowds.

Two sixteen-year-olds were arrested after being observed on CCTV at the ground hurling two red cylinders at Apollon fans, and trying to enter the ground whilst in possession of firecrackers.

A twenty-six-year-old was arrested for abusing police officers during the course of which he attacked one and stole a police radio.

On Thursday 22 March 2012 five thousand APOEL fans, some of whom had slept overnight in the car park, gathered at the GSP Stadium in Nicosia to try to get tickets for a Champions League game with Real Madrid, to be held the following week.

At 11.30am an announcement was made that only a few hundred tickets would be on sale. Following this the size of the crowd dwindled but three thousand fans remained until a ticket vendor turned up an hour later. After just ten minutes he closed the ticket window and left.

Tempers flared as supporters moved towards the main entrance seeking an explanation from the team's management. At this point some forty MMAD officers rushed out of the main entrance and formed a human barrier to prevent the crowds going further. A few bottles were thrown, and abuse hurled, as they then slowly dispersed, amidst rumours that a number of people had purchased tickets in bulk to sell on the black market.

On Friday 23 March 2012 APOEL played Omonia, at the GSP stadium in Nicosia, in front of a crowd of 18,000.

The game finished with a score line of 0-0.

Green and white flares were lit on the stands by Omonia fans, and the air was filled with smoke. APOEL fans responded by raising a huge montage of a group of men lined up, underneath which were the words, *the real terror of Nicosia'*.

On social media 'Mpatsoi Karkino' commented, amongst

other less than polite things, that APOEL fans should, *'stop behaving like penis's, get back in their cage, and shut their mouths'*.

Immediately after the game around twenty APOEL fans, on motorbikes and wearing helmets, broke the rear screen of a moving vehicle with crowbars and then lit a flare and threw it inside the car.

The two occupants had done nothing other than to be wearing Omonia club shirts. The APOEL fans then proceeded to hold the doors of the vehicle closed as the two men, aged twenty-two years and twenty-five years, tried desperately to escape the fire and fumes inside the confined space. This was a life or death situation which could have easily ended up as a double murder case.

Eye witnesses told a local Cyprus TV channel, Sigma TV, that when the occupants eventually managed to escape from the vehicle the APOEL supporters, who had been on motorcycles and were armed with bats, metal bars and knives, threw them to the ground and started kicking them even though their clothes were on fire.

Other fans leaving the football stadium managed to stop the attackers and the two men were rushed to hospital. Their attackers made off from the scene before the arrival of the police and fire service who were called to put out the fire.

Three arrests were made on the day for possession of firecrackers and flares.

A linesman who officiated at the APOEL v Omonia game, was later the subject of a bomb attack.

The CFA later fined both clubs for, amongst other things, allowing fans to chant politically motivated slogans.

On Sunday 25 March 2012 APOEL and Omonia's Under-21 teams played at the GSP Stadium. After the game stones were thrown onto the pitch in the practice areas and, after two people were attacked, other fans turned their attention to the police who were bombarded with stones and hit with bats.

Five police officers were injured and taken to hospital, one of whom suffered a fracture to his head.

In the aftermath police obtained search warrants for both fan club premises and following a search later that evening recovered seven bats, a spray, and two crash helmets, and made fifteen arrests.

One of the APOEL youth team Dioenis Sergides was subsequently fined and banned for one game for causing trouble at the match.

Once again the focus shifted to the Cyprus Football Association and its President Kostakis Koutsokoumnis, who was himself a former APOEL Club President. This was a particularly savage attack and people were crying out for action and for someone to take the lead.

On Saturday 7 April 2012 the CFA hit back at a statement made by President Demetris Christofias on the issue of football violence where he criticised 'football leaders'. They said that whilst they agreed with him that football should not serve economic, or petty political interests, it was clear, *all sociologists agree that sport doesn't produce hooligans, but hooligans who are produced by society act out in sports'*.

On the 11 April 2012 the Cyprus Sports Association put their weight behind the President and said that the CFA needed to do more to ensure that local championships were carried out in a framework of sports ethics and fair play.

On Saturday 5 May 2012 AEL played Anorthosis at Tsirion Stadium in Limassol. They scored the only goal of the match in the 73rd minute to win the game and become League Champions. The goal-scorer, Luciano Bebe, was mobbed by his team-mates as AEL fans went wild in the Stands, in a sea of yellow shirts.

After the game Limassol was full of cars with horns blaring, hazard lights flashing, and people dancing in the streets, and on buildings. Some of them were silhouetted against the darkness of the skyline as fires burnt out of control.

One resident Michael Thomaides told the Cyprus Mail that he had contacted the police and fire service on countless occasions for help but no one came. He said, *'0.1% of the population terrorised the other 99.9%. The Makarios roundabout destroyed, graffiti on shop windows, walls, pavements, roads, explosions of 'home- made' bombs, Bank windows shattered from explosions and stones, alarms ringing, road signs knocked down, public dustbins set alight'.*

Another resident Robert Becks told how he was returning from an event in Larnaca, with his wife and three young children in the car, when as they approached their home near Ayios Nicolaos roundabout, they came across scores of hooligans banging on cars and stopping traffic. His youngest child started crying with fear but despite phoning the police for help he was told to go to the police station to make a complaint.

He continued his account in the newspaper, *'as the evening progressed the situation rapidly worsened with fires being set all around my house and senseless vandalism everywhere. I phoned the police twelve times pleading with them to send some help. On numerous occasions they simply closed the phone. I phoned the fire department numerous times pleading for help. The fire department advised that they wouldn't come because the hooligans threw rocks at them'.*

He and his fifteen-year-old daughter started using a hose and buckets to put out fires surrounding their home but four masked men chased them away.

When asked to comment subsequently on the lack of police response a spokesman said that with 7,000 to 10,000 people out on the streets it was hard to have police everywhere.

On Tuesday 8 May 2012 The Cyprus Football Federation (KOP) began a series of meetings involving the Justice Minister to discuss violence in sport and allegations of match fixing.

On the 12 May 2012 the Cyprus First Division season concluded with AEL crowned as Champions with one game in hand before the end of the season.

On Wednesday 16 May 2012 Omonia beat AEL with a score line of 1-0 in the Coca Cola Cup Final, in an evening game, at the GSP stadium in Nicosia.

Ten thousand AEL fans packed their two allocated stands, but the 'double' was not to be as the only goal was scored in the 16th minute. All this despite the fact that AEL had possession during 56% of the game and had seven attempts at goal, as opposed to Omonia's two.

The GSP stadium is known as the *'damned stadium'* by AEL fans due to their team losing three previous cup finals there since the turn of the century, and now it was to be a fourth.

Yet another night of mayhem and lunacy followed.

At midnight AEL fans gathered near to their fan club and fought with Omonia fans celebrating nearby. At the Ayios Nicholaos roundabout telephone boxes and signs were damaged, and a nineteen-year-old Omonia fan, who was passing on a moped, was struck on the back with a crowbar and knocked over. He remounted and rode off only to be followed in a car and knocked off his moped again before making good his escape. He was able to get away relatively unscathed, but another twenty- year-old was admitted to Limassol General Hospital with head injuries.

Eighteen arrests were made of people aged between sixteen years to thirty- nine years, in Limassol, but when they appeared in Court only one was remanded in custody as the Courts decided that the police had not properly provided either grounds for arrest, or specific evidence as to their individual wrong doing.

In Nicosia fifty hooded men gathered outside APOEL's clubhouse near to the Hilton Hotel and threw stones at passing vehicles, and in Makarios Avenue Omonia fans gathered outside Lykavotis Police Station and caused disturbances leading to seven arrests.

On Wednesday 1 August 2012 UEFA fined AEL 8,000 euro when fans, who were seated in the aisles, for a game with Belgrade Partizan, refused to move, and the team delayed the start of the second-half by two minutes.

On Wednesday 8 August 2012 the CFA questioned the motives of the islands Player Association (PASP) which threatened the national team with a boycott if three recently naturalised foreign nationals were called up to the squad.

The CFA said the PASP were being 'borderline racist' and urged them to withdraw the threat if they were, *truly interested in the welfare of Cypriot footballers and the national team'*. In turn the PASP said that they had nothing against their colleagues but were concerned about the future of local players who were featured less and less in top-flight football.

On Thursday 9 August 2012 Anorthosis played the Georgian side FC Dila Gori in a UEFA European League third qualifying round match at the Antonis Papadopoulos Stadium.

With the score line at 3-0 to Dila Gori, in the 88th minute, a twenty-year-old Anorthosis fan with no shirt on, and carrying a rucksack on his back, ran onto the pitch and confronted the Anorthosis goalkeeper.

Police intervened and after a struggle, involving up to nine helmeted police officers, some carrying shields, he was arrested. This sparked a pitch invasion by up to forty Anorthosis fans who ripped out corner posts, covered their faces with clothing and confronted the police.

One fan on YouTube commented, *'Georgia scored the first goal which was actually offside, and then they scored two further goals due to mistakes by players. One fan ran onto the pitch to the Anorthosis keeper to tell him to 'fuck off'. Police came and tried to pull 'our brother' off the pitch and arrest him. We had to try to help him. We went onto the pitch and the press rooms and changing rooms and there was a riot with the police for about an hour'.*

The referee was forced to abandon the game.

Violence continued outside the stadium with stones being thrown at people and cars. Four cars, including a police vehicle, were damaged and five police officers slightly injured.

An eyewitness commented on the stadium security team and said, *'The authorities just stood there'*. He was advised not to leave the area until after 11pm for safety reasons.

Police later made four further arrests and circulated pictures of four other suspects who were captured on CCTV images. UEFA subsequently fined Anorthosis 50,000 euro and ordered them to play the next three European games behind closed doors for the fans' behaviour.

Also on the 9 August 2012 a twenty-year-old fan was arrested for setting fire to plastic seats in the GSP Stadium in Nicosia during a game between Omonia and Erythros Asteras.

On Saturday 18 August 2012 the CFA laid charges against Omonia in respect of incidents at a previous Super Cup match where fans had spat at the fourth referee, threw missiles, shouted abusive and political slogans and interrupted the game for three minutes. The team manager Michalis Kavalieris was also charged after being sent off the pitch for verbally abusing the same match official.

On the 1 September 2012 the seventy-fifth season of the 2012/13 Cyprus First Division began with AEL as the defending

Champions.

On Wednesday 5 September 2012 a Larnaca District Judge sentenced a twenty-two-year-old man to four months in prison for his part in the pitch invasion involving the Anorthosis game on the 9 August 2012.

The Larnaca District Court Judge had already sentenced three men, aged 26 years, 20 years, and 27 years, convicted of football violence at the same match, to four months imprisonment and commented at the time that, *'playgrounds should harbour entertainment, sportsmanship and healthy competition, as they did in the past'*.

Three more men awaited sentencing, in respect of incidents at the same game, and also faced charges of damaging a television camera valued at 50,000 euro. These sentences however were seen very much as the exception to the rule rather than the norm.

***

Postscript to this incident: On the 24 December 2012 details were posted on YouTube of a, *'coming home party for the brothers who*

273

had completed their prison sentences'. They were driven in convoy in darkness to a location, with a banner draped over a road bridge welcoming them home, fireworks, and lines of supporters on either side of the road holding flares.

***

On Sunday 7 October 2012 APOEL played Omonia at the GSP Stadium in Nicosia, in a game which ended in a 0-0 draw, in front of a crowd of 14,011 fans.Once again the centre of the stand occupied by Omonia fans was filled with green smoke from numerous flares, which then turned into grey smoke and drifted in a large cloud across the pitch.

Four arrests were made, namely a twenty-year-old for throwing a firecracker, a twenty-seven-year-old who abused a police officer, and a twenty-eight-year-old, and thirty-year-old who were drunk, and resisted a body search, as they entered the stadium.

On Sunday 21 October 2012 Omonia played Anorthosis at the Antonis Papadopoulos Stadium in Larnaca in front of a crowd of 8,500 fans.

At 4pm hooded fans attacked a police car patrolling Papanicolis Avenue and smashed the windows. Larnaca Police Chief Christos Andreou said an hour later a group of Omonia fans approached the stands with lit flares in their hands. MMAD units intervened and arrested a nineteen-year-old in possession of two flares.

During the course of the game, which Anorthosis went on to win 2-0, an Omonia fan threw a large firecracker onto the pitch, narrowly avoiding players and medical staff who were on the pitch with a stretcher. It was a miracle that no-one was seriously injured as play was stopped with players holding their heads, and officials milling around as swirling smoke enveloped them on the pitch.

Three further arrests were made of men aged 22 years, 19 years, and 20 years, for damage, assault police, and throwing stones. Four other vehicles were damaged.

One Omonia fan aged twenty-nine years went to hospital with an eye injury as a result of being hit by a missile.

After the match fans exchanged messages on the internet which showed the sheer depth of their hatred for each other, examples of which were: *'Always Omonia are faggots and gays. Fuck you Turkish arseholes. Cyprus is Greek, Cyprus is Greek – Fuck Turkey, Fuck England, Fuck America. Cancer to all anti-antifa pussies. Omonia my love. Death to APOEL and Anorthosis pussy fans. The only thing you can do is attack girls – see you soon in GSP. Gate 9 Antifa action. Your end is near. Pussies you throw firecrackers to the players and outside the stadium. You run like rabbits. But okay it was better fucking at the end. We won 2-0 with ten players once again. So don't mess with us. Fuck the Capital. Fuck Nicosia. Freedom to our brothers. ACAB'.* (All Coppers Are Bastards).

On Thursday 25 October 2012 there was finally some good news when 10,000 AEL fans gathered at the GSP stadium to play a match against the Turkish team FC Fenerbahce in a Europa League match.

More than 1,000 Turkish Cypriots came from the north to watch the game and with four hundred police officers on duty the match was played out with only a couple of minor incidents. Before the game two men from Turkey were caught trying to cross from the north, and a Turkish Cypriot was detained on a 2007 arrest warrant for burglary. During the match some Fenerbahce fans tried to unfurl a TRNC flag but police moved in quickly to confiscate it.

Nicosia Police Chief Kypros Michaelides hailed the policing operation as a complete success and said, *'we are truly proud because we proved once again that we are a European state, which can police football matches as well as any other significant event and we proved wrong all those malicious forecasts waiting for us to fail'.*

The police commented positively on how officials from both clubs had displayed hospitality towards each other and fully supported the police. The Turkish press commented that whilst the Turkish fans were waving Turkish flags the AEL fans were only waving AEL flags. Commentators hailed it as, *'sports victory over politics'.*

Prior to the game between APOEL and AEK at the GSP stadium, on Sunday 18 November 2012, police asked fans to respect each other and to show sportsmanship.

The game was played in front of a crowd of 9,652, and AEK

beat APOEL with a score line of 2-1, as stewards in high visibility yellow tabards were visible and seen to be trying to keep order. One twenty-eight-year-old fan clearly did not get the message as he was observed on CCTV in the ground lighting a firecracker and throwing it towards the pitch. He was duly arrested.

On Thursday 6 December 2012 eleven Marseille fans who had come to Cyprus to watch their team play AEL were arrested for shoplifting, at Larnaca Airport, after they were observed on CCTV stealing perfume and cigarettes valued at 2,000 euro which were stolen from the Duty Free shop.

On Tuesday 11 December 2012 the CFA and the Turkish Cypriot Football Association met to try to attempt to unify football on the island with again the focus being on *'football not politics'*. Further meetings were promised.

On the 15 December 2012 it was announced that Cyprus football clubs owed 13 million euro in taxes despite sponsorship and sizeable budgets. The plight of Omonia in particular was highlighted who owed money to both ex and current players and coaches.

During the course of 2012/13 three police officers from the

Republic of Cyprus attended a EU/UEFA Pan-European Police Training Programme in relation to dealing with sports related violence.

Chapter Eight

2013

On Thursday 17 January 2013 the CFA and the Turkish Football Association met again, together with officials from UEFA and FIFA, in order to try to make progress on the issue of unifying football on the island.

On Saturday 19 January 2013 APOEL played Omonia at the GSP Stadium, which ended in a 1-1 score draw, in front of a crowd of 15,727 fans.

At 2.15pm a twenty-six-year-old man was arrested in possession of two smoke bombs as he tried to enter the stadium. An hour later a twenty-nine-year-old was arrested in possession of two rocks, and at 4.30pm a nineteen-year-old was arrested for throwing a rock at the police. At the same time two sixteen-year-olds were arrested for abusing and assaulting police. Despite these efforts numerous flares were lit on the stands throughout the game with no response from the authorities.

A bus carrying fans was later stopped in Strovolos, after they were spotted lighting and throwing firecrackers from the moving vehicle. Inside the vehicle police found a plastic bag containing five firecrackers and a smoke bomb. All eighteen occupants were detained for a while at Strovolos Police Station before being released.

In a separate incident a woman reported damage to her vehicle after being stoned by fans.

At the end of January 2013 the Police Chief Michalis Papageorgiou gave a media briefing on how the Force had performed during 2012. He highlighted that murders, robberies and cases of blackmail had all increased on the previous year. In commenting about the fact that there had been eighteen cases of murder the previous year, in comparison to only eight in 2011, he provided something of an insight into the mind-set of some Cypriots when he said, *'several Cypriots have become ill- tempered, they have become aggressive arbitrary, they have become violent people who easily take the law into their own hands'.*

He highlighted that the debt crisis which started in 2009

coincided with a recorded increase in crime, and that there was an increase in the availability of drugs, with young people aged between nineteen years to twenty-four years being the biggest 'at risk' group. It was perhaps not surprising that this age group also fitted into the profile of many football hooligans and no doubt contained a few of the *'angry men'*.

In highlighting the Force's capacity to deal with these increases Papageorgiou pointed out that due to austerity measures the police had their budget reduced by eighteen million euro, and had three hundred and sixty five fewer members of staff, despite an increased workload due to Cyprus taking up the presidency of the European Council.

On Sunday 3 March 2013 extensive damage was caused to the fountain, at the roundabout by Larnaca Port, by APOEL fans, just before a game with AEK at GSZ Stadium, which was attended by just 4,322 supporters. Just after 3pm, before the match started, they left their fan club near to the port and started throwing fireworks and stopping traffic.

They then proceeded to damage the fountain, daub the area in slogans, and set fire to dustbins. Police arrived but it took them twenty minutes to restore some sort of order. Two officers were slightly injured, when missiles thrown by fans hit them, and a twenty-seven-year-old was arrested.

The match itself was won by APOEL with a score line of 1-0.

Larnaca Mayor Andreas Louroudjiatis said that they would demand compensation for the damage to the fountain which had cost 1.5 million euro to construct.

On Saturday 6 April 2013 violence took place at two matches, one between Omonia and APOEL in Nicosia, and another between Anorthosis and AEK in Larnaca. Both had a familiar ring to them with cars damaged and flares, firecrackers and Molotov cocktails being thrown by rival fans.

At the game in Nicosia some Omonia fans filmed themselves riding on bikes, in convoy, on their way to the ground, again very few of them wearing a helmet, horns blazing, and waved on by a police officer doing traffic duties.

As the second-half was about to start the two sets of fans tried to get into the moat which circles the stadium and teargas was deployed by police, three of whom suffered injuries

Police made four arrests, including one for possessing a sharp instrument, and two for damaging a police vehicle with a firecracker.

Omonia won the game 3-0 in front of a crowd of 13,757.

After the game 3,000 APOEL fans gathered outside their clubhouse in Nicosia and threw stones and bottles at passing cars leading to the arrest of two men aged twenty-one years and twenty-three years.

Ten minutes after the game in Larnaca finished a group of Anorthosis fans put hoods on and headed towards the AEK stand. Police intervened and one officer was hit by stone throwing. A hundred Anorthosis fans then made their way to the team's training ground where they damaged twelve cars.

In a separate incident five AEK fans in a vehicle were stopped by Anorthosis fans, in three other vehicles, and were attacked and injured. The following morning three men aged 21 years, 20 years and 18 years were arrested, and on Monday 8 April 2013 a further six arrests followed, all of whom were remanded in custody for three days.

AEK beat Anorthosis with a score line of 3-0 in front of a crowd of 5,500.

Between the 11 and 14 April 2013 Cyprus played host to a six-person delegation from the Council of Europe Standing Committee on Spectator Violence who were looking at how compliant the country was in terms of delivering the aims of the European Convention on spectator violence, and misbehaviour at sports events, and in particular at football matches.

The visit was focused on Nicosia and during their stay the delegates visited the GSP Stadium on two occasions to observe two matches, one on the 10 April 2014 between Omonia and AEL, and the second between APOEL and Anorthosis on the 13 April 2014.

Both matches were classified as high-risk and for the second game 230 police officers, and 170 stewards, were on duty which delegates noted in resource terms was far higher than most other European countries, for a crowd of 12,000, would deploy.

The delegates also met with key players involved in trying to solve the problems of football hooliganism and observed that, in addition to the fact that the National Committee for Violence did not have decisive powers, there were also key stakeholders such as football supporters groups, and communities and businesses, who lived adjacent to grounds, missing from the table.

The absence of dialogue with supporters groups in particular had led to a polarization of positions and a lack of trust between the police, clubs, and supporters.

They also noted that the police and the Justice Ministry were not closely involved in meetings held by the Committee. The report they subsequently published later in the year said that many people had commented, *'there were a lot of talks over the last twenty years about the problems, but not about the implementation of the solutions',* and people agreed that the real problem was the implementation of the law and putting theory into practice.

The delegation commented on the extremely low percentage of people who were actually punished for their behavior, which was estimated at being in the low single figures and reiterated that, *'a lack of sanctions leads to a lack of incentive to change behaviour'.*

At the match they observed on the 13 April 2013 no serious incidents took place, although at one stage APOEL fans unfurled two provocative banners aimed at the opposition and no intervention took place by either stewards or police.

At the conclusion of the report twenty-nine recommendations were made, and an action plan produced, which stipulated maximum time periods of two years for the Cyprus authorities to complete.

On Saturday 27 April 2013 APOEL played AEK at Nicosia GSP stadium during the course of which police deployed teargas to quell trouble, some of which effected innocent bystanders. Fourteen thousand spectators were in attendance and the score finished 0-1 to AEK.

APOEL fans published videos of the trouble on the Internet on Ultras-Tifo.Net headlined, *'Police wanted to enter APOEL tribune with teargas but supporters threw them outside where riots continued'.* The videos showed a stand-off with police carrying riot shields, a kiosk which had been trashed, scrub set on fire as smoke rose over the stadium, and seats smashed up.

The Justice Minister Ionas Nicolaou apologised afterwards, on behalf of the police, and said, *'this is the reason we have taken certain decisions today with the aim of improving our ways and our behaviour as a police force. Teargas should only be used in extenuating circumstances when there is imminent danger and for that we recognise that problems were caused due to our lack of training on the subject'.*

He said that a special investigation team had been set up to identify suspects from photographs and that new measures would be introduced in conjunction with the CFA. He also promised to look into allegations of police brutality towards Omonia fans the week before.

The following day Nicosia police started an investigation into a burglary at the Technical College, next to the APOEL club, where fans had been celebrating their team's success at being crowned champions. A fire was started in the college and chairs and a computer stolen, and nearby traffic lights smashed.

On the 19 May 2013 the Cyprus First Division season finished with APOEL as Champions having won two match weeks before the end of the season.

On Wednesday 22 May 2013 AEL played Apollon in the Cyprus Cup Final in Limassol. During the match the stadium was full of smoke from flares and looked more like a fireworks display. Above the Apollon fans on the terraces was a huge banner which read, *'ready for the fight. Not even a step back'*.

Apollon went on to win the game 1-0, and afterwards the *'Gate 3'* yellow shirts of AEL and the *'Gate 1'* blue shirts of Apollon confronted each other in the streets outside the ground, and surged backwards and forwards, as they tested each other's strengths. One AEL fan commented on the Internet after the game, *'Apollon ran like the hare'*.

In July 2013 a UEFA training programme for stewards was scheduled to take place in Cyprus.

At 7.30pm on Friday 12 July 2013 a so-called 'friendly' game took place in Larnaca between the host team Anorthosis FC, and Apollon FC, at the Antonis Papadopoulos Stadium. There were special entrances for away fans but they were apparently not used on the night in question.

At about 7.45pm, fifteen minutes into the game, approximately two hundred Apollon fans approached the stadium, in one body, carrying Molotov cocktails, flares, firecrackers, bats and stones and were confronted by four-hundred Anorthosis fans who streamed out of the stadium to face them.

About twenty police officers present initially tried without much success to quell the ensuing violence which went on for more than an hour. They were eventually joined by a further twenty officers, and eight officers incurred slight injuries, with two officers being treated at Larnaca Hospital before being discharged.

Events were described through the eyes of a *'Maxhtec'* Anorthosis fan which were posted onto social media, together with a video, on the 18 August 2013 – *'Anorthosis fans were inside their own curva shouting for their colours, when 100 supporters of Apollon arrived. Taking advantage of our absence they managed to move down towards the central shuttle. This riot could have been the best riot and could have been played as real men with the use of only hands but Apollon fans approached us with flares, crackers, stones and all the other things they had carried with them. Our answer was immediate though as you can see one of their fans gets on fire from the first item thrown by our side. Watching the video you can realise that as soon as we got out from our curva Apollon fans have withdrawn 400 metres from their original position before we got out. You can also notice that during the whole time many of our lads are showing their naked hands towards them but they continue not to follow and continue throwing items. Basically they aimed to take vengeance for several lost riots in the past but not only did they failed but they withdrew to the back, one of their lads was severely damaged and burned, they lost many of their personal items and once more showed to us that they are not planning to ever start a riot with hands.....Messing with us. Way too risky!'*

The video choreographed with stirring music showed scenes of group violence with Molotov Cocktails crashing onto the ground amongst supporters and exploding in flames.

Three parked vehicles were damaged by stone throwing youths, and a twenty-year-old sustained second-degree burns, classed as serious but not life threatening. He was initially taken to Limassol General Hospital but then transferred to Nicosia Hospital because of the level of his injuries and placed on a respirator in Intensive Care due to inhaling fumes from the mix of flares, Molotov cocktails, and volleys of tear gas fired by the police.

Apollon won the match itself with a score line of 5-0.

Nine Apollon fans were arrested on Sunday 14 July 2013, in connection with the trouble, and Larnaca District Court remanded two of them for five days, and the other seven for three days.

The police chief investigator Marios Papachristophorou told the court that the twenty-year-old had suffered second-degree burns as a result of being struck by a Molotov cocktail. There were counter-claims that a firecracker that he was holding had in fact burned the individual, but the police did not support this theory, saying, *'Apollon fans behaviour was inexcusable and it would appear that they planned the whole thing'*.

One seemingly enlightened Anorthosis supporter, Christos Andreou aged fifty-nine years, told the media at the time, *'there are no friendly games in Cyprus. Police should have taken measures knowing what fans in Cyprus are like and they should have learnt from previous mistakes. Hooligans will always exist and police need to take more severe methods to dissuade them and come down hard on them. I went to Stamford Bridge to watch Chelsea play APOEL in the Champions League a couple of years ago and we were told to keep on the pavement. One APOEL fan decided he was going to walk on the road at which point he was asked to get back on the pavement. He refused and within seconds a police car pulled up and officers told him he was either going to continue walking on the pavement or he was going to be put in the car and taken away. Unsurprisingly he got back on the pavement and didn't get off'.*

In truth this was *'zero tolerance'* being put into real practice.

The Justice Ministry said that it was discussing new measures to prevent this type of violence and on Thursday 1 August 2013, following a meeting involving the Deputy Police Chief Andreas Kyriacou, the Justice Minister Ionas Nicolaou announced a series of measures in response to violence at the 'friendly' games.

These included the creation of a software package designed to assist in identifying offenders taken from video and photographic material, the provision of an additional three days training for police riot teams in order to better equip them in dealing with crowds calmly, and the use of undercover officers in stadiums. He said that a Bill would be introduced to ban previous troublemakers from going to matches, and that an amendment would allow court cases to be fast tracked within twenty-four hours to enable strict bail conditions to be put into place as well as encouraging the use of banning orders following conviction.

In the week previous attention had turned to issues of safety at the GSP Stadium in Nicosia as the manager warned that thousands of lives could be put at risk if police did not do something to stop a number of sandwich vans from blocking the emergency exits during matches.

Phivos Constantinides complained that despite letters to the Justice Minister, and pleas to the police, these vehicles were still routinely blocking access for people to leave, and crucially for fire engines to get in. He was quoted as saying, *'experts came from England, a country which has seen its fair share of tragedies, and they have told us on numerous occasions what measures to take, but instead of learning from their mistakes, we are acting like we want to learn from our own mistakes'*. With complete disregard for the law the vendors even put chairs out for customers to sit on adjacent to the exit gates.

Coupled with this, instead of fans using the car park at the stadium, which had 2,278 spaces, cars were abandoned on pavements, roundabouts, or even at stop signs, forcing people to walk in the roads.

It was all part of the collective chaos that reduced still further any sense of good order, and made it easier for the hooligans to operate.

On Saturday 10 August 2013 a game took place at Pelendri between Omonia and Aris of Limassol, in a pre-season friendly, which was refereed by Leontios Trattos, the chairman of the Cyprus Referees Association, and which Omonia won with a score line of 3-0.

Neither club had asked for a police presence at the match, which is usually the case with friendly fixtures, but during the course of the game an Omonia supporter went on to the pitch and said to Trattos, *'we have not forgotten what you did to us in 2004'.*

This referred to a match between Omonia and Enosis Neon Paralimniou which they drew 1-1 but resulted in them losing the seasons title.

At the end of the game, according to the general secretary of the referees' association Marios Panayi, the referee was approached by a group of some thirty Omonia fans and attacked by three of them.

Trattos had to leave the stadium in a police car and was later taken home by another referee. Despite being injured he declined hospital treatment but gave a statement to the police.

Omonia President Stelios Mylonas attempted to shield the referee, as the attack took place, and the CFA later said that it would act decisively to prevent *'acts of terrorism'* which caused damage to football on the island. Some might have said at the time that the use of this particular word was extreme but given later events in 2014 against the same referee it was perhaps entirely appropriate.

Three days later warrants were issued for the arrest of two Omonia supporters, as a result of being identified from photographs taken on the day of the incident, and evidence gathering was being pursued by police in respect of a third person.

On the 31 August 2013 the 2013/2014 season of the Cypriot First Division began. It was the 76th season of the Cypriot top-level football league made up of eleven teams from the 2012/13season, plus three promoted teams from the 2012/13 Second Division. APOEL were the defending champions.

On this date Anorthosis played Omonia, during which Anorthosis fans choreographed a huge blue and white card display on the terracing, sometimes known as a *'tifo'*, which was followed by pyrotechnics and tickertape. Anorthosis won the game with a score line of 3-1.

On social media afterwards Ultras from opposing clubs then continued to trade insults:

Anorthosis Ultras Famagusta, *'our club has had the most arrests than any other team the last years, just recently 7 of our brothers got jail sentences 4-7 months, no other supporters in Cyprus have received such treatment....It is APOEL who have good treatment from the police and justice we have always received the worst. 4 of our supporters received bans for yesterday's match too*

as well as Omonia fans. *Fuck Ionas. Fuck Cyprus Justice. ACAB'.*
and *'Ban us all son of a bitch Ionas'.*

Green, *'it's pathetic how these pricks show white power and Waffen SS flags, while they don't know shit about the history of these things and only show them to provoke and seem tough while they're all massive pussies'.*

Response from a Greek, *'it's still better than stupid flags with Che, Bob Marley, Soviet Union etc. It's absolutely illogical for people from Greece or Cyprus. Just Greek nationalist spirit is why we can still find Greece on the map. If you don't like it you can move to Turkey. I'm sure that after few months your mind will be full of white power ideology too'.*

On Friday 1 November 2013 five police officers were injured during a basketball game between AEL and Apollon in Limassol. Just before the end of the game AEL fans started assaulting Apollon's coach, and players on the bench, and up to three hundred AEL fans invaded the court and confronted the police. The injured officers suffered neck, knee, and head injuries, and one officer was detained at Limassol General Hospital.

As the Authorities yet again exercised their minds about what to do, one person using the pseudonym *'disqus'* commented in the media, *'so the score was: 5 policemen to hospital, 0 hooligans arrested. Looks like the hooligans won yet again. Same score as always'*.

On Thursday 19 December 2013 seven police officers were injured as fans tried to force their way into a match between Dighenis and APOEL, at Oroklini Community Stadium, without paying. No arrests were made and all of the officers were treated at Larnaca Hospital, one of them receiving eight stitches.

The game finished with a score line of 2-2.

The season was due to finish on the 18 May 2014 but little did anyone know at that time that this was not to be the case.

Chapter Nine

A Profile Of 'Hooligans' In Cyprus

There is some confusion about the use of the word fan but some of its origins can be traced to followers of boxing in England in the nineteenth century. The first use of the word hooliganism is unknown but appeared in a London police report in 1898 with reference to Irish street gangs.

Numerous studies have been undertaken into the nature of football hooliganism, including a project undertaken by The Cyprus Sociological Association in 2002, but there are two things in Cyprus that add a unique dimension to the complex mix of indicators which make up a profile, namely politics, which has been covered earlier in the book, and location.

In prefacing everything that follows in this chapter it has to be stressed that the vast majority of Cypriot football supporters are decent people who just want to enjoy the game and that the so-called football hooligans represent a small, if not significant, minority.

If you look at a map of Cyprus you will see that the main centres of population are Nicosia, Larnaca, Limassol, and Paphos. The residents of those towns and cities have long standing views on each other, which in one way could be deemed as rather humorous but often belies more serious and deep-rooted negative overtones.

People in Limassol will often comment that the men from Nicosia are *'children of their mothers'* – meaning that *'the men are under their mothers skirts'* or even worse *'Poutti'* which is a very unflattering word for part of the female anatomy. They resent the fact that Nicosia is seen as the place of central authority for Cyprus.

Those from Nicosia will say quite simply that Limassol is a *'Fuck Town' whilst* residents from Larnaca are sometimes referred to as *'Gypsies'*.

If you come from Paphos other Cypriots refer to them as, *'being far back from civilisation',* and there is a joke that when the tunnel from Paphos to Limassol was completed on the highway that the people from Paphos used to, *'stop at the Duty- Free'* as they got to the other side of the tunnel.

There is clear evidence that these 'locality' issues form one of the layers that influence hooligan behaviour and whilst it is clear that football plays a major role in this type of cultural behaviour, it might explain why other sports such as basketball have been affected as well. There have even been instances of confrontations on school excursions between students from different locations.

In the four areas mentioned Paphos appears to have the lowest numbers of football fans, which is not surprising given that no major teams play in that locality, whilst the other three share broadly the same levels of interest in the game.

Overwhelmingly genuine football fans in Cyprus highlight fan violence and 'fanatic mentality' as being the biggest problem affecting the game.

In keeping with the UK, and other countries, there is clear evidence that the majority of people in Cyprus involved in football violence are male, with very little involvement of females.

In 2007, psychologist and sociologist Antonis Raftis said that hooliganism was a, *universal problem with many people behaving 'normally' when not at sporting events. When they get together at football or basketball matches for example they all have one thing in* common - their team and it easy for them to express their frustrations when they are in groups rather than individually'.

He added that, *'many people follow a select few ringleaders who 'spread the virus of violence'. Emotions run high. There is lots of aggressive chanting and people simply get carried away'.*

In 2009 another academic Dr. Dino Domic, an Assistant Professor in consumer behaviour at the European University Cyprus, said, *'hooliganism fulfils a primitive human need. The need to express oneself...The question we need to ask is why do these young men have so much 'bottled up anger'.* He added that older generations should have a hard look at themselves and said, *'we've raised young people who have no cause – no objectives. If we look at the past we had World War II, the Hippy movement, the feminist movement. Nowadays there is no common unifying objective...it's about who wears label jeans and has the fastest car. The kids are totally lost'.*

In a damning indictment he blamed parents for pampering children and said, *'we haven't taught the value of work. We've made it too easy for them. And yes it reflects our failure as a society'.*

Many Cypriots have a natural aversion to 'authority' and figures of authority. This is why you see so many people routinely flouting road traffic laws, such as not wearing seat belts or crash helmets. They want to be free to make their own choices and simply do not like being told what to do especially by a police force that they see as being politically biased, and one where people are not always treated impartially.

Given the difficulties the police have in enforcing traffic law it is perhaps therefore not surprising that trying to exercise it in a public-order situation is even harder. Thus those involved with football violence are as likely to be concerned in other forms of low-level criminality or anti-social behaviour.

A classic example of this type of behaviour was reported in the Cyprus Mail on the 19 July 2014 when it was reported that the Mayor of Engomi had asked for speed cameras installed on Nicosia's Grivas Dighenis Avenue, to stop young drivers using the road as a race-track, be switched off during the daytime.

His argument was that too many local residents were 'absent mindedly' exceeding the 50 kph speed limit during the day and many of them were receiving tickets. Somewhat surprisingly the Chief of Traffic told the Mayor that he would submit his request to the Minister of Justice for consideration.

***

Football hooliganism, in keeping with other countries, is very 'tribalistic' in Cyprus and each of the clubs express loyalty to differing symbols some of which are attached to the hooligan history of that particular club.

Omonia fans wear green and white colours, and are often referred to as *'the Chinese'* because there are so many of them. Green is said to be the colour of 'hope' and white the colour of 'joy'. The club uses a green 'shamrock' shaped leaf as one of its emblems which again is seen as an emblem of 'hope and power'.

Many Omonia fans see themselves as being involved in a social struggle against fascism with one of their mottos being, *'Smash Fascism and Goodnight White Proud'.* In the 2011/12 football season they even choreographed an enormous picture of a 'hammer and sickle' in a football crowd.

Their hooligan element lay claim to the North Stand at the GSP Stadium in Nicosia where they can be heard chanting, *'I am telling you, you are the best medicine, you are the best drug. You take my mind. I am singing for you'.* and refer to themselves as being members of *'Gate 9'* and revere the year 1992.

They also used to have a regular spot in the old Makarion Stadium during Omonia's home games back in the 1980s.

The reference to the term *'Gates'* has existed for many years and, whilst at first glance, you might assume that this was always something to do with the gates that certain sets of fans used, to enter grounds, the reality is that in some cases the gate number does not even exist. Number nine was in fact also the team shirt number for one of their most revered players Sotiris Kaiafis.

'Gate 9' claim to have one thousand members with at least eight branches around the world, including one in the UK which had two hundred members in 2005. A number of their members have met untimely deaths through being involved in road accidents and they claim to make efforts to provide some support to their families.

They have also organised protests in relation to the death of sixteen-year-old Alexis Grigoropoulos, who was killed in Greece during clashes with the police, and in 2007 members travelled to Israel to establish a link with Ultras Hapoel part of the 'ANTIFA' movement who are said to have helped people from Sudan and people with disabilities in their country.

Hapoel means 'workers' and one of their aims is for, *'workers of the world to unite'*. They claim to be left wing and not anti-Arab, with whom they seek peace.

They are at pains not to be confused with APOEL who they regard as being fascists.

Omonia class their two main rivals as being the police and the *'unnamed'*, which is how they prefer to call their club rivals.

The Ultra groups within each of the top five clubs share the same mentality in relation to four core points:

. 1) They never stop singing, or chanting, during the match no matter what the result.

. 2) They never sit down during the match.

. 3) They attend as many games as possible, home and away, regardless of cost, or distance.

. 4) They have loyalty to the Stand in which the group is located – also known as the *'curva'* or *'kop'*.

Not all of the so called *'Ultra'* groups in Cyprus are automatically connected to violence, indeed one message, posted on a social website on the 1 September 2012 by the Ultras AEM from Moutayiaka Village in Limassol, referred to the setting up in 1983 of the 'Athletic Union Moutayiaka', and in some ways gave a message of hope amongst all the despair, *'our goal as a loyal group is to be away from the 'modern football' dominated by the mainstream. Seeing that the only true football that remained is the rustic Lower Division Championship. There not dominate, nor the financial, nor the lie. There need not be the political. But playing for the jersey of a village that it supports'.*

***

Apollon fans refer to themselves as *'Gate 1'*.

Anorthosis Ultras traditionally occupy the North Stand at the

Antonis Papadopoulos Stadium, in Larnaca, and one of their regular chants is, *'Always fight for the blue and whites'.*

AEL fans refer to themselves as *'Gate 3'* or the *'Super 3'.*

For many years supporters of the clubs in the First Division League have organized into fan clubs and gather in clubhouses which are treated as 'hallowed premises'.

If you go to AEL's second clubhouse, and more recent acquisition, which is situated on a traffic roundabout near to 'My Mall' in Limassol you will see the stark reality of how fans ignore the rule of law.

Previously known as the *'Swordfish Inn',* cars are parked routinely on double yellow lines, on the roundabout itself, and all of the new road signs have been graffiti sprayed with AEL insignia. The whole of the front of the clubhouse has been sprayed with a huge picture of a *'roaring lion'* taking pride of place. A long concrete wall adjacent to the property has been spray painted with slogans with the word 'hooligan' unashamedly in bold lettering. There is no evidence of any enforcement activity taking place whatsoever, as groups congregate with impunity.

The police seem unwilling, or unable to confront the situation which is not unique in Cyprus.

Another example of how laws are routinely flouted relates to smoking in restaurants, bars, and the like, which was completely banned in Cyprus in January 2010 but 'lip service' is paid to the law which is infrequently enforced by the police.

***

Footnote: *In February 2014 some Deputies in the Parliament building were themselves accused of smoking in the building and flouting the very law that they had passed.*

***

Little surprise then that this type of behaviour emboldens the hooligans on match days when they continue to push the boundaries of anti-social behaviour to the point where it is now just seen normal. This is the picture presented to visitors to 'My Mall', which is a brand new shopping centre, and leisure centre, with designer shops to attract tourists and local families. The contrast could not be starker and does nothing positive for the image of Cyprus as a whole.

As you move through Limassol, and onto the highway, there are constant reminders of football related graffiti on hoardings, walls, and road signs, and such efforts as have been made to remove the graffiti have failed. AEL supporters are alleged to have several three-man teams, whose role is to graffiti, and they do it with apparent impunity.

At the other end of Cyprus, on one of the main arterial routes into the capital city Nicosia, a similar scene greets you at the clubhouse of APOEL which rises like a pyramid, at the roadside, and is likewise plastered in slogans, graffiti, and street artwork extolling the virtues of the club. All of this designed to mark out their 'piece of territory' in much the same way as that seen by other species living on the planet, and to be defended just as ferociously.

When I first went to Cyprus in 2003 it was relatively rare to see graffiti in public areas and although there was a tradition amongst youths entering National Service to spray paint areas, with the date of their intake, there was little in the way of football related graffiti.

By 2007 this had changed, and by 2014 it had reached epidemic proportions in some areas. Municipalities were obliged to clean public areas but not private property but they were fighting a losing battle with locations like the showcase roundabouts built in Limassol to ease traffic problems, a frequent target for graffiti.

Police put the blame on youngsters and football fans, with one fan spraying a slogan, which would then be sprayed over by someone from an opposing team, or a counter slogan added. Whilst the police confirmed that graffiti was classed as a Malicious Damage offence with sentences up to three years imprisonment and a fine of 1,500 euro, the reality was that prosecutions were rare.

In the UK it has long been acknowledged that graffiti is a 'precursor crime' to encouraging other forms of criminality, and that it needs to be actively addressed to reduce the fear of crime within the community. This is clearly not the case in Cyprus and adds to the football hooligans' feelings of being untouchable. They have even used social-networking sites to promote pictures of their handiwork which on the one-hand mirrors some of the 'street art' seen in America, and the UK, to the basic and blatant messages of hate all too often sprayed along household walls such as, *all the Police Force will go under the ground. Whores, Lesbian Police – Fighters ACAB'*.

Cypriot hooligans come from all social classes, but many come from the middle-class, and the majority will be well educated men in their twenties, with jobs, and in some cases their own families.

The younger element will be in their late teens seen as the 'up and comers' striving for recognition, and acceptance, in a strictly hierarchical structure where there is a recognised 'pecking order'.

The older element will be in their early-thirties, some of whom will have a history of involvement in violence, which has established their reputations.

Mixed in among these age-groups will be the socially inadequate looking for a 'sense of identity' and the opportunity to belong to something tangible, that will give them friends and sometimes status, within a society where traditional values, and structures, are being challenged more routinely.

This group is particularly vulnerable to 'grooming' because they will be desperate to please and fit into the hooligan structure. They will be tested and the fear of rejection will play strongly in their efforts to be accepted.

As parents struggle to maintain a coherent family structure there is some evidence that their influence and ability to divert sons away from criminal behaviour has diminished over the years.

A struggling economy will have provided another fertile recruitment ground for youngsters who can see no future for themselves, and more importantly no money in their pockets to socialise in the more traditional ways through visiting restaurants and Bouzouki.

It should not be assumed that all of those involved in violence will have come to the notice of the police, in fact many will have not surfaced on their 'radar' at all, and even fewer will have been convicted of football violence, especially given the nature of how protracted justice can be in Cyprus. Even those that are convicted will invariably receive what are deemed to be 'light sentences' leaving them free to continue their activities but with an additional 'badge of honour' to their credit.

Some hooligans will actually seek the company of police officers, in social- settings, in order to try and solicit information in relation to police tactics, or to try to establish 'connections' which they think might afford them a level of protection should they be arrested.

At the same time there is clear evidence that the police are seen as targets for acts of violence with the added potential for acts of intimidation given the fact that 'everyone knows everyone' in Cyprus and it is not particularly difficult to find out where a police officer lives.

In Cyprus everyone knows a police officer, or a politician, in a position of influence. It is the norm and when problems occur their advice is routinely sought with an expectation that they will assist if at all possible. Remaining impartial in such a small society is very challenging to say the least.

The casual use of cannabis, in a society where smoking is still widely practiced, and alcohol, is evident amongst those involved in football violence, although as yet there is no clear evidence of hard drugs being routinely accessible. However in 2014 drug seizures on the island appeared to be on the increase, and this is a factor which might change in the future, as more addictive drugs such as heroin and cocaine become more widely available, and hooligan groups provide a ready- made focus for dealers.

Hooligans are absolutely dedicated to their chosen team and invariably go to all home, and away, games entering the ground early, wearing club colours, and occupying particular terraces. In some cases, when travelling away, for example, to Larnaca, they will travel even earlier and occupy the centre of some unsuspecting village en route for several hours, before a game, creating havoc, blocking roads and intimidating the locals.

Generally the local police in small numbers will feel powerless other than to appeal to the better nature of fans who will invariably consume more and more alcohol by the hour. There is a parallel to this with UK hooligans who traditionally take the opportunity to occupy seaside resorts at weekends when their team is playing nearby, although they are less likely to display identifying scarves.

APOEL based in Nicosia, Anorthosis based in Larnaca, but representing Famagusta in the 'Occupied Area', and Apollon in Limassol, are widely considered to be affiliated to the 'right wing' of politics, whereas Omonia based in Nicosia, and AEL based in Limassol, are seen as leaning towards the 'left wing'.

In more recent times AEL fans have sought however to de-politicise themselves to some degree.

In a comment on a social networking site on April 7 2011 'Isovias3' said, *'we are the only team in Cyprus that the fans go to the stadium only for the support of the team and not for politics. In 2009 the newspaper reported in a neighbourhood in Limassol there were 400 voting cards on them 'EVIVA AEL'. We are fanatics only for our love AEL. Always Faithful Gate 3 Limassol 1989'.*

The fans of right-wing teams APOEL -The Portocalli, and Anorthosis - Machites/Fighters or *'Macedonian Fighters'*, make use of the Greek flag, Greek colours, and the two-headed Byzantine Eagle.

There is a certain irony in the behaviour of fans from the extreme right-wing in that they will applaud their teams enthusiastically from the stands, albeit there is a real racial mix of foreign talent, all of whom would require residency permits, whilst at the same time on the streets they espouse strong anti-immigration views.

Racism in sport in Cyprus is not well documented, which to some extent is a reflection of the reporting systems which exist in Cyprus as a whole, where some might say that racism does not exist.

In 2013 the Ombudsman Institute had a record of only four cases of racism in football. However in a report entitled *'Racist Violence in Cyprus'* published in March 2011 there are references to the fact that in 2009 APOEL was charged by UEFA due to the racist behaviour of their fans, and on the 19 February 2009 a group of Turkish Cypriots were attacked, after a match, by Apollon fans, as they sat stationary in vehicles at a traffic junction.

Black players in Cyprus have been subjected to *'monkey chanting'* from crowds and one player in particular, Seyni N'Diaye of Senegal, who has played for both AEL and Omonia has suffered from this behaviour with little or no sanctions being imposed.

The fans of left-wing teams Omonia- Gate 9, and AEL –

Gate 3, sometimes make use of the Cypriot Flag, and pictures of Che Guevara as a post-communist symbol.

APOEL fans consider their arch-rivals to be AEL and Omonia. The first because they are based in Limassol, and have an intense dislike of each other, and the second because of deep-rooted political differences are considered the *'eternal enemy'*.

APOEL fans are considered by their opponents to be *'politically connected'* and to have close connections with the police in Nicosia. Anecdotally they will point towards the provision of heavy police support for convoys of APOEL fans to travel to away-games, which are not always replicated elsewhere.

Omonia fans consider all right-wing teams as their enemy. They have an intense dislike of APOEL fans, with whom they share the capital city, and the GSP stadium.

AEL fans consider all right-wing teams to be their serious rivals but in particular Apollon, who are also based in Limassol, and with whom they share Tsirion stadium, and APOEL with whom there is a traditional 'vendetta'.

Anorthosis fans consider Omonia to be opponents due to their long-lasting political rivalry and refer to themselves as *'The Warriors'*.

Hooligans will de-personalise their acts of violence by referring in the third person to their rivals i.e. *'We did AEL last week and gave them a good beating'* and portray themselves as *'Lions'* or *'Warriors'* distancing themselves from the reality of their own real character and identity.

They have a rank structure with leaders, second lieutenants, spotters, intelligence gatherers and photographers. They will have people who provide weapons, medical support, and transport and spokesmen.

Observers will recognise this structure because it is the same structure that the police have. The difference is that the hooligans can mobilise with much greater speed than the police in a live situation and are not hindered by the need to follow legal processes in what they do.

***

Footnote: In 1987 I watched from a surveillance point as an organised fight took place between two sets of fans in the city-centre of Birmingham with more than one hundred people involved. It lasted less than two minutes, once the fighting started, and one youth was stabbed and nearly lost his life. By the time uniformed police arrived it was all over.

***

Football hooligans love the history of violence and will relate to incidents time and time again. It provides status to the individuals involved, and anniversary dates which need to be revered, and celebrated if possible, with further acts of violence, as they constantly seek to outdo each other.

Some hooligan groups will moralise over the use of 'hands and feet' as being the 'noble' way to fight as 'real men' but the reality is that rocks, stones, bottles, flares, firecrackers, iron rods, wooden staves, and Molotov Cocktails are actually the norm for these occasions.

They love to keep memorabilia about their activities such as newspaper cuttings, photographs, and video. The advent of social media sites, and the use of mobile camera phones, allows them to promote visual material using stirring music to excite the minds of those who might be attracted to getting involved. This is however also one of their downfalls, as it also provides potential evidence with which to prosecute them retrospectively.

Given the mix of politics, and localism, between these five clubs it is impossible to see how any fixture between them could not be regarded as a 'high-risk' fixture.

Added to this, many fans believe that the potential for violence is increased by poor refereeing, perceptions of match fixing, linked with betting, and in some cases the poor behaviour of team players themselves, all of which on occasions has been 'blown up out of all proportions' by a local media who themselves were often seen as politically biased.

There is a saying that *'there are no free meals in Cyprus'* and as such for every action there is a consequence. There is a general lack of trust amongst all of the parties involved in football on the island, in particular the fans, who are not convinced that 'fair play' and 'even-handedness' are the norm within the game. It all adds to the violent mix.

Having said all this once you start to understand through profiling what essentially makes 'normal' people do 'abnormal' things you can then start to tackle them.

Football hooligans feel power when they are in 'faceless' and anonymous groups.

Once you can strip away that anonymity, and start to isolate them as individuals, they are no longer untouchable.

Chapter Ten

A profile of MMAD

If you view social media on the Internet it will not take you long to find incidents of violence, filmed by hooligans in Cyprus, which are usually accompanied by 'war- like' music or modern 'rap'. Within the content you will frequently see scenes of police officers carrying shields, embroiled with crowds with no apparent ability to secure static-lines, or to maintain a sterile distance, between the police, and those intent on fighting.

Hooligans approach the police often with impunity and all you can see is a swirling mass of people where individual officers are sometimes isolated and exposed to punches and kicks.

In one such video I saw a youth, at the head of a mob, who was wielding a long white pole which he used to poke at police officers, who seemed unable to contain him, and indeed were forced to retreat.

All of this belies the fact that the Republic of Cyprus police actually have a very highly-trained public order force (Rapid Reaction Unit or Emergency Response Unit) known as MMAD who characterise themselves as officers who are disciplined, obedient and work well together as teams.

The team was established in 1978, in response to an increase in terrorism in the Middle East Region, and in particular three terrorist acts that took place in Cyprus, namely the murder of Joysef El-Sepai, Chairman of the Afro-Asiatic Union, at the Hilton Hotel in Nicosia, the kidnapping of Achilleas Kyprianoy, the son of the ex-President of Cyprus, and rioting which had taken place in the Central Prisons.

Based in Nicosia, but with an island-wide remit to act independently, they were placed under the direct control of a Commander who reports to the Chief of Police. They use training facilities near Analiontas Village, which includes the provision of a 'police combat simulator', and are highly- trained in anti-terrorism techniques.

Their main mission is to confront organised acts of violence and terrorism, with a secondary mission to provide help in cases of calamity or disaster, and to carry out VIP protection and public order duties.

To achieve this aspect of policing they operate five 'security squads' each one of which has three teams of officers within it.

Within their fourteen operational aims there is a specific reference to the repression of disturbances and the policing of sporting events using anti-riot teams.

Without doubt MMAD have been at the forefront of many of the violent confrontations which have taken place over the years, at sporting events and, as is normal with such specialist teams they have been the subject of high praise for their professionalism, and criticised for using excessive force in equal measures on many occasions.

They are the 'hard-edge' of policing within the Republic and in my purely personal opinion the situation at many problem fixtures would have deteriorated still further had it not been for their presence and courage. I have seen first-hand in the UK that small well-trained teams of dedicated officers can often overcome much larger numbers, in the face of adversity, and history has shown that having faith and trust in one another is the key. I would call it the *'Spartan'* concept.

The very nature of their work however means that they are never very far away from controversy.

On Christmas Eve 1993, Lefteris Andronicou, and his fiancée Elsie Constantinou, were killed after MMAD officers stormed a flat in Chlorakas, outside Paphos, where Andronicou was holding Elsie hostage, following a domestic dispute. He was hit by twenty-nine bullets, and she was hit by twenty bullets, after two MMAD officers forced their way in. One of the officers was injured.

The families of the deceased lodged an appeal with the European Court of Human Rights in August 1994 claiming that the government had violated Article 2 of the European Convention which stipulates 'no one shall be deprived of his life intentionally'.

A government enquiry absolved the two officers of any wrongdoing and in October 1997 it was announced that five judges had rejected the appeal at the European Court of Human Rights, against four judges who had upheld it, one of whom was the Chairman of the Cyprus Supreme Court.

The solicitor for the Andronicou family said, *'I am rendered speechless by the decision of the five Judges despite the fact that he had been shot ten times when lay on the floor and the gun had been on the couch, not in his hands'.*

At the beginning of May 1998 a special task-force was set up at Larnaca Airport, by the Chief of Police, who had described the security operation as a *'shambles',* and criticised the weak leadership in Larnaca police, which he alleged had failed to instill discipline. The head of security was replaced, and a MMAD team was deployed with a Senior Inspector from the Unit being put in charge.

In October 1998 the Unit hit the headlines again following a riot which occurred in holding-cells at Larnaca, after fifty-one Arab and Nigerian asylum seekers set fire to mattresses in their cells.

In scenes that were captured on television, MMAD officers tossed teargas into the cells, forcing the occupants into the police courtyard of the old police station, where officers wearing gas masks were filmed clubbing and kicking prisoners. A total of fifty-six MMAD officers were deployed to the operation.

On Sunday 24 January 1999 a police officer under training

with MMAD was arrested on suspicion of starting twenty-five grass fires in the Buffer Zone, near Xylotymbou, during the early hours of that morning.

In February 1999 it was announced that the Attorney General had decided to charge MMAD's Deputy Commander Charalambos Mavros with dereliction of his duty following the beatings at Larnaca Police Station. No-one else was to be prosecuted as all of the other officers involved had been wearing gas masks, and all of them had remained silent when subsequently interviewed, but nevertheless the Police Association were up in arms about the decision.

Mavros was the Acting Commander of MMAD at the time of the incident.

On the 7 July 1999 MMAD came to the notice of the media again when it was announced that fourteen members were under investigation for attending a party with a group of foreign 'strip tease artists' at a cabaret club in Ayia Napa.

The group were supposed to be on a covert training exercise in the Protaras area, but announced their presence somewhat by parking a Mercedes motor car, and an Opel Vectra, both bearing MMAD number plates, outside the premises. They were spotted by local plain-clothes police officers, and reported to their superior officers, who immediately ordered them back to their Units.

MMAD Commander Yiannakis Phillippou was said to be *'outraged'* by the incident, and appointed an, 'in-house', investigator.

At the start of the proceedings, in relation to the police station riot, on 16 September 1999 Larnaca District Court Judges refused to accept a copy of the TV footage as being admissible evidence.

On Friday 14 July 2000 Charalambos Mavros, who by now was the Head of the Force Drug Squad, was acquitted by Judges in a Larnaca Court of using excessive force. In a 127-page decision, that took them three hours to read out, the Judges vindicated the actions of the officer.

In 2002 a survey conducted amongst fans concluded that the police were not sufficiently trained to confront incidents of football violence and that they were insufficient in numbers to police effectively. They believed that the police often behaved provocatively towards fans by treating them 'all the same' instead of focusing on the hooligan element, and that in some cases certain fans were discriminated against dependent on their political allegiances.

In April 2002 speaking on behalf of MMAD Iakovos Papacostas said, *'for a policeman, football and bad experiences go hand in hand. Whenever there is a match we are always waiting to hear how many fans end up at police stations and how many end up in hospital'*.

On Saturday 5 October 2002, in a clear example of the challenges faced by police officers trying to operate impartially in a community of less than a million people, where everyone knows each other's business, a fragmentation grenade was thrown at the home of a MMAD officer in Nicosia, at 1.15am in the morning.

Both of his vehicles, and that of a neighbour, were damaged in the attack.

On Thursday 6 April 2006 police denied reports that MMAD Units were going to be disbanded because of video footage recently released showing two students being beaten by officers in an incident in Nicosia on the 20 December 2005 after they were stopped for ID checks.

MMAD officers, together with other Headquarters staff, were engaged in plain-clothes, on a surveillance operation for a serial rapist when they had cause to speak to the two and maintained that they had resisted arrest.

Whilst the police admitted that they were going to reshuffle departments they denied that MMAD would be closed down. Several TV channels broadcast the camera footage at a time when the Force was receiving a high level of bad press. Eight officers were under investigation.

In 2007 in a further survey conducted amongst eighty-seven MMAD officers they drew a comparison between their role as a rescue and major incident support unit, dealing with floods and fires, a common occurrence in Cyprus, and their role in public order and conflict situations.

In the former they believed that the public were supportive and obedient, and recognised and respected their role in situations where they were invariably working closely with sections of the community, who at that time were feeling particularly vulnerable and at risk.

In the latter the officers cited a number of high-profile public order situations, some of which had cast them in a negative light, as well as events at football matches. Words such as 'reactionary, irritable, aggressive, disobedient, and generally un-cooperative and undisciplined' were words used to describe how people were transformed in such situations.

The officers highlighted the fact that many Cypriots would not adhere to regulations and laws believing that they only applied to others.

There was a general feeling amongst the officers that although they had made mistakes the media was largely to blame for fermenting a negative image with the public, as it did not always objectively report the facts.

The age-group normally most negative towards them were in the sixteen years to twenty years age-group, but officers felt that part of this was due to people's prejudices towards the police, problems at home, and lack of respect, education, and lack of role-models.

Against this background it was not difficult to see how football hooliganism was alive and well amongst some sections of the population and provided an ideal outlet for them to vent their frustrations and anger on the police, particularly by hooligan elements from the left who saw the police as politically biased against them.

In the first five months of 2008 thirty complaints were made against the police, to the Independent Authority for the Investigation of Claims and Complaints.

Just one of those was made against a MMAD officer.

On Monday 1 September 2008 the media were given a rare insight into the workings of MMAD when one hundred officers in full riot-gear, and carrying shields, were put through their paces at the GSP Stadium in Nicosia.

Following the introduction of new legislation to combat football violence, the exercise, which involved the use of a 'mock' unruly crowd, was designed to show how they prepared for matches. All of the MMAD officers had also attended a two- day seminar designed to increase their awareness of the new powers available which were aimed at being much more proscriptive. For example national symbols such as the Greek flag would only be allowed into stadiums providing that they had not been altered in any way.

On the 30 October 2008 MMAD celebrated its 30th anniversary and marked it with an event showing a series of drills, some of which were open to the public, and some to family members of the officers only. Deputy Commander for Operations and Training Simeon Papadopoulos explained the work of the two hundred strong unit to the press.

On Thursday 19 March 2009 the Unit came under the spotlight again when ten police officers, including four MMAD members, were acquitted at Nicosia District Court of beating the two students in 2005.

In a 158 page verdict, which took five hours to read out, three Judges, who had reached a unanimous decision, declared that the guilt of the officers had not been established beyond doubt, this despite the fact that the whole incident had been recorded on a forty-three minute video.

The following day hundreds of people blew whistles outside

Nicosia District Court to demonstrate against the decision, against a backcloth of condemnation from several quarters, including from the Attorney General.

The State Prosecutor Savvas Matsos said in the aftermath, *'Officers make false allegations and incriminate citizens and knowingly commit perjury in court'*, and a furious Attorney General announced that he would mount an appeal against the decision.

It was not a good day for the police, and the officers still faced disciplinary proceedings.

In September 2009 it was announced that, during the first six months of the year, a total of fifty-seven complaints had been made against the police, to the Independent Authority for the Investigation of Claims and Complaints.

Just two of those complaints involved officers from MMAD.

In February 2011, following a successful appeal in the Criminal Courts, by the Attorney General, eight officers subsequently received suspended prison sentences for their part in the attack on the students, but further controversy followed, within a couple of months, when they were fined just eight days pay by the Police Disciplinary Committee, and remained as serving police officers.

This decision was then itself appealed by one of the Assistant Chief Constables.

On the 8 April 2011 the Attorney General announced that Police Association spokesman, and MMAD officer, Andreas Symeou would be prosecuted for 'inhuman and degrading treatment of people', following events involving a group of residents, at the football match on the 30 October 2010, between Apollon and AEL.

The officer claimed that he was being picked on because of his union involvement, and said that after making four arrests, he had been attacked by a man wielding a stick, and his wife, who had put her nails into his throat.

He claimed to have received more than one hundred blows to his body, during the ensuing struggle, and that a DISY Deputy who was a lawyer, and friend of the family, had turned up at the station and allegedly tried to interfere with the course of the case.

The Cyprus Police Association highlighted the fact that Symeou had many times led an anti-riot team against hooligans, suffering injury, and on one occasion nearly losing the sight of his left eye.

Whatever the truth, or otherwise, of these specific allegations, the reality of policing football in Cyprus is that a relatively small Unit of officers play a disproportionally larger role in trying to prevent trouble.

They are in essence Cyprus's equivalent of the, *'thin blue line'*, without which authorities would simply have lost control on many of the occasions researched within this book.

On Friday 3 August 2012, seven years after the incident in 2005, three of the officers involved in beating the two students were dismissed from the Police Force at a hearing of the Police Appeals Board. This was something of a milestone for the Force where dismissals were extremely rare.

On Monday the 9 September 2013 the Justice Minister Ionas Nicolaou visited the Headquarters of MMAD where he asserted that the Justice Ministry was fully supportive of police efforts to build a new Force that would be dignified and professional. He said to officers, *'we want you to stand proudly in front of the public. We wish through your correct behaviour you have managed to enforce the law as it should be enforced'.*

He commented further on the training which MMAD officers had been receiving to find the best course of action in dealing with violence during football matches and said that he expected the same level of engagement and professionalism from the CFA and Stadium Managers. He commented, *'as you are aware, the greatest punishment for hooligans is to be banned from stadiums as they do not really care whether they go to jail'.*

He also highlighted that due to the economic climate the police service was struggling to be able to fill 450 staff vacancies and that the emphasis was on maintaining front-line policing.

A total of 145 complaints were recorded against police in 2012, against 132 the previous year. With the figures increasing this could either point to the public having greater confidence in the system, or the fact that the police were facing greater challenges in terms of maintaining standards.

On Saturday 8 March 2014 at about 10am, a Pakistani male was stopped whilst walking in Nicosia, by four MMAD officers. It was alleged by KISA, a monitoring group, that the male was hit by one of the officers, who demanded to see his papers.

It was established that he was lawfully in the country but when he challenged the officer as to why he had hit him the officer was alleged to have said, *'if you don't like it you can go wherever you want. But I will find you. I will plant drugs on you and you will go to jail for the rest of your life'.*

The individual later made an official complaint against the officer and KISA called for the practice of stop-checks based on racial profiling to end. This was a scenario that had something of a familiar ring to it with similar debates on the use of 'stop and search' in the UK.

Chapter Eleven

The SBA Police Experience

The British Sovereign Bases consist of two, fifty square mile, areas, with one focused around RAF Akrotiri near to Limassol, (WSBA), and the second further north in Dhekalia and near to Larnaca (ESBA).They were retained by the British for military use, and strategic purposes, after Cyprus was granted Independence from Britain in 1960.

Some 15,700 people are resident within the SBA's, which are regarded as British sovereign territory and comprise 3% of the island's landmass.

It has its own police force, which provides a range of policing services, within the areas of the two Bases.

Akrotiri has no public order issues relating to football to speak of, but in Dhekalia a new ground known as the Dasaki stadium was built in 1997 with a capacity of 7,000 seats, which became home to Ethnikos Achna FC, a First League Club, with right-wing political allegiances.

The SBA Police also had responsibility for policing arrangements for seven Minor League Clubs.

Although the total strength of the Force hovers around the two hundred and forty mark, it does train officers in UK public order techniques, and can deploy fully operational Public Support Units, which are used to police some of the games at Ethnikos Achna, the only 'designated' sports stadium on the Area.

The top management-tier of the force consists of former senior British police officers, but the majority of the staff are Greek-Cypriots, or Turkish-Cypriots, who speak fluent English, and wear British police-style uniforms.

On Tuesday 3 July 2001 the SBA Police faced a major public order threat of a different kind when a riot occurred at Akrotiri, as up to one thousand Cypriots demonstrated in response to protests about the construction of military masts near to RAF Akrotiri, and the arrest of a prominent MP.

In the violence that ensued, as the demonstrators confronted one hundred and forty officers, at least fifty-five police officers were injured, as well as three fireman, ten soldiers, and five protesters.

Thirty-five of the injured were hospitalised.

Thirty-five police vehicles were damaged, or destroyed by fire, and Episkopi Police Station, and the Signals Unit in Akrotiri, suffered severe damage as troops were deployed to support the police in restoring order.

The total bill for damage came to £500,000 pounds.

A British military spokesman called the protests, *'one of the most violent and abhorrent acts of lawlessness ever seen in Cyprus'*, and Chief Constable Eric Vallance pointed to a number of those involved having come from the criminal fraternity in Trachoni Village.

***

Footnote: Prior to 1974 Trachoni was a village of just sixty people but following an influx of refugees from northern Cyprus had grown to 2,400 by 2002.

Chief Superintendent Jim Guy, then Divisional Commander from ESBA, who was a colleague of mine for eighteen months, said, *'I watched defenceless police officers attacked for no reason other than trying to do their lawful duty. I watched while missiles were thrown and people struck on the head. People were kicked and dragged out of the crowd. If that is not criminal and hooligan I do not know what is?'.*

Two SBA police officers subsequently received the Queens Commendation for Bravery, in respect of this incident, notwithstanding the fact that in December 2001 the SBA Attorney General Peter Visagie announced that it had been decided not to prosecute any of the offenders on the grounds that it was 'not in the public interest'.

Whatever the rights and wrongs of a decision, which was clearly complicated by political necessity, it meant that many guilty people went totally unpunished for their actions.

In the SBA Police Annual Report for 2001/2, Eric Vallance made note of the fact that there was ever-increasing crowd violence at football matches, which had presented serious public order challenges, and had led to an agreed overspend in the budget for policing sporting events in the SBA areas.

He also highlighted that the SBA police had been involved in major football tournaments, involving staff and pupils at most schools in WSBA and ESBA, along with numerous sporting events, all of which were supported through external sponsorship.

The SBA Police Annual Report for 2002/3 again highlighted concerns about football policing, as well as highlighting further violence in July 2002, when a further demonstration in Akrotiri resulted in one police officer being injured, three cars being damaged by fire, as well as extensive fire damage to Fassouri Police Station.

In the SBA Police Strategic Plan covering that period - Aim Number Two in relation to Crime and Community Safety, the force outlined efforts at dealing with violence in sports grounds which included debrief letters being sent to the CFA, and Clubs after each game, and a 'Statement of Intent' being signed up to, outlining the responsibilities of clubs, the police and the CFA.

A briefing card for individual officers was introduced, games were graded in terms of risk, and common policing tactics with the Republic of Cyprus Police, which complied with EU directives, were looked at.

***

At 10am on Sunday 2 March 2003, whilst the Divisional Commander at Akrotiri, I attended a mini-football tournament in Limassol, organised by the Cultural Committee of Trachoni Village.

It was organised to raise funds for the expenses and needs of the Cyprus Team for the upcoming Special Olympics Games in Dublin in the summer. Two hundred and fifty people attended and watched the team play the SBA Police. They also raised 1,350 Cyprus pounds through sponsorship. This was one of the nicer days for football in Cyprus.

At 2.30pm on Friday 14 March 2003 I attended a football match between the ESBA and WSBA Divisions of the SBA Police. It took place at the British military sports ground in an area known as Happy Valley. The SBA officers loved their football just the same as any other Cypriot, and in much the same way that they loved their food!

On Wednesday 2 July 2003 I attended a Republic of Cyprus Police 'passing out parade' at the Police Academy in Nicosia for new recruits. Soon many of these young officers would be on the front-line of policing football, but controversy was never far away as senior officers were prone to comment about the number of female officers, who would go on to occupy office-jobs, thus avoiding confrontations on the streets.

The fact was that they were also more likely to pass the promotion examinations and in a *male dominated* society such as Cyprus this did not always sit well with their male counterparts.

At midday on Thursday 3 July 2003 I met with Nicos Nicholaou, the president of Anagenissis FC, regarding the possibility of Apollon FC building a football stadium within the area of Trachoni. Although at that point it was just an idea it was causing concern in the community and were it ever to come to fruition would have placed great strain on policing in the area.

On Thursday 7 August 2003 I attended another football match in Happy Valley but this time it involved a team from

Trachoni.

Past differences were put aside for the duration of the game.

On Wednesday 24 September 2003 I attended a presentation at Erimi Village and then presented a number of medals to a football team.

On Monday 27 October 2003 I held a further meeting with officials from the Anagenissis FC.

On Tuesday 4 November 2003 at 7pm I attended a mini football tournament at Zhakaki, which was supported by SBA Police Community Officers, and was aimed at trying to bring local youths together in the name of sport. The Justice Minister from the Republic attended to present the winning trophy.

On Sunday 9 November 2003 I was the Silver Commander again for another protest against the Akrotiri antenna when a demonstration was organised by the Green Party, with some involvement from Turkish Cypriot groups.

Although we deployed in full PSU kit, with reserves on hand, I kept the affair low key in terms of our policing style, and officers wore baseball caps instead of riot helmets.

By 1pm, about one hundred protesters had dispersed peacefully, after a speech from the Green Party Deputy George Perdikis, where concerns were again raised about potential health risks and environmental pollution.

I am not sure what sporting events were taking place that day to divert the attention of any hooligan fringe but was grateful not to be engaged in confrontation as we blocked the main gate to the Antenna site with a police cordon.

Operating in temperatures of over 30 degrees was no joke, but fortunately the helmets stayed on our utility belts and were not required.

On the evening of Monday 10 November 2003, I arranged a meeting in a coffee-shop between officials from the two teams based in Trachoni, one being Anagenissis FC and associated with the left, and the other Costantinos and Evripides FC who were associated with the right of politics.

Both of them played in one of the lower leagues. Somewhat

naively I explained that I was trying to find ways to improve the status of Trachoni as a village and pointed out that they both had good players in each team, which if merged together into one unified team could lead to better promotion prospects.

They listened intently and respectfully and promised to consider my proposal. Needless to say the idea did not progress but our policing style of presenting a firm public order image, blended with constant community engagement was definitely the right approach.

***

Andry Christou-Layton was a police officer who served with the SBA Police for six years between 2000 and 2005, and this is her recollection:

"On the afternoon of Sunday 15 February 2004 I was posted to a Police Support Unit to be deployed at the football ground at Akhna. The match was between Ethnikos Akhna FC and AEL. We were deployed in full public-order kit which consisted of dark blue overalls, a helmet with protective visor, heavy boots, gloves, and a utility belt attached to which was an Asp, (extendable truncheon),

and handcuffs. Even with all this kit on I remember that it was a cold day and I was freezing. Normally it was the opposite because in addition to the uniform we also wore protective padding around the chest, elbows, shins and kneecaps, as well as a fire resistant neck and face protector. Trying to work sometimes in temperatures of 40 degrees on a hot summer's day was really challenging.

I was one of only a few female officers trained in public order, at the time; and part of the requirements to pass the course was to be able to run 500 meters carrying a full protective shield which weighed seven kilos.

I was working at Akrotiri at the time and we left in the police bus in the morning to get to Dhekalia. We worked in serials and my Sergeant that day was Hadjiloucas. He was quite a tough guy but very good to have next to you in difficult situations.

When we got to the ground we deployed to the football pitch facing the AEL fans on the terraces. I cannot remember much about the game but we were trained to work together and not to get isolated.

One of the AEL fans started teasing me making sexist

comments like, 'Hey you with the red hair. I like you. You look beautiful in uniform'. He carried on but I ignored him. My nephew was in the crowd and heard what was going on. You have to remember that with less than a million Cypriots living in Cyprus, which in itself is a small place, everyone knows everybody so you are always likely to see people you know.

After the interval and the second-half started the same man came over to me again but this time he apologised for his behaviour. It was obvious that my nephew had spoken to him and put him right!

There was some trouble but I cannot recall how it started. Spectators were coming up to us saying that there were others waiting outside to fight. The gates were locked and we needed to get outside to see what was going on. I ran for the keys and threw them over a fence to other officers. Hadjiloucas caught them and they opened the gates to deal with the problem outside. We also had police dogs at the game. They were good to have because the fans were scared of getting bitten.

At the end of the day there wasn't a lot of trouble but you could feel the tension and it wasn't a nice feeling. When we did the *football we felt that we were doing a good job. We were disciplined and I think that the fans realised this and were more cautious about causing problems than they were in the Republic.*

I also attended AEZ Zakaki football ground, which is near to Ladies Mile in Limassol. It was just within the Akrotiri Base area. They were a second-league team and usually two of us would go as a double-crewed car. We were there to show a presence on the pitch and prevent trouble. You normally got between fifty to a hundred spectators.

Football is something that the majority of Cypriots are very passionate about. Most of them support their own Cypriot team as well as supporting a UK team such as Arsenal, Manchester United or Chelsea. Some supported Greek teams and others Spanish, or Italian teams. Mostly they follow English football. Lots of children in Cyprus play football within school teams or village teams.

One of the saddest occasions I experienced whilst an SBA police officer was when I attended the funeral of a young boy in Akrotiri Village, together with a number of other officers, and the Divisional Commander. The boy had been playing football when he collapsed and died from a previously undiagnosed heart condition.

He was just a child and the whole community were consumed with

grief."

***

I was that Divisional Commander and the memory of that funeral on Friday 20 February 2004 remains with me to this day, as people collapsed in the church, overcome by events.

I left Cyprus a few months later, in June 2004, and at that point I was of the firm belief that I would never return.

I had learnt my lesson the hard way that you could not simply apply UK policing methods in a country that faced Europe in one direction, and the Middle-East in another.

In Cyprus the relationship between the police and the public is in many ways quite different and there is no doubt it is one of the factors that has made the problem of hooliganism difficult to stamp out.

***

During the period 2004/5 the SBA police were invited to join the Cypriot National Committee which was formed to combat football hooliganism. In trying to engage and educate young fans the SBA Police mounted high- profile media opportunities at the Achna Ground, like the occasion in which young people occupied the space in front of the centre circle of the pitch displaying placards spelling the message, *'No violence in football grounds'*.

In the 2005/6 review of performance the SBA Police highlighted that they had been congratulated by the media and commended to *'CyPol'*, (The Republic of Cyprus Police), for their handling of public-order events and the policing of sporting events.

In 2007 arrangements were made for Leeds United to play a friendly game with Achnas, at the Dasaki Stadium, and in the same year they received a European trophy after winning the Intertoto Cup.

On the 20 May 2009 the Control of Violence in Sports Grounds Ordinance 2009 appeared in the Sovereign Base Areas Gazette Number 1539 and replaced the previous legislation used to address football violence, namely the Control of Violence Ordinance

1999.

It was enacted by the Administrator J.H. Gordon and took account of an updated *'Handbook'* used by the Council of the European Union to deal with measures to prevent and control violence and disturbances in connection with football matches which had both international as well as EU involvement.

It listed thirty-one measures aimed at preventing violence which included the use of CCTV and the appointment of an experienced and trained club safety security manager for the stadium. It listed various powers that the Chief Constable of the SBA Police could call on, and requirements such as clearing the stadium of building materials at least two days before any game.

It also called for the creation of a database to be maintained by the SBA Police of persons where a football banning order had been implemented, as well individuals who posed a substantial risk to public order at events, and a list of people who had legal restrictions placed on them in attending sporting events within the EU.

All of the measures listed related to activities both inside the stadium as well as within 500 meters of the ground.

In a positive step the new Ordinance allowed the SBA Police to exchange information with the Republic of Cyprus Police, in preventing and suppressing football related violence, and the use of dedicated football liaison officers, and in January 2014 the Ordinance was updated to provide a direct link to the corresponding Republic of Cyprus Law number 48 (I) 2008(c) (Prevention and Suppression of Violence in Sports Ground Law 2008).

Multi-Agency co-ordination was seen as a key feature of the process and the Chief Constable was nominated as the chair of Event Co-Ordination meetings with full risk-analysis processes being implemented.

Thirteen offences were listed such as threatening behaviour and the use of inflammatory slogans, symbols or expressions, together with the relevant maximum sentencing for each offence.

In Cyprus the throwing of firecrackers is a popular pastime, not just at football grounds, and the ease of availability is a real problem for the police. At Easter celebrations huge bonfires are built, often adjacent to Churches, and I have personally experienced the solemnity of an Easter Service conducted to the background of huge fireworks being let off and firecrackers being thrown liberally amongst crowds and into the fires.

In order to combat the issue of the possession of offensive weapons the Ordinance went into some detail and in typical Cypriot fashion offered up some unique versions.

An offensive weapon was defined as any article made, or adapted, for use for causing injury or fear of injury to others or intended by the person having the article with him for such use by him or by some other person.

This could be any article capable of causing injury to a person struck by it such as a bottle, tin can or portable container but not one used for medicinal purposes. It could be an object made of metal, wood, stone or otherwise capable of being thrown at or being used to strike another person other than a walking stick, crutches, or other similar aids for a disabled person.

Most importantly it classified fireworks within this offence classification as something which had the main purpose of emitting an illuminating flare or the emission of smoke or visible gas such as distress flares or fog signals but did not include matches or cigarette lighters.

***

At some point in December 2009 the SBA Police in Dhekalia said that, following discussions with clubs and referees, they would no longer guarantee to police football matches at Achna due to a lack of finance, unless they were compensated.

For the period 2010/2011 the SBA Police announced in their Annual report that, despite the introduction of new measures, problems continued with the policing of sporting events. That said they were able to reduce police overtime costs significantly when Ermis, one of two clubs using the Achna Stadium, moved to Larnaca to play their home games.

In addition, they reviewed the use of overtime before the start of the new season in a bid to cut costs still further, by achieving a closer balance between the identified risk of trouble, and the number of officers required to deal with it. The combined effect was a reduction overall of 51.6% from 91,916 euro to 44,452 euro.

During the period 2010 to 2013 the SBA Police announced in their Annual Reports that there had been no major problem with football violence in the SBA areas, and this was attributed to a robust searching regime aimed at ensuring that the favoured hooligan pastime of throwing missiles inside grounds was drastically reduced, as well as a *zero-tolerance* approach to policing as articulated within the 2011/2014 Strategic Plan.

This phrase originates from an approach taken by an American Police Chief who advocated coming down hard on all types of 'lower-end' anti-social behaviour in order to make life uncomfortable for criminals. Many police forces have adopted the phrase but not all have actually fully implemented its intended meaning.

In 2012/13 a brand new police control room was also completed at the Achna ground, which enabled staff to operate a closed circuit television system.

Twelve months previously a major multi-agency 'table-top' exercise based on the 'Bradford Fire' scenario in 1987 was held to test the engagement of the emergency services.

Whilst it is absolutely clear that the SBA Police have nothing like the scale of the problems to deal with, in relation to football hooliganism, than the Republic of Cyprus Police, the question remains as to why they have managed to remain relatively unscathed over the years.

Chapter Twelve

2014

No Change

At the end of January 2014 the Justice Minister Ionas Nicolaou held a closed-door meeting, lasting several hours, with the CFA and the Cyprus Sports Organisation, (KOA), at the Justice Ministry,

The Minister said, *'Our job is not an easy one, but we must all take responsibility for our respective part in taking more effective measures'*.

The debate focused on the installation of turnstiles, and an upgraded CCTV system, that would enable fans to be photographed upon entry to the GSP, Tsirion, Antonis Papadopoulos, and GSZ Stadiums. They would be photographed with their ticket-stub, and then details entered onto an online database to assist the police in tracking down offenders. It was also announced that a list of stewards for each club would be available from February 2014.

Whilst these appeared to be positive steps forward, it was hard to see how such an intrusive scheme could in fact be introduced given the ongoing resistance to the concept of even having a fan identity card.

On Sunday 9 February 2014 three people were arrested after police checked a bus carrying Apollon fans from Limassol to the GSP stadium in Nicosia for a match with APOEL.

Two people aged twenty-nine years, and twenty years, were detained after twenty-seven flares, eleven smoke bombs, and a small quantity of drugs were found.

A twenty-three-year old was also arrested in connection with possession of one gramme of cannabis, and possession of a flare-gun and a flare.

On Friday 28 February 2014 a sinister development took place in the form of a bomb which exploded under a vehicle at 2.45am in an underground car park in an apartment block in Latsia.

Damage was caused to the windscreen, bonnet, and engine as well as to an adjacent vehicle, although fortunately no one was injured. The owner of the vehicle was again Leontios Trattos, the chairman of the Cyprus Referees Association, the well-known Cyprus First Division and International referee.

The attack came days before he was due to referee a game between AEL and Apollon, and sent shockwaves through the sport.

As the police looked for a motive it was said that he had a good friend who was an AEL supporter and that it was thought that he would show favouritism towards them. At the same time police did however rule out any link to any international football games bearing in mind that Trattos was due to referee a friendly game in Cyprus, between Ukraine and the USA, during March 2014 which had already been moved once for security reasons.

All top tier fixtures were suspended for that weekend as referees refused to officiate in any games in protest.

On Friday 14 March 2014 a volleyball match was held in Limassol between Omonia and Anorthosis.

The Anorthosis fans were granted general right of entry to the game and twenty-seven Omonia fans were given a pass to enter.

Fans began screaming abuse at each other, and after the game ended, a glass panel above the heads of the Omonia fans was shattered by a missile.

Someone then opened a door on the west side of the court and up to one hundred people, wearing motor-bike helmets and hoods, stormed in brandishing sticks, bars and throwing flares. Police moved in and made eleven arrests.

One of those arrested was found to be in possession of 2.5 grammes of cannabis, and a later search of his home address revealed a further eight grammes of the drug.

The following day, all of those arrested were remanded in custody for three days by a Limassol Court.

On Wednesday 2 April 2014 the Justice Minister Ionas Nicolaou, and Acting Prison Director Eleni Vatiliotou, launched a football tournament to be played at Nicosia Central Prisons under the banner *'Building Bridges'*. With the support of the Referees Association, and some of the major clubs, prison teams were to play veteran teams from Omonia, APOEL, AEL, and Apollon in a ten match tournament.

On Saturday 5 April 2014 Omonia played APOEL at the GSP stadium in Nicosia, in front of a crowd of 12,800 supporters. The game finished in a 0-0 draw with the usual round of flares filling the air with white and green smoke.

At one point the smoke was so thick that the pitch could not be seen from the stands. During the match a small group of APOEL fans waved a Greek flag, and then climbed fencing in full view of spectators, and burnt a Turkish national flag in protest at the alleged support of AC Omonia by Turks.

The incident came amid a European Union and American official's visit to the island to revive peace talks between Greek and Turkish Cypriot leaders. The Turkish Foreign Minister later condemned the act and said, *'while negotiations for a comprehensive settlement are underway it is our hope that the disrespect shown to our flag is not approved of by the majority of the Greek Cypriot community'.*

On Tuesday 22 April 2014 APOEL played AEL at the GSP stadium in Nicosia. Everyone knew that this was a high-risk game, with real potential for violence between rival fans, and three hundred police officers were on duty including MMAD public order teams.

Before the game both sets of fans clashed on the motorway adjacent to the stadium. A Police spokesman said that club representatives had agreed that supporters would not travel en masse, without a police escort, but a section of AEL fans gathered at the exit near Pera Horio, outside Nicosia and headed to the GSP.

They refused to be escorted by police and also used a bus to transport fans without agreement by police. At the same time APOEL fans failed to follow the agreed routes to the stadium and many travelled to the game in a large convoy of motorbikes, and scooters.

APOEL fans subsequently confronted AEL fans at the Orphanides roundabout, near the Mall of Cyprus. There was traffic chaos as fans cut traffic and hurled abuse at innocent drivers trying to negotiate a way through the milling throng. The keys were snatched from one vehicle leaving it stranded in the middle of the road. Grass in nearby fields was set on fire as flares, firecrackers, and volleys of teargas fired by the police filled the air.

Traffic came to a halt for about half an hour as one eye-

367

witness described how, *'AEL fans cut off the roundabout over the highway using cars and motorbikes and were verbally abusing passing drivers, as they drove around it several times. They regulated traffic themselves, deciding who should pass and who should stay. With each firecracker going off the cars would tremble......and all the time I was thinking why there were no police officers present'.*

During the ensuing confrontation, rocks and flares were thrown, and a twenty- seven-year-old APOEL fan lost his eye after being hit by a rock. As is often the case the man was an innocent victim who was on his way to the game with his father and was apparently hit as he sat in his vehicle. Six further members of the public were injured, and treated at Nicosia General Hospital before being released, as well as six police officers, one a MMAD officer. Ten people were arrested on the day. Police blamed a core-group of up to fifty people for causing most of the trouble.

A large number of firecrackers were also seized before the game as APOEL fans raised a large banner in the ground stating *'The Terror of Nicosia',* and at least two Ultras climbed high up the netting separating the pitch from their stand which was occupied by massed ranks of orange shirts.

Police reinforcements were rushed to the stadium, before the end of the game, to keep fans segregated. A total of 15,985 supporters attended the match, which APOEL won 3-0, following which the whole of the APOEL team lined up before their fans to take a bow.

All the headlines were however made off the pitch.

As had happened all too often previously the 'blame game' started very quickly afterwards with both clubs accusing the police of failing to handle the situation properly, and failing to follow the plan agreed with clubs.

AEL said, *'we want to report the police about the incidents on the 22nd. We are against any kind of violence which has no place in football. The attitude of the police played an important role. Security was ineffective despite three meetings with them before the game. Fans of the two teams were to be led from different routes with fans from AEL being met from the Highway and APOEL fans coming from the Orphanides traffic lights. In spite of this 200*

APOEL fans with motorcycles were found on the Highway next to the parking spot for AEL fans. There was not enough police and no police at the parking lot. A few police in the area were just looking away helpless and without any intention of reacting. When police arrived at the incident the police threw gas into the parking lot. Some fell inside cars and broke windows. When fans complained about broken windows the police threatened to arrest them. We are calling for an investigation of the police'.

The police themselves admitted that having reviewed their planning that there were some 'weaknesses and omissions' that possibly existed, but in turn pointed towards the fact that the two clubs had rejected a suggestion for AEL fans to use the southern stand, which faces Limassol, which would have provided easier and more secure access for the Force to police.

The Chief of Police ordered an investigation and police made the point, *'It is high time for all of us to engage in self-criticism and have the will to take measures. Supporters must isolate those individuals who create trouble inside and outside stadiums'*.

One supporter said, *'they should lock these hooligans up. It's because of people like them that people are afraid to go to football matches anymore. My father used to bring me to see all APOEL home matches but now I can't do the same for my kids for fear that they would be hit by a flare or a rock'.*

A newspaper commentator put it more succinctly at the time by saying, *'It would be wrong to say that club officials never blame the fans at all but in almost all cases there is a 'but' at the end. The statement usually goes something like this: 'We as (insert club name) condemn most strongly our fans' behaviour BUT we should not ignore the fact that they were provoked by refereeing decisions/police/opposing coach/bad weather etc'.* He concluded that hooliganism in Cyprus was rife and blossoming and all concerned should tackle the problem before it's too late.

He observed that just two months previously one club official had congratulated fans on their immaculate behaviour, whilst in the same game an assistant referee was twice hit by projectiles thrown from within the very same set of fans.

AKEL politicians again waded in with calls for the resignation of the Justice Minister Ionas Nicolaou, who they alleged had previously committed himself to dealing effectively with football violence. He declined saying that he would not be held accountable for other people's mistakes, nor would he accept seeing the police made into 'scapegoats'.

On Saturday 26 April 2014 at a Gala Dinner to celebrate sixty years of the founding of Apollon FC, the President of Cyprus Nicos Anastasiades said on the subject of football violence, *'It is time to act like England in the Margaret Thatcher years'*. He noted that, *'Violence at Sporting Grounds was one of the main obstacles to the mass reach of sports to the Cypriots',* and concluded that, *'The Government approach was to eject the hooligans from clubs and force them to watch games from afar. That is the only thing that can regain the trust of families and young people who need to find a healthy hobby rather than be exposed to incidents such as the ones we have seen recently'.*

Whilst this was indeed very laudable it did not cater for the point that in keeping with their English counterparts much of the organised violence took place away from football grounds, in locations where there was a reduced chance of detection. Whilst the

President referred to them as being 'brainless' there was clear evidence that many of them were far from it as they planned their violent activities.

At the same time the President confirmed that he was pressing ahead with the concept of a new stadium in Limassol, to replace Tsirion Stadium, which would meet European safety standards.

On Wednesday 30 April 2014 a number of still photographs, taken from CCTV, were published in the Cyprus Mail, of suspects involved in the trouble at Nicosia on the 22 April 2014. The chatter on Facebook was all about why those shown were, in the main, wearing the colours of AEL and reinforced the view that the police in Nicosia were biased.

Notwithstanding this it was clearly a positive step forward.

On Saturday 3 May 2014 police arrested a twenty-year-old for throwing a flare, during a game between APOEL and Apollon, at Tsirion stadium in Limassol, attended by just 2,844 supporters who saw Apollon win with a score line of 2-1.

He was subsequently remanded in custody for three days.

On Sunday 4 May 2014 a twenty-eight-year-old man was questioned in respect of the disturbances on the 22 April 2014. He handed himself in after recognising himself in one of the published photographs. A Limassol police spokesman Ioannis Soteriades confirmed that they would be filing charges.

On Wednesday 7 May 2014 a twenty-year-old man was arrested by police in relation to an investigation into football related violence and public swearing. He was arrested before a championship game between AEL and Apollon, in Tsirion Stadium, began. They said that they had also located two school bags in the stadium containing eight flares and an improvised firecracker.

The game was won by Apollon with a score line of 1-0.

An impressive win by Apollon over leaders AEL threw the championship wide open, with just two games remaining, and the AEL Chairman accusing the referee of, *'officiating at another game'*. It was not unusual for heated verbal exchanges to take place between club officials at press conferences, and whilst passion is clearly an element within the game of football, the very level of these exchanges did nothing to calm the behaviour of the hooligan minorities.

On Tuesday 13 May 2014 it was announced that a meeting between AEL and APOEL, the Police, and the Cyprus Football Federation, had failed to reach agreement on the ticket allocations for fans attending the final championship game of the season, at Tsirion Stadium in Limassol, with a seating capacity of 13,331, which would decide the winner.

It was clear that frustration was building as the CFF had already changed the kick off time three times at the request of the police so that it could be held in daylight.

It was now due to kick off at 5pm on Saturday 17 May 2014 and the police said that although they could cope with a full-house at the ground it was clear that policing would be affected elsewhere on the island as they would need seven hundred to eight hundred officers to keep order; quite an astonishing figure in comparison to the total number of fans attending.

Although negotiations were ongoing it was anticipated that AEL would receive 5,000 tickets as the home team and APOEL about 2,500.

A police spokesman said, *'the real problem for the Force is spreading itself too thin. The problem lies with staff deployment. We will have to pull officers from Nicosia to effectively police the game. This means that Nicosia will be somewhat weakened when it comes to keeping order. What will happen if something happens in Nicosia? This is the problem that the teams, fans and politicians don't seem to grasp'.*

In any event this would not be welcome news for AEL fans who already took the view that officers from Nicosia naturally favoured their home team of APOEL and showed it in the manner in which they dealt with them.

At the same time fan websites were in overdrive on both sides gearing up for a *'war',* and each promising that the game would end in violence.

The Cyprus Football Association issued a plea for fans to tone the rhetoric down saying, *'We can have a game worthy of the names of the two big clubs away from any sort of violence and for fans to drive back home safely after the game'.*

The motto of the Cyprus Football Association is *'Through Football we make friends'*. – an irony that could surely pass no-one by as others waded in with criticism as to how referees policed matches and showed favourable treatment to some teams.

All of this increased the tension in the build-up to the game.

As if the Republic of Cyprus Police did not have enough to worry about the press went into overdrive in relation the visit of the US Vice-President Joe Biden, who was visiting Cyprus on Wednesday 21 May 2014.

He was to be afforded *'Head of State'* protection which would involve several hundred police officers, including the deployment of MMAD teams.

This date coincided with the football Cup Final match, this time between APOEL and Aradippou Club Ermis, and concern was raised about the fact that Mr Biden was due to stay at the Hilton Hotel in Nicosia, which was adjacent to APOEL's clubhouse, with the potential security risk posed once fans congregated there after the match.

It was perhaps no surprise that he was re-located to a hotel in Limassol, although yet again the police found themselves in something of a no-win situation.

When police spokesman Andreas Angelides was asked to confirm that arrangements had been changed for this reason he would neither confirm or deny it in the knowledge that the Force would be criticised for its inability to control a few hundred football supporters, or even block them from gathering altogether.

Chapter Thirteen

The Finale

In the run up to the AEL versus APOEL game on the 17 May 2014
police stepped up disruptive activities against hooligan elements, as
well as trying to put extra control measures in place for fans
attending the game.

During the evening of Thursday 15 May 2014 police officers
raided the fan clubs of both teams in Nicosia, and Limassol, acting
on information that the respective premises were being used to plan
and organise violence.

Nothing was found but the police action was designed to
send a clear message to those who were seeking to disrupt the event.

On Friday 16 May 2014 four football fans accused of inciting
violence, some of it on the internet, were banned from attending the
actual game with the threat of fines and prosecution should they
breach that order. They were contacted by email and the police
claimed that they had credible information that they were planning

violence, although one of them told a news outlet that he had merely posted a picture of AEL fans carrying flares.

Fans with tickets were told that they would only be allowed entry to the stadium with ID cards, the number of which would be placed on the back of their ticket. The ground itself was to be open from 2.30pm, with kick off at 5pm, and fans were advised to arrive early. It was made clear by the police that they would not allow entrance to the ground to anyone found carrying a flare, or firecracker, or anyone carrying motorcycle helmets.

Streets around the stadium would be cordoned off and AEL fans had been instructed to gain access to the stadium from the eastern side, whilst APOEL fans would use the western side.

The police confirmed that they were deploying seven hundred officers, with four hundred at the stadium itself, and three hundred performing traffic and monitoring duties in the surrounding streets.

A police spokesman said, *'we are using every tool at our disposal. More staff, more checks, everything. We want to make sure that the law-abiding fans enjoy the game without feeling threatened by hooligans'.*

It was the highest risk game of the season – the stage was set.

Before the game started two TV technicians on duty at the game were hit by a flare and were taken to hospital.

Just six minutes into the second half with the score at 0-0 the referee Demitris Masias suspended the game after firecrackers thrown by AEL fans hurt an APOEL player and a doctor.

Brazilian defender Kaka, and Dr Costas Schizas were hurt by a firecracker thrown into their team dugout from the stand occupied by AEL fans, in the 51st minute of the game. They were put on stretchers and rushed to hospital by Ambuline with Kaka placed in head and neck supports as a precautionary measure, and in obvious pain.

Three minutes earlier fans from the APOEL stand, standing in front of a banner proclaiming, *'The Pirates',* had thrown other objects onto the field. The perimeter track around the ground was littered with projectiles many of which had come from a kiosk in the ground which had been damaged by APOEL fans.

As the referee and his assistants consulted, and then started to walk off the pitch, they were surrounded by a melee of agitated players from both teams remonstrating with the referee and seemingly anxious to play on.

Several police officers, with radios anxiously clasped to their mouths, needed to provide a shield to enable them to leave in the highly charged atmosphere. This was their worst-case scenario coming to life in front of their eyes and someone needed to quickly assert authority before the situation deteriorated still further.

Police officers were moved into the ground in large numbers, including MMAD Units with shields, and after an hour's deliberation the referee and his assistants decided the game would be suspended using a rule which dictates that if a player is injured by disorder the game can be stopped.

Police reported that fans were leaving the ground quietly but as a precautionary measure it was announced that roads around the APOEL club in Nicosia would be closed to traffic to reduce the potential for disorder.

Ultimately the Cyprus Football Association, in the form of

their judicial committee, would now have to decide who would take the championship, or alternatively whether it would be replayed in some form.

During the inevitable inquest into what went wrong the question would be raised as to how firecrackers had got into the ground with such a strict search regime.

The firecracker that injured the player and the doctor was described as an improvised 'egg-shaped' device with a fuse attached to a duct-taped ball of gunpowder. It transpired that two similar firecrackers were later found in the stadium, having been lit and thrown at the pitch but failing to ignite. A senior police officer suggested that they could easily be carried in *'ones private areas'* in an effort to explain how they might have avoided detection.

In a bid to distance itself from the violence AEL FC quickly released a photograph of the main suspect for throwing the firecracker who was a young male wearing a skeleton mask. They also offered a five thousand euro reward for information leading to his arrest.

On Monday 19 May 2014 President Nicos Anastasiades

again raised the issue of football violence during a meeting at the Presidential Palace to discuss the construction of a new stadium at Limassol.

He once again mentioned the approach taken by Margaret Thatcher in the 1980s and said, *'After Saturday's incidents our imminent proposals become more urgent and relevant, so that the next season we can incorporate the new arrangements'.*

Deputy government spokesman Victoras Papadopoulos confirmed that proposals and Bills would be submitted in the following days.

Football federation President Kostas Koutsokoumnis said, *'the President has very strong opinions on the future course of football, which we will discuss with him and the Justice Minister. We have hit rock bottom. The federation's board will convene on Tuesday to make decisions that will amend disciplinary regulations so that any club that allows such behaviour is punished severely'.*

Justice Minister Ionas Nicolaou again came under fire from AKEL for what was perceived to be a failure on the part of the police to ensure that a violence-free game took place despite all of their planning.

Despite announcing the creation of a robust search regime it transpired that many searches were actually sporadic and nominal, and a two-minute video showing AEL fans entering the ground, which was posted on YouTube confirmed this.

Police spokesman Andreas Angelides said in their defence, *'searches were performed to the extent possible. Whether searches could be performed differently, that is a different issue. You can only perform so many body searches in one hour'*.

AEL's Chairman Andreas Sophocleous, smarting at the prospects of losing the game, and the title by default, if APOEL were to be awarded the three points, said at the outset that in his opinion the person who threw the firecracker was not an AEL fan. He went even further in implying that this could be a case of provocation and said, *'we consider this person to have nothing to do with AEL. No AEL fan would do such a thing at that time. This person was fiercely trying to stop the game'*.

Only an arrest would clarify that point, but at that stage the police were making no promises.

On Tuesday 20 May 2014 the Cyprus Football Association announced a series of measures designed to punish football clubs for the behaviour of violent fans, following an extraordinary meeting.

It announced that disciplinary regulations would be amended for the following season to include a three-strike rule against football clubs when 'dangerous objects' were taken into stands. Three such offences would trigger the closure of part of the club's stands at their next home game. An additional offence would trigger a 'closed doors' match, to which only pensioners and children under twelve-years of age, accompanied by their mothers, could attend.

Where objects were actually thrown onto the pitch, or at opposing fans, similar rules would apply, and after three instances there would be a deduction of points with the number of points deducted increasing with each additional offence.

The CFA also proposed that a 'fan identification scheme' should be put in place at Nicosia's GSP stadium, Larnaca's Antonis Papadopoulos stadium, and Limassol's Tsirion stadium, with a fan card that was different for each club.

Finally the CFA proposed the immediate trial of offenders

arrested for football violence and the banning of hoods and masks in stands.

After years of frustration, and perceived inertia, it appeared that things were starting to move at a fast pace. Some of the recommendations had a familiar ring to them but this appeared to be a genuine attempt to apply a *'Cyprus solution to a Cyprus problem'*.

Time would tell, but this was the type of tough talking that the community had been waiting for.

On Wednesday 21 May 2014 the 72nd Cyprus Cup Final took place at 7pm at the GSP Stadium in Nicosia, between APOEL and relative newcomers to top-flight football ERMIS ARADIPPOU. A crowd of 11,463 were in attendance.

APOEL would play the game without their defender Kaka as he was still recovering from his injuries.

Normally this fixture would be described as the showcase match of the end of the season but the weekend's events had dampened the usual exchange of pre-match hype between the clubs. Had things really changed for the better, or was this just a pause for breath, on the part of the hooligan element as they considered their next moves?

The majority of the new proposals were focused on improving behaviour at stadiums but it was clear that this would only address part of the picture. Changing the mind-set of a minority who steadfastly refused to comply with the law would require determination and courage, but that is the price of resisting anarchy. Were the police, the government and the clubs now going to blow the whistle for full-time on the hooligans or would they go into 'extra-time' again.

APOEL went on to win the match with ERMIS 2-0 and their retiring team captain Marinos Satsias, who was given a hero's send-off at the end of the game, dedicated the result to Kaka as they celebrated winning their 20th cup win by saying, *'this cup is dedicated to my team mate Kaka who was not able to be here'.*

Police arrested four people before the 7pm kick off, for possession of firecrackers, and a further six arrests were made after the match when celebrations by APOEL fans outside their club got out of hand. At about 11.30pm, after most people had left, some fans started throwing stones at the police and two police officers were injured.

At the same time police in Limassol announced that they had arrested a twenty-five-year-old man from Ayios Nicholas on suspicion of throwing the firecracker which injured Kaka.

It remained to be seen whether in fact he was an AEL fan or not, as the debate went on as to who was to blame. There was even a difference of opinion as to whether the firecracker had pierced the glass covering of the team dugout, or whether it had dropped through a hole where the glass had already been broken.

Whilst to the casual observer this type of debate changed nothing in relation to the injuries sustained it was a clear illustration of how animated and focused people were with regard to scrutinising every bit of detail and how easy it was for conspiracy theories to develop.

On Thursday 22 May 2014 a decision was made that the APOEL v AEL game would be replayed in full at a neutral ground, namely Antonis Papadopoulos stadium in Larnaca, on Saturday 31 May 2014 without fans being present.

Just to complicate matters for the clubs it was already apparent that five players from the two clubs had already gone to Japan to play in a friendly game. They were eventually recalled.

On Monday 26 May 2014 the police announced that the twenty-five-year-old man arrested in connection with the suspension of the AEL v APOEL game had been released after posting a ten thousand euro bail. He was due to appear before Limassol District Court on the 20 June 2014 charged with igniting and throwing the flare which struck the player Kaka.

Significantly in media reports he was described as being an AEL fan.

Police had published a photograph which differed from the initial description in that the suspect was described as wearing a hoodie, sunglasses and a bandana to cover his face.

At the same time APOEL fans voiced their anger following the decision to replay the match, arguing that the CFA should have ruled in favour of APOEL given that the reason cited by the referee for the suspension of the game was the throwing of the firecracker.

In a press statement issued by the team's fan club they demanded justice and said that the CFA should not equate, *'the guilty with the innocent'*. They also announced that a protest march would be held at 7.15pm on Tuesday 27 May 2014 at the Kolokassides roundabout in Nicosia.

On Tuesday 27 May 2014 the Auditor General Odysseas Michaelides published a fifty-two pages report on the activities of various athletic associations that had taken two years to complete.

Michaelides asked the government to find a way to cover policing expenses, saying that it should not be up to the taxpayer given the dire economic circumstances the country was in.

According to the report almost a million euros (953,575) was spent each year in policing football matches, of which 400,000 euros came from the Cyprus Sports Association –funded by the government, and the rest from the State.

In 2009 a suggestion was made by the CSO to the CFA that the policing bill be paid by taking one euro from the price of each match ticket. This was rejected by the CFA who in 2010 suggested that the money should come from TV rights.

In 2013 the CFA received just 72,842 euro from TV rights for policing purposes, leaving it far short of the amount required.

Michaelides said, *'if the CFA doesn't want to enforce this measure then it's up to them. But that doesn't mean that the taxpayer has to shoulder that expense. If football clubs want extra policing then they should pay for it out of their own pockets. This might act as a counter incentive for football clubs to rein in their most troublesome fans'.*

He reminded people in his report that the CFA had previously undertaken with the teams to cover half the costs of policing but that this agreement had never been fulfilled.

The CFA were not immediately available to comment as some members were in Japan for the friendly game with Cyprus.

On Tuesday 27 May 2014 thousands of APOEL fans marched to the headquarters of the CFA, in Makedonitissa, in front of a banner which read, *'The Judicial Committee legalised Violence'.*

The march passed-off peacefully and the APOEL Club

Chairman Prodromos Petrides assured fans that he would do his best on, and off the pitch, to vindicate the club. He indicated that the club had filed an appeal against the decision to replay the game with AEL, whose own supporters had held their own march in Limassol during the week.

In contrast, in addition to replaying the game, the CFA announced that AEL would have to play two games without fans, and were fined 58,100 euro, whilst APOEL were fined 19,200. Another CFA official said that the fines were too lenient and that an appeal would be made to increase the sanctions.

To add to the mix APOEL boss Giorgos Donis slammed the football community for failing to prioritise the injury of his player Kaka over the outcome of the title race.

He said of Kaka, *'his life was in danger, he had stitches, he has lost part of his hearing, he can't train or play football, and is still in a state of shock. But the strange thing to come out of this is the fact that more people are concerned about what will be the outcome of the ruling as opposed to the wellbeing of the player. The situation became almost comical when some people accused him of making up his injuries'.*

Another Brazilian player with APOEL, Gustavo Manduca, threatened to go home because of the lack of security at games saying that he feared for himself and his family.

Donis concluded, *'this ruling is in some ways encouraging all those wanting to cause trouble'.*

On Wednesday 28 May 2014, in a further twist to the ongoing saga, the entire Football Appeals Board collectively resigned refusing to make a decision as to whether the appeal against the replay between APOEL and AEL would take place or not.

They issued a statement accusing both teams of publicly attacking and humiliating them in order to put pressure on them. They insisted that despite a plea to the clubs that they should issue statements supporting the CFA in order to calm things, neither team had responded, and the *'war of words'* had continued.

The Appeals Board was due to meet on Thursday 29 May 2014 but it was now unclear as to what the next course of action would be as pressure mounted to find a way out of the impasse. The outcome of this game would not only decide the Cyprus Championship, but would also decide which team would be put forward to the Champions League, and the CFA were operating under strict timescales to provide the name of a team to UEFA by the first week in June.

On Thursday 29 May 2014 the chairman of the CFA Costakis Koutsokoumnis called a meeting in the afternoon with APOEL, AEL, Omonia, Apollon, Anorthosis and AEK to try to find a solution.

In an apparent exercise in brinkmanship he announced that in the absence of a new appeals board the match would go ahead on Saturday and that UEFA would be informed of the Cyprus team nomination by the following Monday at the latest. He did however still leave the door open for an appeals process to take place in June 2014.

On Saturday 31 May 2014 the game between AEL and APOEL went ahead and a goal on the stroke of half time, by Northern Irishman Cillian Sheridan, playing for APOEL, was enough to give them their second consecutive championship title.

He slid a shot past AEL's Moroccan keeper Karin Fegrouche to clinch the game. This was APOEL's third trophy of the season after winning the Super Cup at the beginning of the season, and the Cup ten days previously.

It had been an exhausting process, but now that the football on the pitch was out of the way the police, the clubs, the CFA, and the Government had three months to try to start making an impact on the problem of football violence. Would it be a success story or would it be more of the same.

***

As if spelling a message of doom, *'Lions Radio'*, an unofficial website for AEL fans, started carrying messages on their site on the evening of the 31 May 2014, together with a picture of MMAD police officers in riot gear and wearing balaclavas.

The postings claimed that, *'AEL fans 'The Lions' had gathered at Enaerios, by their clubhouse in Limassol, to pass the night together and to drink beer and sing. They were doing nothing wrong. Suddenly women and men in the parking area started to get attacked by MMAD without any reason. Somebody came out of a*

Kebab house and they were attacked too. Whoever wore yellow was being hit with Asps, by police wearing masks and carrying shields'.

At 2150hrs they updated the posting to say that the police were entering coffee places and hitting people and throwing them out.

At 2205hrs a further update stated that a person sat nearby had told Lions Radio that the police were going into shops and demanding that people remove anything yellow even shop staff who wore yellow uniforms. The parking place was full of police and also at the Ayios Nicholas roundabout.

At 2230hrs another update said that the police had gone on foot by Debenhams looking for AEL in coffee places and in the side roads and by TJ Fridays.

A final update at 2345hrs said that at the police in Limassol were, *'very happy beating people up'.*

In such situations facts and fiction very easily get blurred into one as you contrast this with the police version of events as outlined by Police spokesman Andreas Angelides in a briefing which appeared on Cyprus TV Channel ANT 1.

He explained that shortly after the game finished some four hundred AEL fans, some of whom had covered their faces, gathered at the Ayios Nicholas roundabout and proceeded to start causing damage to local property throwing stones and Molotov cocktails.

Two police officers were injured in the disturbances.

The windows of a bank were smashed causing damage valued at 20,000 euro, and six police cars were damaged, as dustbins were set alight in the area. Three MMAD teams were already deployed to Limassol, in anticipation of trouble, and further MMAD support was summoned from Larnaca.

Police said that they were expecting to make retrospective arrests.

In Nicosia two people, aged twenty-two years, and seventeen years, were arrested for throwing stones at the police during celebrations by APOEL supporters, and one thirty-nine-year-old man was arrested for abusing police officers.

Police were also investigating a case where three APOEL

supporters in a vehicle on their way to the celebrations were attacked by thirty people wearing green and black and with hoods on. They forcibly removed the three occupants from their vehicle and removed the team jerseys that they were wearing.

On Sunday 1 June 2014 police spokesperson Andreas Angelides said, *'no plan to combat hooliganism can be effective on its own and the competent authorities must take a holistic approach to addressing the problem. This has now advanced to alarming levels'*.

On Tuesday 3 June 2014 the focus shifted again to the CFA Head, Costakis Koutsokoumnis, who had been pictured presenting the championship trophy to the winning Turkish Cypriot team in the occupied north. Whilst his visit was not a secret, and was seen as part of the efforts to reunify football on the island, it nevertheless drew massive criticism from football clubs, who demanded his resignation, and noted that he was not present to award the championship cup to APOEL, the previous Saturday.

Fan clubs from APOEL, Anorthosis, AEK. Olympiakos, and Paralymni based ENP issued a joint statement calling for his resignation and said that they would organise marches to protest about the level of his engagement with Turkish Cypriot football, even though in November 2013 an initial agreement to unite had been signed in Zurich.

Politics was definitely back on the agenda at a time when Koutsokoumnis was also getting the blame for the problems resulting from the AEL versus APOEL game. On Thursday 5 June 2014 the Belgium based match fixing watchdog Federbet, with a mandate to report matches with irregular betting patterns, published its annual report to the EU.

As part of its findings it said that as many as one hundred and ten matches had been fixed across Europe in the 2013/14 season which was a rise of 20% on the previous year. The previous month Reuters had reported that match fixing was a major issue, especially in Greece.

Specifically in relation to Cyprus it was suspected that seven matches had been fixed, all of which were in the first division.

A police spokesman Andreas Angelides said, 'we are keeping a close-eye on match fixing but we have yet to officially *receive any such report'.*

DISY MP Andreas Michaelides later commented that in the four years that UEFA had been implementing a 'red-file' reporting system there had been thirty-one cases of suspected match fixing, fifteen of which had been deemed as unsolvable by the police and filed, whilst investigations on the others were still ongoing.

Up to now no person, or team, in Cyprus had ever been convicted of match fixing.

In a final twist to events, on the 6 June 2014 the CFA's disciplinary committee, acting as an appeals board, unanimously cancelled the CFA council's decision to replay the Championship final between AEL and APOEL and awarded the original match to APOEL 0-3.

Whilst it added nothing to the eventual outcome it was yet another illustration of the turmoil taking place within the game.

***

On Friday 13 June 2014 Government spokesperson Nicos Christodoulides confirmed that a draft bill aimed at preventing violence at football matches was with the State's Legal Services and would be ready to be tabled with the House on Thursday 19 June 2014.

The Bill would call for an extension of football banning orders, and an increase in the length of prison sentences. It would also call for the introduction of a 'fan card' to end the issue of anonymity so that fans would be required to produce a card as identification when purchasing tickets, which would then be matched to a specific seat in the stadium.

On the same date it was announced that FIFA President Sepp Blatter had praised Cyprus for the manner in which efforts were being made to reunite football on the island, and in particular the work of the Cyprus Football Association, and the Cyprus Turkish Football Association (KTTF) in pursuit of this aim.

It was hoped that an agreement to integrate the KTTF with the CFA would be reached by May 2015 and it was said to have the full support of the President Nicos Anastasiades.

On Thursday 19 June 2014 Justice Minister Ionas Nicolaou held a press conference to announce that the Bill had been introduced to the House and said, *'today we are taking the first step in our journey to change the unacceptable state our football is currently in. This journey won't be easy or short but it's one we have to see through to the end. I know that the Bill will get some of the fans and teams upset. We are willing to discuss some improvements on the Bill but will not render it ineffective because some fans reacted. Our only option is to work together and take decisive action without hesitation. What we won't accept is turning this bill into an 'a la carte' menu where everyone can take provisions off and add restrictions'.*

The following week, seventeen hand-picked Greek and Turkish Cypriot teenagers aged fourteen years to eighteen years, who were members of the Peace Players International Cyprus (PPI-CY), spent a week in Norway involved in coaching, learning about conflict resolution, and making Norwegian pancakes. The aim of the organisation is to create strong, confident, and happy children who can become well rounded leaders of tomorrow. Their common-bond is sport and a love of basketball.

Sometimes, when surrounded by a sea of negativity, it is easy to miss the small signs of hope and to remember that for the silent majority sport is still a very positive experience.

The aim was to introduce the new Bill in time for the next football season, and on the 1 July 2014 the focus shifted very much back onto how it was progressing, when it was announced, by the Chair of the House Legal Affairs Committee Soteris Sampson, that it would be put to a plenum vote on the 10 July 2014, despite growing objections from the CFA, who perceived a transfer of control of some elements of managing football from the CFA to the Justice Ministry.

In addition to this the CFA, and representatives of clubs, objected strongly to proposals that they should start paying for some elements of providing policing at matches, at a time when a number were in severe debt, and earnings from games were allegedly down by five million euro in 2014. It was anticipated that if the Bill were passed that they would have to start paying twenty euro per hour, per police officer, at matches.

Justice Minister Ionas Nicolaou however said that the Bill was, *'well on its way'*.

Just twenty-four hours later Soteris Sampson announced that the Bill was facing a number of challenges from Deputies who had taken a step back following the objections.

AKEL MP Aristos Damianou told the press that football clubs should not be expected to pay for policing as it was the police's job to keep the order and preserve public safety. He also wanted further discussions on the implementation of a fan ID card which it was anticipated would cost fifteen euro each to issue.

AKEL's youth branch EDON was also strongly opposed to the introduction of an ID card system, along with other fan clubs, who argued that it was an excuse for the police to 'monitor people'.

For his part the Justice Minister stood his ground and said that the fan card system would remain in the Bill along with all the other measures as a package, even though politicians accused him of a 'take it or leave it' attitude, and EDEK MP's also asked for further time to talk about the provisions.

It seemed that politics, and the need for more seemingly endless discussions, was yet again coming to the forefront but on Friday 4 July 2014 the Justice Minister announced that the Bill would be put to a vote on the last day of the Parliament before the summer break and said, *'lifting anonymity is a major component of this Bill'.*

On Saturday 5 July 2014 Anorthosis fans interrupted the team's first training session by hurling smoke-grenades on the pitch, and missiles at members of the clubs management.

On Monday 7 July 2014 the Justice Minister Ionas Nicolaou said that the government had done its duty preparing a comprehensive Bill and now it was the parliament's turn to do the same. He went on, *'any delay in approving the legislation will allow certain people to continue with behaviour like those we saw over the weekend during a team's training session. It will also allow those who react to continue with the behaviour they displayed in recent years, covered behind anonymity and the mob'.*

The new Police Chief Zacharias Chrysostomou confirmed his support for the proposed Bill and when asked whether he would consider withdrawing the police from stadiums if not passed he said, *'It is our duty to be there. Surely reaching the point where matches are not policed isn't our priority. This is something we will have to talk about if the need arises'.*

In a most telling statement he concluded with the message, *'It is in that spirit that the House should set voting on the Bill as its highest priority. I'm sure that all citizens not only want, but actually demand that MP's rise up to the challenge, so we can put an end to this unacceptable phenomenon and not reach the point when we have to mourn victims'.*

On Wednesday 9 July 2014 three people were placed under investigation by police in connection with alleged match fixing after their homes were raided and eight computers, four external hard drives and other evidence was seized. The three were suspected of being engaged in match fixing by betting large sums of money on Cyprus First Division games, on an unauthorised betting website.

A police spokesman confirmed that it was part of an investigation involving sixteen cases which had been referred to them by the CFA, none of which had resulted in a successful prosecution. Andreas Angelides said, *'It's very hard to build a case in this kind of investigation. But we will try, since we received a report from the CFA we are obliged to investigate'.*

On Thursday 10 July 2014 the vote was set to take place on the new legislation, despite objections from the main opposition party AKEL, who wanted an adjournment to discuss serious reservations.

The ruling party DISY wanted the Bill passed, in its entirety, whilst the other parties said that they would seek amendments. One AKEL MP Aristos Damianou said that the Bill included provisions which were, *'unacceptable in a modern society',* and complained that existing legislation had not been enforced because those held responsible did not show the necessary will to do so.

On Friday 18 July 2014, during a session of the House Legal Affairs Committee, it was decided to proceed with the proposal to set up a Fan ID Card system but to allow for a transition period between September 2014 and the 1 January 2015 when it would become mandatory.

Between those dates fans could still get a card and whilst most parties accepted this compromise AKEL still refused to do so on the grounds that forcing fans to register violated their human rights. They also maintained that the ID card system had been introduced in Britain during the Thatcher years but had since been abandoned.

AKEL also maintained their objections to a provision which stated that football teams should be billed by police for supervising matches.

In a further compromise the provision requiring a person banned from entering grounds, due to repeated offences, to stay at home with an ankle monitor was also removed, as was the provision making it a criminal offence to stand up, or move around the stands.

It was agreed that the Bill would go back before the House for a vote on Wednesday 23 July 2014 but despite this AKEL MP Aristos Damianou said that his party had still not decided how to vote and would not do so until Wednesday's plenum vote. He characterised the Bill as *'Thatcherite'* and proposed the setting up of a new national anti-violence committee consisting of psychologists, sociologists, and other experts, to map-out a comprehensive strategy on battling football violence with emphasis on prevention.

Also on Friday 18 July 2014 Jerome Valcke, the general secretary of the international football governing body FIFA, wrote to the CFA to ask them to remind the House Legal Affairs Committee that, according to articles 13 and 17 of the FIFA statutes, that members must, *'manage their affairs independently and without influence from any third party'*.

The letter was a reference to provisions in the new Bill which stipulated that clubs would be punished in the event of a violent incident, if the actual perpetrators were not brought to justice. This supported the view of the CFA, which was that they were the competent and recognised authority for punishing clubs, and that they could not be replaced by the state.

For FIFA to consider that its statutes took primacy over the laws passed by the Government of any country seemed a rather strange approach.

In something of a reminder of what was actually trying to be achieved, once all the political arguments had finished, a twenty-four-year-old from Limassol was arrested the day before in possession of three grammes of cannabis, fourteen smoke- bombs, thirty firecrackers, and twelve flares at his home address.

It would not be unreasonable to suggest that these would

have found their way into the stadiums at the start of the new season.

On Tuesday 22 July 2014 some fans held marches to protest against the proposed Bill and Omonia fans, in particular, turned in their hundreds to demonstrate on the streets.

The top 'Ultra' groups from different clubs also came together in Nicosia to protest outside Parliament. Nicosia is extremely hot in the summer months and some said that temperatures reached up to 50 degrees Centigrade.

The police attended but the march passed off peacefully.

On Wednesday 23 July 2014 the House approved the new Bill after making even further amendments, including removing the provision requiring clubs to meet some of the costs of policing football matches, and much to the annoyance of the Justice Minister Ionas Nicolaou, who at one stage was prompted to say that the legislation had been rendered, 'toothless'.

Only the main opposition party AKEL voted against it.

On the same day Apollon and Anorthosis played a 'friendly' match at Tsirion stadium. The Apollon Ultras did not enter the ground in protest at the introduction of the proposed fan ID card, and minutes later, a group of Anorthosis Ultras also appeared.

After cautiously 'eyeing each other up' for several minutes, both groups joined together and marched in the streets, chanting against the police, politicians and the CFA.

Apollon won the game 1-0.

At an AEL game with Zenit St Petersburg, on Wednesday 30 July 2014, supporters displayed a large banner saying, *'Privacy is not a crime',* and held up another large banner depicting the face of the Justice Minister with the words *'Wanted Dead'.*

For their part APOEL displayed a large banner in Nicosia saying, *'Fans Card equals Football's gravestone'.*

Apollon, AEL, and Anorthosis Ultras later announced that they would boycott games in the new season as part of a protest against the introduction of fan cards.

What would the 77th season - 2014/15, bring? Only time would tell, and the clock was already ticking away, with the first two First Division games due to be held on Saturday 23 August 2014.

For the first time the league would consist of twelve, rather than fourteen teams, as some of the major teams were set to slash their budgets by up to 30% in order to keep their finances in order. That said there were clearly still huge disparities between clubs, with APOEL boasting of having the highest budget of around ten million euros, whilst newly promoted Othellos Athienou only had a budget of 650,000 euros. Not exactly a level 'playing field' with which to contest the football championship.

By way of a reminder of the thoughtless behaviour of some, on Friday 22 August 2014 the press reported on the case of a Greek Cypriot student, aged twenty- two years, studying at University in the UK, who was arrested on Thursday 15 May 2014, as he was about to board a flight to Cyprus from Stansted Airport in the UK.

He came to the attention of the police when a member of the public saw him some time earlier, on a train, reading an electronic version of the *'Anarchist Cookbook',* a terrorist manual which contained instructions on how to make a car bomb.

When detained at the airport, officers also found a box contained inside his luggage, which was already in the plane's hold, which held eight distress signal mini flares.

They were mistakenly returned to him by police, but later recovered and formed part of the evidence in relation to two subsequent charges.

Pierides subsequently appeared at the Old Bailey and pleaded guilty to an offence under the 2000 Terrorism Act of possessing the electronic book, and a charge of possessing a dangerous article in an Airport, in relation to the flares, under the Aviation Security Act 1982.

The Prosecutor in the case accepted that Pierides had been 'stupid and naïve' and that he did not associate with terrorists. The court heard that he was an Omonia football fan and that he had intended using the flares at football matches.

His legal representative Jeremy Ornstein said, *'There is very widespread use of different types of flares at football grounds as part of the underlying political nature of football supporting culture there'*.

He added that the flares glowed for five seconds after being fired into the air and only posed a 'theoretical risk' after it was claimed that they would only have exploded if there had been an external fire.

The case was adjourned for pre-sentence reports to allow the Judge to consider whether or not to impose a custodial sentence.

On the 29 August 2014 the Cyprus Mail reported on the arrest of a twenty- seven-year-old man found drunk outside the GSP Stadium in Nicosia. He appeared at Nicosia District Court, on that date, and under the new legislation was required to post bail of one thousand euros and to hand his travel documents in.

He was also required to appear at a police station every time that his team played a match and to stay there for the duration of the game, until the date of his court hearing in September 2014.

According to police he was a passenger in a vehicle which had been reported for being involved in a disturbance. He agreed to take an alcohol-test, which showed that he was three times over the legal limit.

This was the second case reported where these provisions

had been implemented, following the arrest of a thirty-one-year-old from Limassol, on August 25,when he tried to gain access to a football match without purchasing a ticket.

The only comments on the article were from individuals complaining about civil liberties – not one comment was posted in support of a more robust police response.

Towards the end of September 2014 the Justice Minister Ionas Nicolaou highlighted the latest problems surrounding efforts to implement the legislation, regarding the introduction of a fan ID card, when he announced in the press, *'Everyone condemns football violence but when the time comes to turn words into actions, an unofficial alliance kicks the ball offside'*.

His comments came as the Cyprus Sports Association, as a semi-government organisation, maintained that they did not have the necessary funds to implement the scheme. An alternative suggestion that the Cyprus Football Association should take it over were dismissed by AKEL politicians who cried foul on the basis of civil liberties and the fact that the CFA was an independent body answering to no-one.

At that moment it looked as if certain sections of society within Cyprus really did have the power to stop the properly elected Government from carrying out the basic function of implementing legislation passed lawfully, and for the benefit of the wider community.

The Justice Minister concluded, *'everybody knew that the CSO did not have the means of implementing the fan card by January. As long as fan anonymity is protected, football violence will continue. Some political parties, or individual party members, some media outlets and football teams caved in to the pressure from organised fan clubs.... the pressure from that small portion of fans whose violent behaviour they previously condemned'*.

As if another reminder was required, at about 3.30am on Monday 13 October 2014 a small pipe bomb, containing small density explosive material, exploded outside the offices of the Cyprus Referees Association in Nicosia.

Weeks earlier a fire bomb had been thrown at the home of an assistant referee in Limassol.

On the 14 October 2014 the head of the Cyprus Sports

Association announced to Parliament that in fact they would assume responsibility for the 'Fan ID Card' scheme, albeit because they were short of funds they would seek an extension to its implementation date, as they simply did not have the money.

It looked like there was still a long way to go before this issue was to be resolved.

On the same date the Cyprus Mail reported that the House Watchdog Committee had heard evidence that, during the last two years, one employee from the Cyprus Sports Organisation had taken fifty-five trips abroad, and been absent for one- hundred-and fifty-five-days. The Chair of the committee said that they had been waiting since February for the CSO to submit financial statements to them in relation to work trips carried out by Board members over a three-year period. They were also said to be looking at bad planning and mismanagement relating to budgets.

Violence, politics and a hint of corruption – it was the stuff that books are made out of, and just three months later the issue of corruption became much more than a hint.

Chapter Fourteen

Offering Solutions

In trying to find solutions to the problems of football violence in Cyprus it is important to make three points:

Firstly to re-emphasise that the vast majority of people who attend football matches are decent law-abiding citizens who usually want nothing more than to support, and enjoy with some passion, a sporting activity which brings people together in a common bond.

It is an experience that is often passed down through families, from fathers to sons, and mothers to daughters. Whatever we do we therefore need to make sure that we do not criminalise the innocent majority and it is vital that they feel engaged and part of any solutions. This is achieved by way of effective marketing and communications. They should not be made to feel part of the problem but part of the solution.

It is important for the public however to see football hooliganism as a crime and not some form of sub-social activity.

Secondly football hooliganism is not an insolvable problem.

Perhaps it would be naive to say that it can be eradicated completely in any country, but it can certainly be managed and reduced in size.

There is no, *'one size fits all'*, solution, rather it needs a basket of options all of which contribute to attacking the issue. The most important thing is to remove the veil of anonymity which often exists with such individuals. These people need to know that their identities are known, and that there are consequences to their actions, which in turn increases the fear of detection.

Finally there is clear evidence in this book that the Republic of Cyprus Police, and Government, as well as sports-bodies have engaged, over a period of years, with other colleagues abroad in an effort to identify good practice and to implement plans which are fit for purpose in Cyprus. My observations on how the situation could be improved are therefore based on the premise that some of my proposals have already been tried.

I do believe however that in 2014 the timing was right to stop prevaricating, to stop blaming each other, to put politics to

one side, and to actually work together in implementing
proposals, such as those listed below in a bid to end the cycle of
violence:

All activity needs to be 'intelligence-led' with formal Football Intelligence Tasking Meetings taking place and a comprehensive approach to intelligence analysis using the services of qualified Intelligence Analysts and Researchers.

These individuals would be required to produce Problem Profiles on priority hooligan groups, Target Profiles on individuals, and also to identify 'hot spots' through historical analysis and to make predictions.

This would allow the police to make operational decisions as to where to deploy staff based on reasonable assumptions. This should apply to activity at different phases of an operation i.e. before, during the game, and afterwards.

Such staff should also be deployed to assist with Post Incident Investigations so that 'Time Lines' and 'Sequence of Events' charts can be created to assist with the formulation of evidence.

Apply the *'Al Capone'* philosophy - he was finally dealt with and sent to prison for tax evasion although he was involved in serious organised crime. There are many ways of restricting and marginalising the activity of a football hooligan and if it proves difficult to charge them with public order offences then we should look at other ways. Do they have outstanding fine warrants, do they drive an uninsured car or not wear a seat belt? Do they drink and drive or take drugs? Do they regularly park on double yellow lines? Do they carry weapons or engage in illegal hunting?

A Target Profile will identify these issues and create enforcement opportunities aimed at disrupting the individual to the point where they either give up their anti-social behaviour to get out of the limelight or go to prison.

I would describe any hooligan structure as that of an 'apple' with the hard- core group generally being made up of no more than one hundred hard-line hooligans who will be happy to engage in serious close contact fighting either with fists, feet or weapons.

There is then a second layer made up of *'up and comer'* individuals who are prepared to join in with the hard-liners when the odds are right, and then finally an outer layer of people who are happy to run around at the back trying to look as if they are fighting but actually doing nothing apart from adding to the chaos.

Whilst it is the hard-core who should be treated as a priority you also need to cut off roots and branches in relation to the other two layers to stop them becoming part of the core.

Apply stringent bail conditions when someone is arrested for football-related matters such as not to enter any designated football grounds in Cyprus, not to enter defined areas such as clubhouses or town centres, signing on at police stations on match days, and curfews.

This is where the present system of 'slow justice' could work in favour of the police as the bail conditions would remain in force until the case was concluded at court. The important thing is to make sure that the police rigorously enforce such conditions.

Address the issue of graffiti, much of which is football-related and goes largely unchecked in Cyprus.

Criminal damage of this nature raises the fear and perception of crime not only for the local population, but as importantly for tourists. More needs to be done to educate, prevent and enforce in partnership with local authorities who need to be proactive in carrying out cleaning operations.

Stop the 'blame culture' and start working in partnership. If the clubs, the police and the government come together this should ultimately lead to increased gates, increased revenue and less policing, therefore less costs.

Speed up the justice system and put the emphasis on addressing the needs and expectations of victims rather than the offenders. Minimum timescales should be set for case disposals to ensure that the 'public interest' is not lost.

Re-examine the law in Cyprus in relation to the use of CCTV and hand-held video cameras in public places to ensure that their use in gathering visual evidence is maximised upon. The innocent have nothing to fear from being viewed on camera but visual evidence provides irrefutable evidence in a court of law and also acts as a real deterrent when people know that they are likely to be filmed.

Adopt a 'two ejections' policy where you are out and banned

from a ground for a set period of time by the relevant club.

Increase the political willpower to legislate quickly and to support the judiciary in terms of having an effective deterrent sentencing policy. Offenders should expect to start going to prison.

Review the effectiveness of the current stewarding arrangements in grounds.

Increase the numbers of trained police spotters/evidence gatherers, using dedicated resources who are less likely to be the subject of targeted intimidation.

Increase the use of the removal of club membership for convicted hooligans.

Post Incident investigations to be conducted within agreed timescales and Investigators to be held accountable for the quality of their enquiries and the ensuing results.

The use of informants should be encouraged.

Confidential Phone Lines to, *'shop a hooligan'*, to be supported with media campaigns.

Visits to known football hooligans to be conducted the week before high-risk fixtures to make them aware that they are known and being watched.

The use of dedicated staff to conduct pro-active operations to target the most troublesome groups. To reduce the risk of intimidation, or of operations being compromised, it is suggested that serving, or retired officers, from the EU policing family should be employed on secondments, or fixed-term contracts, who would serve on a two year basis in specific roles dealing with the gathering of evidence through to court finalisation. These operations would be conducted away from main police buildings.

Maximise results in the media through an open press partnership with the police and the use of a nationally recognised *'anti-hooligan'* logo. Everything should be done to stigmatise the hooligan rather than to glorify them.

Club websites and match programmes to adopt the same logo and to contain 'standing items' condemning violence or racism and highlighting the 'hotline' numbers.

There needs to be an increase in diversion at an early age

through better inputs to schools and colleges on the effects of anti-social behaviour in general.

Review to be conducted in relation to football-related arrests over the last four years to identify good practice, and poor practice, in relation to tactics and outcomes. This review should ascertain the levels of success, in terms of convictions, and ascertain the rationale when cases are withdrawn or still shown as pending after lengthy periods of time.

A review of current police public-order tactics regarding football policing to be carried out to ensure that current tactics are fit for purpose. Such a review would also need to establish whether there are sufficient numbers of officers trained.

Football briefings to be developed for police officers, to assist in building the intelligence picture, based on a structured intelligence requirement.

Football clubs to appoint, 'Community Engagement Officers', to work on diversion projects and in collaboration with each other, rather than in competition.

The costs to Hospitals in treating injuries relating to football violence should be highlighted given the strain that hospitals are already operating under. The media should be allowed to publish 'shock' photographs of injuries to fans and police officers.

Reformed hooligans should be used as 'champions' to spread the message that being a 'thug' is not cool.

EU funding to be sought to support initiatives.Sponsorship from corporate Companies to be sought to support initiatives.A 'National Action Plan' to be created to pull together all of the actions and to allocate lead owners.

A National Co-Ordinator to be appointed who should not be a political figure but would be answerable to the Justice Minister for delivery.

One of the Cyprus Universities to launch an academic study, using previous studies as benchmark documents, to examine the culture and causes of football violence in Cyprus, which would assist in more long term planning.

Look at raising the voice and profile of women in relation to a campaign. Women have a powerful voice in the home that should not be ignored.

Music also has a popular and powerful voice in Cyprus and leading singers should be engaged in developing *'Say No To Hooliganism'* campaigns.

Police should actively seek to close down social-networking sites that advocate football violence.

Do more to stem the flow of 'firecrackers' into the hands of hooligans by ensuring that appropriate legislation is applied to supply sources.

Develop more robust search regimes at stadium turnstiles and ensure that submitting to a search is a condition of entry to the stadiums.

Solicit support from UK clubs to reiterate the message that there is no place in the modern football world for hooliganism.

Harness the use of voluntary organisations to provide mentoring for those youngsters most at risk at becoming involved in football violence.

Employ 'saturation' policing at selected high risk games with 'zero-tolerance' and dedicated arrest teams deployed as 'snatch squads'.

Encourage companies who employ people convicted of football hooliganism to consider dismissing them on grounds of bringing their company into disrepute or make it a condition of service with government departments that such sanctions will be applied.

Make use of 'disinformation' in a selective manner to leave hooligans 'second guessing' as to the tactics of the police.

Encourage the Greek Orthodox Church to have a greater voice on the subject.

Agree a costing formula with the CFA for policing costs that more properly reflects the actual costs, and realign the influence and control that the CFA exercises in such matters.

Police football intelligence officers to be nominated for every team in the First Division.

The law to be reviewed to ensure that fans inciting violence via the internet can face prosecution.

Review the makeup of the current football leagues to find ways of reducing the number of so called 'local derby' games involving the 'Big Five' clubs by for instance expanding the number of teams in the First Division.

Look at re-branding and re-naming the other sports linked to the 'Big Five' clubs with a view to diversifying the fan-base and distinguishing them from 'hooligan' elements.

Introduce an independent Disciplinary Review Body to deal with matters relating to conduct issues involving club officials and players, with at least half of its members being non-Cypriot.

Improve segregation within stadiums and the creation of permanent sterile areas.

Increase the availability of both technical and human resources in the field of covert policing of sporting events.

Introduce mandatory prison sentences for assaults on police during sporting events.

Introduce an offence of 'aggravated' possession of articles used to throw missiles at the police with a mandatory minimum sentence on conviction.

Review the use of community service orders for convicted football hooligans.

Consider setting up one special island-wide criminal court to deal with all football related offences of violence, that attract sentences normally dealt with within District Courts, in order to support consistency in sentencing.

Increase the conditions for the legal sale of firecrackers including a requirement for the details of purchasers to be recorded, against production of identity cards, and increase sentencing options in relation to breaches of such laws.

In order to reduce instances of damage to police vehicles secure sterile car parking areas to be provided at each stadium which should be covered by CCTV.

A policing provision funding element to be 'ring fenced' within any government subsidies paid to clubs via the Cyprus

Sporting Organisation.

Support the development of *'Respect'* programmes.

Deploy 'Explosives' police search-dogs at high-risk games to complement search regimes as fans enter stadiums, as well as 'General Purpose' dogs to assist with crowd control.

Improve the systems for logging police information at grounds during matches and ensure that CCTV operators routinely create a 'montage' of supporters on film prior to the commencement of each game to assist in offender identification.

Design out issues relating to the use of vehicles, and in particular motorcycles, in the vicinity of grounds in an effort to regulate safe parking and reduce their criminal use to convey hooligan elements.

No-one holding any form of political office at either a local or national level should be allowed to take up any formal, or honorary positions, on the Boards of Football Clubs in Cyprus which should be deemed as a 'conflict of interest'.

Create an 'aggravated' offence of causing criminal damage to emergency service vehicles i.e. police, fire, and ambulance.

Make use of dedicated CID documentation/charging teams during high-risk games to free up uniform resources at the earliest opportunity.

Epilogue

On Sunday 4 May 2014 the Sunday Mail in Cyprus carried the front-page headline,

'Hooliganism action plan – naming, shaming and relentless pursuit crucial says former top UK police officer'.

Following an interview with me the previous week, whilst I was on a visit to see family in Cyprus, a reporter Constantinos Psillides, outlined my thoughts on the ongoing problems in an extensive article reproduced in full as follows with the kind permission of the Editor Jean Christou:

'Lifting the veil of anonymity surrounding football hooligans, relentlessly pursuing them and engaging the public in a targeted media campaign are just some of the actions police should take to effectively deal with football violence in Cyprus, according to a former Chief Superintendent of West Midlands Police in England. "This is not an insolvable problem", Michael Layton told the Sunday Mail adding that football violence can be reduced to a

manageable level.

"It would perhaps be naive to say that it can ever be eradicated completely in any country but it can certainly be managed and reduced in size".

The April 22 clash between APOEL and AEL fans which resulted in an innocent bystander losing an eye when he was hit in the face by a rock is just the latest incident in the ever rising menace of football hooliganism.

Layton, a frequent visitor to Cyprus, is no stranger to issues of football violence. A veteran with more than 40 years in the police service and a former director of intelligence and operations with the British Transport Police (BTP), Layton was directly involved in the British Police fight against hooliganism.

He managed an undercover police operation called Operation Red Card which targeted Birmingham City's football hooligans, known as Zulu Warriors.

According to the book 'Football Violence and Social Identity' by Richard Guilianotti the 1987 operation ended when 180 police officers swooped in the homes of 67 youths suspected of belonging to the hooligan group.

Twenty-one were remanded in custody for one week while others were bailed not to go within one mile of a football ground. Fort- nine were charged. Fifteen were jailed, the maximum sentence being 30 months.

Asked by the Sunday Mail, Layton produced a twenty point list on how to deal with football hooligans, clarifying that a basket of solutions should be offered so the police can pick those that fit the situation best.

In his action plan Layton pointed out that anonymity was one of the main problems to tackle.

"They need to know that their identities are known and that there are consequences to their actions which in turn increase the fear of detection", said Layton.

In the past authorities had asked the clubs to cooperate with them by issuing a 'fan ID card' which fans would be required to present to enter the football grounds.

The suggestion never materialised as clubs did not want to antagonise fans who vehemently opposed the suggestion.

Police then tried to use other deterrents, such as publicising photos of hooligans. This measure has also proved ineffective, as the latest clash showed clearly. Police issued eleven pictures of hooligans but no arrests have yet been made.

Sergeant Michalis Herodotou head of police anti-hooliganism office, agreed with Layton that an anonymity ban could be an important weapon. "Once these people feel that their anonymity is at risk, they won't set foot in a football field. Anonymity is their greatest weapon", he said yesterday. "The cards would be issued by the clubs themselves. We won't have access to personal data, except when it comes to criminal investigation. We don't care who issues a fan ID card, as long as they are issued", he said.

But Herodotou told the Mail that clubs had initially been in favour of the measure but backed down when the story broke in the media.

Following the anonymity ban Layton argued that the justice system needed to speed up with emphasis put on addressing the expectations of victims rather than offenders. Politicians, he said, should support the judiciary system in terms of having an effective deterrent sentencing policy".

"Offenders should expect to start going to prison", said Layton. The former Chief Superintendent also suggested that the law governing CCTV and hand held camera footage should be re-examined. Currently the admission of video footage is a 'grey area' for Cypriot Courts.

"The innocent have nothing to fear from being viewed on camera but visual evidence provides irrefutable evidence in a court of law and also acts as a real deterrent when people know that they are likely to be filmed", Layton argued.

Stringent bail conditions should also be applied when a suspect is arrested for football related matters. These could include not being allowed to enter any designated football ground in Cyprus or areas such as clubhouses or town centres, signing on at police stations on match days, and curfews.

Layton's action plan also calls for an 'intelligence led task force' to gather and assess intelligence on a regular basis so as to produce problem profiles on priority hooligan groups, create target profiles of individuals and identify 'hot spots' through historical analysis.

All of these, according to the former Chief Superintendent, would enable the police to make operational decisions as to where to deploy staff.

A historical data analysis would have indeed have saved the police a lot of trouble, if it had been applied before the APOEL – AEL game. It wasn't the first time the area near to the futsal fields next to the Nicosia Stadium had seen football related violence. On November 15, 2009 fans of APOEL and OMONIA clashed at that very same spot, armed with knives, baseball bats and wooden sticks. The incident resulted in an APOEL fan being seriously injured when fans of the other team almost beat him to death.

When dealing with football hooligans, Layton said that police should be relentless and not just when it comes to football related activities. He cited the 'Al Capone philosophy' referring to the famous Chicago mobster who was arrested not for his numerous criminal activities but for tax evasion. "Do they have outstanding fine warrants, do they drive an uninsured car. Do they not wear seat belts? Do they drink and drive or take drugs? Do they regularly park on double yellow lines? Do they carry weapons or engage in illegal hunting?" asked Layton "A target profile will identify these issues and create enforcement opportunities aimed at disrupting the individual to the point where they either give up their anti-social behaviour to get out of the limelight or go to prison".

Layton described the hooligan structure as that of an 'apple' with the hard core group generally being made up of no more than a hundred hard line hooligans who will be happy to engage in fighting. The second layer consists of 'up and comer' individuals who are prepared to join in with the hard liners when the odds are right, and then finally an outer layer of people who are happy to run round at the back but actually doing nothing apart from adding to the chaos. "Whilst it is the hard core who should be treated as a priority, nevertheless you need to cut off roots and branches in relation to the other two layers to stop them becoming part of the core", he warned.

Although most of the measures he suggested are suppressive,

Layton made it clear that an effective media campaign is absolutely crucial.

Layton stressed that law-abiding football goers should not feel targeted. "The vast majority of people who attend football matches are decent law-abiding citizens who usually want nothing more than to support and enjoy a sporting activity which brings people together in a common bond", he said. "Whatever we do we therefore need to make sure that we do not criminalise the innocent majority, and it is vital that they feel engaged and part of any solutions".

Responding to those that said that police should withdraw from policing matches and leave the security to the clubs, Layton said that this was simply not an option for any civilised society.

"Once you start withdrawing from one element of policing, it is inevitable that the community will try to fill the void to police themselves and anarchy prevails with only the strongest winning", he said.

***

On Sunday 13 July 2014, following the developments in relation to the proposed new Bill, I participated in a further article which was published in the Sunday Mail in Cyprus under the headline, **'The true cost of hooliganism'**. The article is again published in full as follows:

'Well over 200 police officers and around 130 members of the public, match officials, and football players have been injured in sports related violence in Cyprus in the last decade, a British former top police officer has discovered.

In a week which saw the House of Representatives fail to pass the long- awaited Bill to tackle rampant hooliganism, the British expert's research has highlighted yet again the desperate need for police to have the means to root out hooligans.

By trawling through media archives, Michael Layton, the former Chief Superintendent of the West Midlands Police Force in England, has collected data going back to 2003.

He cites 77 matches where one or two of the Big Five – APOEL, AEL , Omonia, Apollon, Anorthosis – were playing. Besides football matches, Layton also looked into 13 basketball and volleyball matches during the same period which again involved the same clubs.

In every single one of these games some sort of disorder occurred according to Layton. "More than 211 police officers have been injured whilst policing football matches, and at one fixture an officer died of a heart attack during disturbances. Officers have been stabbed, burnt, suffered broken noses, fractures, and routinely hit with rocks and missiles on at least 43 occasions", said the former Director of Intelligence and Operations with the British Transport Police (BTP), who was directly involved in the British police force's fight against hooliganism.

According to his data, at least 128 members of the public, match officials, or players have been injured or assaulted during the course of these games.

He said that the vast majority suffered violent attacks, with burns, head injuries, loss of fingers, loss of eyesight, and other injuries recorded, many of which required hospital treatment.

The youngest victim of football violence was just twelve-years-of-age.

For Layton, and most experts in the fight against hooliganism, the police's key weapon is that violent fans lose their anonymity.

And it was precisely on this issue – the provision of fan identity cards – that the Justice Ministry Bill stalled on Thursday. Parliamentary parties, with the exception of ruling DISY and former coalition partner DIKO, decided to postpone the vote on the Bill for two weeks, so a compromise can be reached on some of the bill's provisions. The request to postpone voting was put forth by main opposition party AKEL. Party General Secretary Andros Kyprianou told the plenum that he agreed that, "the gangrene of sports related violence had to be dealt with but this Bill contains provisions that were adopted in other countries and later withdrawn."

Kyprianou's comment mirrored those made by party MP Aristos Damianou a week ago, when he told the press that the Bill employed, "Thatcherite practices that the English have abandoned years ago". Damianou promised then that his party would table its own Bill to deal with hooliganism, which they probably will in the coming week.

While AKEL does raise some good questions – a fine for even covering your face partially, in and near the stadium, and for standing up during the match can be characterised as draconian – the party's main opposition is over fan cards.

The fan card – a card issued for anyone who wishes to buy tickets to a sporting event – has also angered fans who view it as a tool to be used by police to keep tabs on them, even though the police will have nothing to do with the registry. AKEL, with its strong ties to Omonia, one of the biggest teams in Cyprus, has always been in the front-line of the war against the fan ID card.

A compromise on the fan card appears impossible. Justice Minister Ionas Nicolaou has repeatedly said that the Bill is a 'package deal' and that he would not give in one inch over the need for cards. He also made clear that the Bill had to pass before the House closed for its summer recess.

Ionas has the full support of the Cyprus' top police officers. Sergeant Michalis Herodotou, head of police anti-hooligan office, told the Sunday Mail that fan cards were a crucial instrument, while Police Chief Zacharias Chrysostomou said they were an absolute necessity.

"We wish we didn't have to go this far but we have to adapt to the situation before us", said Chrysostomou.

For Layton the failure to pass the Bill was a missed opportunity.

"It will leave the public and politicians 'wringing their hands' when violence inevitably erupts again at the start of the new season", he said. "The figures themselves over the last eleven years alone tell a dismal story of constant dialogue, followed by strong messages of condemnation and promises of action, which are all too often not followed through. The new police chief has already made it clear that he does not want to see people mourning the death of someone caught up in this type of violence."

The former Superintendent also notes that not dealing with football violence has an actual monetary cost, since fans are destroying stadiums and private property, while insurance companies are forced to fork out money to cover damages. This leads to increased premiums – the cost of which is passed to fans via ticket price increases – while treating victims of football violence in hospitals also adds to the pile.

In his research Layton also studied how MP's responded to football violence. He noted more than 40 political interventions, with statements from ministers and politicians, and more than 200 meetings and seminars which were attended by members of the House Legal Affairs Committee on the subject.

"Hooligans will see the failure of this Bill as a triumph which is why a strong message needs to be delivered to them at the start of the new season, the 'battle' is actually just starting and that the 'gloves are off', he said.

As for AKEL's opposition to fan cards, Layton pointed to the widespread use of social media such as Facebook and Twitter.

"These give out far more information of a personal nature than a fan ID card ever will" he said "As long as there is a proper and transparent system for dealing with requests for information from the police through using appointed 'Single Points of Contact' it should not be an issue".

He also questioned AKEL's objections that some of the Bill's provisions had no place in a modern society. "I would venture to

suggest that in a 'modern society' people do not go around throwing

rocks at each other on a weekly basis just for the fun of it",

responded Layton.

***

In October 2014 the fan card issue again hit the media with comments from the Personal Data Commissioner, Yiannis Danielides, that the proposed system violated the principle of proportionality, since the trouble was caused by a small group of fifty to one hundred people, and not the vast majority of fans.

Whilst he was certainly right about the latter comments I would question his maths given the numbers I have seen on various incidents portrayed freely on YouTube.

He accused the government of not consulting his office, a fact disputed by the Justice Minister, and suggested that the scheme should be restricted to fifteen to thirty-year-olds as they were the group that included most of the troublemakers.

Although the fan card measure was due to come in on the 1

January 2015 the reality was that with the Cyprus Sports Association and the Cyprus Football Association still saying that they had no money, or resources, to implement it, this piece of legislation was not going to meet its deadline.

On the 30 November 2014 a French-born black Omonia player Mickael Pote, aged thirty-years, suffered *'monkey chants'* which were directed at him by APOEL fans.

The player responded against his tormenters and was booked for protesting. The same thing happened during a subsequent game with Anorthosis, in December, and although a tannoy appeal was made asking fans to stop the abuse it appears that no police investigation took place.

The CFA took action against both clubs but Ombudswoman Eliza Savvidou, who acts as the anti-racism authority, said, *'Racism incidents in Cyprus almost go unnoticed to the extent that one wonders whether binding directions to fight racism in stadiums are enforced'.*

On Thursday 18 December 2014 the 'bubble burst' on allegations of match- fixing as international referee Marios Panayi presented a detailed dossier to the police, alleging extensive 'match fixing' at games in Cyprus.

He spent hours providing written statements to the police at the Headquarters in Nicosia. The day before he held a press conference and claimed to have recordings, documents and other evidence proving that members of the Cyprus Football Association, and in particular the CFA Deputy Head, were involved.

The Chairman Costakis Koutsokoumnis was described by Panayi as a *'straw man'* and he said that as a result of his disclosures to the press he had already received death-threats on his mobile phone. He also asked political parties to 'come clean' as to the extent of their involvement with the CFA.

A police investigation was launched which initially focused on sixteen games, and Aris Football Club in Limassol was the subject of early police investigations.

In the run up to Christmas police seized a number of computers from the CFA's office which were subsequently returned. The former Chairman of Aris made a statement to the police, following which he too reported being threatened with violence.

As calls mounted for the Cyprus Football Association leadership to resign they steadfastly refused, and even went so far as to claim that they were sure that the investigation would come to nothing, and said that they would mount their own investigation, and nominate the individuals who would conduct it.

***

On Saturday 3 January 2015, at 2.30pm, I attended a Second Division match at Zakaki Stadium, in Limassol, between AEZ Zakaki and ELPIDA Xyphagou.

About two hundred supporters, from both clubs, stood on a single dilapidated wooden stand in the freezing weather.

Supporters smoked throughout the game and routinely dropped their cigarette ends through the wooden slats, onto the rubbish-strewn floor below, in scenes which reminded me of the 'Bradford Fire' in 1985 when fifty-six people lost their lives at Bradford City Football Stadium.

Facing the pitch was a single strand fence, with barbed wire on top. The entrance gate was closed so we were literally hemmed-in.

There were two Sovereign Bases Police officers on duty inside the ground, with one pacing the touchline area incessantly, whilst the second in contrast remained in a police vehicle for the majority of the time. When he did come out, hatless, his hands remained firmly implanted in his pockets.

The first half of the game was uneventful, and whilst I don't speak Greek, I do know the favourite swear words and listened to the incessant chants of, *'Gamo tin mana sou'*, which colloquially means *'Fuck your Mother'*.

As my wife Andry sat next to me she was reminded of her previous life in the Force. Near to her was a neighbour from her village, who swore at every opportunity, oblivious to his proximity to a number of women.

Another supporter spread his legs wide, sat next to another female, as he thought nothing of *'invading her space'*.

In the second half, ten minutes from full-time, the mood changed dramatically after the referee sent the coach of ELPIDA

Xyphagou off the pitch. He protested violently but was eventually escorted out of the ground by a very large steward and the police officers.

As he did so he waved and gave a mock salute to supporters, before leaving, as both sets of fans started to abuse each other. A man, in his forties, in front of me who should have known better, moved swiftly towards the opposition, followed by a group of younger 'hangers on' and you could feel the tension palpably rise.

Outside the ground a confrontation developed, and the two SBA officers had to run outside to restore order, before the game restarted, and eventually finished in a 0-0 draw.

The tension remained, and at the final whistle the referee remained in the centre circle, with his linesman, until he was escorted off by the two SBA officers, who had to put themselves in between the officials and a very fat man who came onto the pitch and berated them, excitedly pointing his finger at the referee.

Another great day for the sport which left me feeling cold inside and out.

***

On Wednesday 7 January 2015 the Chairman of the Cyprus Referees Association (CRA) Michalis Argirou, and former CRA member Michalis Spyrou, were arrested on suspicion of match fixing in 2011 and 2012.

They were subsequently remanded by the courts, as police enquiries looked set to continue for some time, and question marks were raised as to the admissibility of some of the evidence presented to police.

***

At this stage of the book I will quote from some genuine fans:

Koulla, from Nicosia said to me, *'I have supported APOEL since I was six- years-of-age. My parents supported APOEL, and my husband, and my son, as well as my sister, and brother. The whole of my village Skillouras, in the Occupied areas, also supported APOEL, and three famous brothers from the village Giorgos, Nicos, and Koullis played for their first team. I love the game and I love to watch my team. I also support Arsenal in the UK, and my son,*

Giorgos, and my husband Phillipos, support Manchester United. I get excited when I watch my team play. Shouting and singing at the games is fun but I don't like hooligans and want to see them out of the stadiums. If I see an APOEL fan behaving like a hooligan I feel that they give my team a bad name and I don't like this. Many people feel like this. We don't want them to spoil everything and want this behaviour to stop'.

Valentinos from Limassol said, *'I have supported Omonia since I was born, and everyone in my family supports Omonia, including my mother, and brothers. My father was an Omonia fan and took me to games. Half of Cyprus supports Omonia and between the 70s to the 90s they have lost only five championships. I watch most of their games on the TV now, because of the economic situation, as it is expensive to go to matches. I also watch a lot of other football on TV as I enjoy it very much and I also follow Manchester United. I think that the problem with hooliganism is that the police are not strict enough. They need to do something more to stop it'.*

Tassos, from Trachoni, near Limassol said, *'I have been an AEL supporter since 1966 when I was ten-years-old. My father, my brother and all of the family are AEL fans. It is the team of my town Limassol and my cousin, Stelios, played for AEL. I used to go to the games but because of the hooliganism I now watch the games on TV. I love football, and the commentary programmes, and watch about two hours a day. I also support Tottenham Hotspur, and my brother is a fanatical fan of Liverpool, and he sometimes goes to the UK to watch them. The situation with football hooliganism in Cyprus is totally unacceptable'.*

The point of the messages are not about which team they support but that they speak with one common-voice for the silent majority of decent people who want to live in a decent society, and to simply enjoy the 'beautiful game' as it was intended to be.

***

On Sunday 11 January 2015 APOEL played AEL at Tsirion Stadium in Limassol in a game which was eventually won by AEL with a score-line of 2-1.At half-time APOEL fans set fire to stadium seats, a fire-escape exit, and a canteen warehouse, causing extensive damage. They hurled missiles at officers and injured four of them, as a pitch invasion caused a twenty-minute delay.

One hundred APOEL supporters were hosed-down by a fire service truck as they attempted to prevent fire fighters from putting out the fire. They formed a human chain around the fire and hurled seats, flares, smoke bombs, stones, ceramic tiles, and toilet bowls at the fire truck.

At the end of the game police led six buses, transporting APOEL fans back to Nicosia, into the ground, and searched everyone.

In the buses they found an extendable baton, a folding knife, several flares, a bag containing cannabis, a three-metre chain, and a slingshot.

A total of forty-one APOEL fans were arrested, nine of whom were soaking- wet.

Police officers identified a number of them as being involved in the disturbances and CCTV was examined to identify other suspects, with a warrant being issued for a further suspect.

Nine of the suspects were subsequently remanded in custody

for three days when they appeared in court the following day.

Justice Minister Ionas Nicolaou said afterwards, *'We will not allow the football fields to become battle fields for any junkie or drunk'.*

He pointed towards a recent reduction in violence but insisted that he was still keen to introduce a Fan-ID card.

On 20 January 2015 it was reported that Justice Minister Ionas Nicolaou was calling for an end to inflammatory comments from football club officials, suggesting that they contributed to the problems of football violence in Cyprus.

His comments came after a bomb blast at the home of a referee's mother.

The sixty-year-old woman was the mother of referee Thomas Mouskos, who had been under police-protection after receiving threats following the Apollonas versus Othellos game which ended in a 2-2 draw.

The previous May his home had been targeted when a hand-grenade was thrown which failed to explode.

It was the fourth incident in twelve months involving referees being targeted with explosives and for a week the Referees Association refused to officiate at any game of the Cyprus Football Association.

On Sunday 1 February 2015 a fight broke out between players during an amateur-league game, between AEN Chlorakas and Chrysomilia Ayiou Amvrosiou in Chloraka, Paphos.

The game was stopped at 5.15pm, due to the fight, and two AEN Chlorakas players in their thirties, were taken to hospital with head injuries.

In February 2015 the results of a survey by the Cyprus Footballers Association revealed that a footballer in Cyprus had a 34% chance of being approached by a stranger, and a 23% chance by an official from his club to fix a match.

On Wednesday 4 March 2015 a thirty-year-old man tried to enter Larnaca's Antonis Papadopoulos stadium, without a ticket, to watch a game between Anorthosis and APOEL. He was turned away by police but then after purchasing one he returned and started swearing at the officers before being arrested. After an initial court appearance he was banned from attending sporting events pending the outcome of his trial.

In March 2015 the Justice Minister Ionas Nicolaou met with members of the Cyprus Referees Association to try to reassure them in relation to the growing list of attacks on members. In the same month a car used by top referee Leontios Trattos was set alight, with a similar incident occurring the month before when a car belonging to the wife of another referee was set on fire.

On Saturday 2 May 2015 a twenty-four-year-old woman was arrested on suspicion of throwing a firecracker at a car, following a game between APOEL and Omonia in Nicosia, which finished with a 3-2 score. Three other people aged 16 years, 21 years, and 24 years were also arrested.

Following the game, amid accusations that the referee had shown bias, a complaint was lodged with police that an unnamed referee had received a threatening text message which said, *'you're finished. Do not mess with Omonia'*.

On Sunday 3 May 2015 a group of about ten individuals, wearing hoods and believed to be Anorthosis supporters, caused damage at the APOEL fan club near the port in Larnaca. A window was smashed and walls spray-painted with slogans before they made good their escape.

On the same date unknown individuals attempted to set light to a new APOEL fan club which was still under construction.

On Thursday 30 July 2015 a twenty-year-old man from Limassol was arrested after trying to carry flares into the Antonis Papadopoulos stadium in Larnaca, which was hosting a Europa League football match. He was spotted on CCTV trying to get a backpack containing sixty-three flares inside for a game between Apollon and Azebaijani side Gabala.

He was seen trying to pull it inside but unfortunately for him it got stuck on a pole and he was arrested at the end of the game, which ended in a 1-1 draw.

He was later banned from entering stadiums until October 2015.

In September 2015 the Cyprus Footballers Association (PASP) announced the results of a survey which revealed that 67%

of football players are aware that matches in the top-flight are fixed, although only 25% of them said that they would be willing to report this to the authorities because of 'insecurity'.

An even larger percentage of players believed that match fixing was rife in the Second Division.

On Monday 21 September 2015 a twenty-one-year-old was arrested at the Makarios Stadium in Nicosia, during the Doxa versus APOEL match, after he pushed a police officer in an attempt to escape, when he was spotted throwing a bag, which was believed to contain flare-guns, off a wall, near the East Stands.

After being told that he was under arrest he attacked the police officer, and punched him in the face.

When he first appeared at court he was banned from attending his team's matches until the conclusion of his case.

On Saturday 26 September 2015 APOEL played Limassol team Aris in a game which finished 4-0.

A 'red-file' was subsequently sent to the Cyprus authorities by UEFA after suspiciously high betting activity was reported during the game, and police launched an investigation.

In October 2015 the Justice Minister Ionas Nicolaou indicated that the police in the Republic were studying the use of police dog units to combat football hooliganism, particularly in cases where they were attacking police officers.

The Minister also attended a large-scale public order exercise, run by the SBA police, at Ethnikos Achna FC, involving more than one hundred and fifty people, which included police, military, and civilians.

The exercise was also witnessed by the Commander of British Forces, Air- Vice Marshall Michael Wigston, who commented, *'football violence in Cyprus is not uncommon and the exercise was aimed at improving the response of officers, ground staff, and safety officials to it'.*

On Sunday 18 October 2015 a game between Apollon and Anorthosis at Tsirion stadium was abandoned after fans from Anorthosis invaded the pitch and attacked the home side's officials and substitutes.

It happened five minutes before the 6pm kick-off.

The trouble began when Anorthosis fans managed to gain access via a gate which had been opened to allow an ambulance into the ground to attend to a fan who had fallen ill.

Apollon chairman Nicos Kyriz said, *'What happened today was a very sad day for football'*.

Anorthosis club official Charalambos Manoli believed that the game should have gone ahead because the fans returned to the terraces and said, *'There is a flip side to the coin that the Apollon players claim that they were hit by our fans. It should be noted that the Apollon officials and players provoked us when one of our fans was being attended to for an injury. There is nothing else to say'*.

Police subsequently investigated the actions of three of the Apollon players, and a member of the coaching team, and a warrant was issued for a twenty-six-year- old Anorthosis fan accused of riot and illegal entry to a sporting arena.

The Football Association's judge later awarded the game 3-0 to Apollon, and fines and other penalties, were handed out to both clubs, as well as to three Apollon players, who took part in an exchange of objects with Anorthosis supporters.

On Sunday 25 October 2015 fifteen fans, aged between fifteen years to twenty-four years, were arrested after they tried to force their way into Tsirion Stadium without tickets.

The group was alleged to have been part of a bigger group of around thirty AEL fans who arrived by bus from Paphos.

They were said to have, *'walked aggressively towards gate 3, wearing hoods and scarves, while some of them were holding wooden sticks, and demanded to enter the stadium without tickets, while pushing at the stadium's metal fences'*.

Stadium security then closed all of the entrances and called the police who then made arrests.

On their first appearance the fifteen, who denied any involvement, were banned from attending their team's matches whilst the case was ongoing.

On Thursday 5 November 2015 APOEL played the Greek side Asteras Tripolis away, and around 1,500 APOEL supporters attended the game at Tripolis which APOEL subsequently lost 2-0.

Before the game Greek police detained six APOEL fans following random searches. Four of them were found to be in possession of flares, and two were in possession of cannabis.

During the game APOEL supporters started throwing flares onto the pitch in the second half, and continued to do so even after the referee threatened to suspend play. At one stage the Austrian referee suspended play for fifteen minutes as he considered safety issues. No arrests took place.

Following the game two APOEL Board members, and the Financial Officer, resigned in protest at the fans' behaviour as the club commented, *'The behaviour of certain brainless individuals irreparably hurt APOEL's name'*.

The club faced the prospect of heavy sanctions from UEFA.

On the 3 December 2015 the referee Marios Panayi, who went public with charges of widespread match fixing in Cyprus, was struck-off by the CFA Judicial Committee, after he failed to pay a 5,750 euro fine for allegedly making offensive online comments against members of the Cyprus Referee Association.

For his part Panayi, regarded by many as a whistle-blower for coming out into the open, continued to campaign for a radical overhaul of refereeing in Cyprus, and for changes in the CFA.

At the beginning of December 2015 some seven hundred Omonia fans, from the organised *'Gate 9'* element, staged a protest outside AKEL's central offices demanding that the party loosened its stranglehold on the club.

For their part AKEL denied having any involvement in the clubs affairs and hit back at the organisers, claiming that they had ulterior motives.

On Tuesday 12 January 2016 two match officials were injured during a district football league game in Limassol between AEM Moutayiakkas and Dierona, when just before the end of the game, with the score at 2-2, the referee awarded a penalty.

This prompted about fifteen people to run onto the pitch and to attack the referee, and a linesman, before running off.

The two men were taken to hospital and released after

treatment.

The following day police arrested three members of the AEM Moutayiakka team, all aged twenty-six years, who were suspected of taking part in the attacks.

At the beginning of February 2016 Justice Minister Ionas Nicolaou stressed the need for the Cyprus Sports Organisation's proposed ID card system to be implemented.

He said, *'We are at the final stages of awarding the contract for the strategic partner that will undertake the issue of cards, installing the ID programme and putting in place all mechanisms required to make our football stadiums operate in a modern fashion'.*

On 14 February 2016 a Facebook post by the organised fans of Omonia FC prompted a police investigation as three automatic weapons, with magazines, were shown laid out on top of an Omonia flag.

Police armed with a court order raided the fans' headquarters, as well as the home of their *'leader'* but found nothing, although a computer was seized.

Posted by *'Gate 9'* fans on Facebook, the picture was captioned, '*and for those who enjoy conspiracy theories: GATE 9 UP IN ARMS'*.

On Saturday 9 April 2016 Anorthosis played APOEL in a match at Larnaca.

One seventeen-year-old was arrested for committing damage, entering a stadium illegally, and using dangerous items in a stadium.

A twenty-five-year-old was arrested for possessing an assault weapon in a stadium and for committing violence.

They were both found guilty in a Larnaca court next day and banned from attending the matches of the team they supported.

On Saturday 23 April 2016 AEL goalkeeper Matias Degra reported to police that he had received a threatening phone call just before midnight, when an unknown individual told him that he was at risk of physical harm if he did not leave Cyprus immediately.

On the same day played Omonia played their arch rivals

APOEL – a game which Omonia lost.

A twitter account going by the name *'Monaha Thyra 9'* which means *'Only Gate 9'* and connected to Omonia, posted a slogan aimed at the *'Orange'* Panhellenic Fans Association of APOEL which said, *'The Orange were always wimps, they should all die in the Panhellenic Association'.*

One man standing for AKEL as a parliamentary candidate posted the tweet on his own account, and after a number of commentators condemned him for doing so he eventually issued a statement distancing himself from the comments.

On Sunday 15 May 2016 APOEL played Anorthosis at the GSP Stadium, following which APOEL were awarded the 2015/2016 Cyta Championship title with 83 points, for the 25th time in their history.

Before the game three Turkish Cypriots alleged that at about 5.15pm they were in Makarios avenue, opposite the Lykavitos Police Station, in a car which was registered in the north. They said that they were surrounded by a group of up to fifteen men wearing orange T-shirts, on mopeds at some traffic lights, who started kicking the vehicle, causing damage valued at 500 euro. The incident was reported to police.

On Wednesday 18 May 2016 the Cyprus Cup final took place between Omonia and Apollon.

Omonia eventually lost to Apollon with a score-line of 2-1.

In Nicosia, before the game, Omonia fans set fire to a number of tyres at about 2pm, outside their fan club in Pallouriotissa. The burning tyres caused thick black smoke to rise, near to the city-centre, and when the Fire Service arrived to deal with the fires some four hundred fans denied them access.

When units of MMAD arrived to restore order they were pelted with rocks, and responded with tear-gas. Eight police officers were injured, and one police vehicle was damaged, as well as a number of other vehicles in the area.

A thirty-year-old woman was arrested for rioting and assaulting an officer.

Later in the day at Tsirion Stadium in Limassol, both sets of fans fought with each other and two of them aged sixteen years, and twenty-one years old, were arrested. The older of the two suffered a head-injury as a result of being hit by an object thrown during the fighting and required hospital treatment.

The Croatian referee had to stop play at one stage when Apollon fans threw tens of flares onto the pitch and seven minutes of extra time were added on.

Just before the match was due to finish four hundred Apollon fans entered the pitch and moved towards the stands occupied by Omonia fans, throwing flares and firecrackers at them. Around forty Omonia fans responded.

The referee blew the whistle a minute before the end of the extra time and raced straight into the tunnel.

Extensive damage was caused to the stadium as well as film equipment being used by TV crews.

Three police officers were injured during the disturbances.

Police spokesman Andreas Angelides said afterwards that there had been a reduced number of such incidents compared to previous years, and he put it down to planning by the police, and efforts to combat hooliganism by all competent agencies.

They later issued photographs of four suspects that they were seeking in respect of the earlier incidents in Nicosia.

On Saturday 28 May 2016 police arrested three men from Nicosia in connection with disturbances that took place at this match.

Postscript

The Hooligans Are Still Among Us

On Friday 3 June 2016 the Justice Minister Ionas Nicolaou confirmed that enquiries into a total of fifty-nine cases of suspected match fixing remained open but that the authorities had no concrete evidence to go on.

He was speaking after a meeting with football authorities, which had been held in response to the large number of so-called *'red notices'* received from UEFA, during which it was confirmed that twenty-one reports related to the current season, with sixteen of them relating to games played in 2016.

At that stage discussions took place about making it illegal for club officials and team players to take part in betting activity relating to their own teams.

The CFA subsequently made proposals for a series of measures designed to discourage such activity starting with a fine of 5,000 euro for any team that was implicated for the first time in a '*red notice*', leading to points being docked and finally relegation after a seventh occasion.

Ultimately the CFA were instructed by UEFA to put stricter measures in place whereby the first '*red notice*' would attract a 50,000 euro fine, with the same for a second plus a deduction of six points from their league table score.

A third notice would lead to expulsion from the league and removal of any CFA grants, with any further notice leading to the imposition of a 100,000 euro fine, being struck off the federation register and no entitlement to be re-registered in a CFA championship for a period of five years.

A number of new notices were received in Cyprus in September and the following month.

***

At the beginning of September 2016 the government provided an update on the proposed '*Fan ID Card*' scheme, which had formed part of a Bill in 2014 designed to combat football related hooliganism.

It was hoped that the scheme would gradually be rolled out at the beginning of next year due to delays caused by an appeal filed by one of the companies that took part in the original competitive tender for its creation.

As previously alluded to, the scheme was opposed by organised supporters of all the major football clubs in Cyprus.

The task of implementation was originally given to the Cyprus Sports Association which in turn asked the CFA to do it because of lack of funds. That decision was then reversed after protests from some of the opposition political parties, in particular AKEL, who raised concerns over privacy and personal data.

***

On Tuesday 27 September at 3am, a car parked outside the home of football referee Yiorgos Nicolaou in Zygi was severely damaged after a bomb was placed in front of the vehicle.

The forty-one year-old had last refereed a game in Limassol on Saturday 24 September when AEZ Zakakiou hosted Nea Salamina, in a match which the home team lost 5-1.

The CFA condemned such *'terrorist'* acts.

***

After a period during which fewer incidents of football related hooliganism had in fact been reported, on Sunday 6 November 2016 rival fans clashed shortly after the end of a game between Apollon and Ethnikos Achnas, at Limassol's Tsirion Stadium, when a group of about thirty Apollon fans gathered outside dressing rooms adjacent to the football field.

As they began throwing stones the police intervened and dispersed the crowd with tear-gas. They in turn set fire to a plastic garbage bin as they left.

During the disturbances one police officer was struck on the head by a stone and received treatment at Limassol General Hospital before being released.

***

On Monday 7 November more than two hundred APOEL fans went on the rampage outside their clubhouse in Nicosia, during celebrations for the football club's 90th anniversary.

The clubhouse itself was engulfed in smoke from firecrackers being thrown as some fans started throwing stones at passing cars, and destroyed traffic lights, whilst traffic officers tried to divert cars away from the area near the Hilton Hotel.

MMAD Public Order Units moved in to stop the violence and a violent confrontation took place as they were subjected to a barrage of bottles, bangers, and anything else the hooligans could lay their hands on, which left three police officers injured.

Following those incidents the Sports Federation Chairman Kleanthis Georgiades spoke about political intervention to free troublemakers saying that it was known to have happened for many years regardless of which club they supported.

For their part the police rejected such accusations and demanded that he provide evidence.

On Wednesday 9 November the police carried out a raid at the Strovolos club- house frequented by APOEL fans in Nicosia and four arrests were made after cannabis was recovered.

The following Saturday, 12 November, the police announced

that they had conducted a similar raid at the clubhouse of Apollon fans in Limassol under the auspices of a warrant. The premises were searched, as well as twenty-six persons present, and some people were reported for breaches of laws relating to alcohol consumption.

***

On Thursday 17 November 2016, at about 2.30am, a bomb was placed at the Limassol offices of Minerva Insurance in Omirou Street. The attack was believed to be connected to a recent statement by the CFA chairman Costakis Koutsokoumnis, who had said that, *'the party is over for the betting mafia'.*

He has an interest in the insurance business.

Police raids followed during the coming days, and a number of people questioned, but without any specific outcome.

***

On the 28 November 2016 the media reported that the police had stepped up security measures after threats were made against the Justice Minister Ionas Nicolaou, following statements that he was looking at taking strict measures against football fan club premises, closing some down if necessary.

It was said that the Cyprus Secret Service (KYP) had also obtained information that attacks were being planned against the Ministers home.

***

On the 18 January 2017 Karmiotissa Polemidion played Aek Larnaca in a second leg cup fixture.

Bets were placed on Karmiotissa losing by at least a five-goal difference, and is it happened the full-time result was 6-1 to visitors Aek.

A 'red notice' was issued and a CFA judge imposed a 50,000 euro fine on Karmiotissa.

On the 22 January a league fixture took place between APOEL and AEZ Zakakiou which the home team won 7-0.

UEFA identified that there had been a great deal of betting activity in favour of AEZ trailing by at least five goals at half time. As it happened the half-time score was 5-0 to APOEL.

A notice was issued and although AEZ denied any involvement this was dismissed by a CFA judge and a fine of 50,000 euro was issued.

***

On the 1 February 2017 a court case involving a twenty-six-year-old woman from Nicosia was finally concluded.

She had been charged following an incident on 2 May 2015 after being found guilty of using firecrackers unlawfully at a football match.

She was given a six months prison sentence, which was suspended for three years, and she was banned from attending matches for six months with a condition that she present herself at a police station for the duration of any games.

***

On Wednesday 22 February 2017 a match took place between Apollon and Omonia in Limassol's Tsirion Stadium.

In the first half of the game Omonia fans invaded the pitch to complain about their own team's performance, and threw flares, as the game was held up for eight minutes.

At the end of the first-half Apollon led with a score-line of 2-1.

During the second-half Apollon scored again in the 72nd minute, to make it 3- 1, and Omonia fans responded by throwing firecrackers and flares. The referee Leontios Trattos stopped the game and went to the dressing rooms for eight minutes before returning to the pitch and restarting the match.

After just two minutes however he abandoned the game completely as disturbances continued.

A week later a thirty-three-year-old man was arrested in connection with the disturbances and interviewed in relation to rioting, improper conduct, and obstructing a football match.

**

On Sunday 26 February a match took place between Apollon and APOEL in Limassol, which Apollon won 2-1.

Shortly after the start of the match a flare was hurled by the home fans in the direction of APOEL fans at Tsirion Stadium, injuring two people who received hospital treatment.

At the end of the match home-fans hurled stones injuring police officers, some of whom required hospital treatment. Two persons aged twenty-seven, and twenty years, were arrested for throwing stones, and a thirty-five-year-old man for hurling abuse at the police.

***

On Friday 3 March 2017 police officers searched an address in Nicosia and seized 11,000 firecrackers which were intended for unlawful use at football matches.

A twenty-four year old man was arrested.

On Sunday 5 March a match took place in Larnaca between Anorthosis and Apollon and at the end of the game, at around 6pm, a group of Anorthosis fans gathered in Lysou Santama Street and started throwing objects at cars and pedestrians.

As police officers arrived the group turned their attentions to stoning the police vehicles and a twenty-three old from Limassol was detained, although he later denied any involvement in the disturbances.

***

On Sunday 12 March 2017 a match took place between Anorthosis and APOEL in Larnaca.

After the game up to one hundred and fifty Anorthosis fans gathered in Papanikoli Avenue and started to fight with another group before police intervened.

Stones were thrown at the officers which resulted in four officers being injured, three of whom were treated in hospital for chest pains, a wrist injury, and a leg wound.

Five people, aged between sixteen years and twenty-six years, were arrested and appeared at Larnaca District Court the following day when they were remanded for two days pending further enquiries.

Four members of the public in Larnaca also reported being attacked by APOEL fans after the match, two of the victims receiving hospital treatment.

***

On Tuesday 28 March, at 3am in the morning, an improvised device exploded under a vehicle in the Nicosia suburb of Engomi, destroying the front-end. No one was injured.

The media speculated that the vehicle was being used by a forty-five-year-old man who had previously been the chair of the APOEL fan club.

***

During the spring of 2017 the debate about match fixing rumbled on with further *'red-notices'* being received about matches of concern.

***

On Saturday 8 April 2017 a twenty-nine-year-old man was arrested during a routine search as he tried to enter a game between Anorthosis and Apollon at the Antonis Papadopoulos Stadium in Larnaca. The man, who was an Apollon supporter, was found to be in possession of two cannabis *'joints'*.

In a separate search of the Apollon teams fan bus, four flares were recovered by police.

***

On Wednesday 19 April AEL and APOEL played at Limassol's Tsirion Stadium.

A few minutes after the start of the second-half APOEL fans in the western stand set fire to the toilet block. Members of the fire brigade, with police protection, moved in to put the fire out, and were attacked by APOEL supporters who threw plastic chairs, flares and other objects at them.

Teargas was deployed by the police and two arrests made, one aged thirty- seven from Limassol, and a twenty-one-year-old from Nicosia. During a violent struggle to restrain the two men four officers were injured, as well as those detained. All six were treated at hospital and one of the officers was detained overnight.

***

At the beginning of May the Justice Minister announced that he hoped that a bill aimed at combatting match fixing would be in place before the summer recess.

Cyprus was described as having one of the worst problems in Europe and that it was hoped to provide punishments of up to seven years in prison, or 200,000 euro fines for those found guilty.

The proposed legislation was also designed to afford some protection for *'whistleblowers'* who had exposed wrongdoing.

***

On Thursday 11 May 2017 the police announced that they had arrested two persons, aged forty-one years and thirty-one years, in connection with violence after a game the day before between Orfeas Nicosia and Posidonas Yiolou.

The lower-league clubs played in Limassol in a match which Orfeas lost, and after the final whistle the referee was attacked by two members of the Orfeas team. As he fell to the floor others joined in punching and kicking him, whilst the assistant referee was also attacked.

Both subsequently received treatment at Limassol General Hospital.

On Tuesday 23 May, at about 8.45pm, a group of Apollon fans were making their way along *'28th of October Street'* when they were confronted by a group of AEL fans at the Enaerios traffic lights in Limassol.

The AEL fans, with hooded faces, had been hidden in bushes, and behind shops, and a fight commenced during which Molotov cocktails, flares and fireworks were thrown, as garbage bins and traffic lights were set on fire, and windows smashed.

A thirty-nine year old man was arrested after he hit a twenty-four-year-old man as he drove through crowds in the Enaerios area of Limassol. He claimed to be trying to avoid the fans who were throwing stones and police took possession of video footage of the incident, some of which was widely circulated in social media.

MMAD Public Order Units were deployed and teargas was used to disperse those involved.

One nineteen year old at the scene was treated in a private clinic after he received an injury from a firework. Three other people aged eighteen, nineteen and twenty-four received treatment at Limassol General Hospital and released.

Further disturbances then took place at the Apollon fan clubhouse, near to the traffic lights at the New Port, as fires were lit and flares thrown.

Upon the arrival of the police Apollon fans threw stones and flares resulting in damage being caused to four police vehicles.

Following these disturbances the police reviewed their security measures for the Cup Final and highlighted the fact that they had three *'crisis'* centres in place to deal with any problems.

Six men aged between eighteen years and twenty-nine years were arrested and interviewed at Limassol Police Station by midday of the following day, in connection with the trouble.

***

On Wednesday 24 May 2017 the Cup Final took place at the GSP Stadium in Nicosia between APOEL and Apollon.

During the match police found a large drum containing ten fireworks and ten smoke bombs in the northern block of the stadium.

A twenty-two-year-old was stopped entering the stadium and

found to be in possession of a smoke bomb. He was later fined 500 euro and banned from attending matches for six months.

Apollon went on to win the game with a score-line of 1-0 and watched by a crowd of 13,906 people.

A video subsequently emerged showing APOEL fans firing a flare-gun towards Apollon fans.

Director of the GSP Stadium Phivos Constantinides published a statement which appeared in the media saying, *'I wonder if someone has to die before the state and the competent authorities take action and kick hooligans out of stadiums. Tolerance, coverage, funding, support, and protection of those who cause trouble, as well as the mockery of the public by the state must be stopped'.*

He went on, *'Political parties serve the interests of teams which are in the sphere of influence. These phenomena are constantly increasing, people stay away from the stadiums and football clubs go bankrupt'.*

On the same day some forty APOEL fans on motorcycles, and wearing hoods and helmets, attacked the Omonia clubhouse in

Lakatamia.

The attack occurred about an hour after the Cup Final and Molotov cocktails, firecrackers, and stones were thrown resulting in minor injuries to those inside.

A passing motorist, who had a child in his vehicle, was also injured in the incident and a motorcycle with no plates on was found abandoned afterwards bearing an emblem of the Nationalist Party ELAM.

The Omonia Lakatamia club made a statement on their Facebook page next day which was published in the media, *'We cannot stay silent on the provocative attitude of the police which when arrived at the club after the end of the incident tried to arrest some of our club members'*.

The Justice Minister, in response to the problems, highlighted the fact that since 2014, when the Football Bill was passed, the courts had been imposing tougher sentences for football related violence.

He did however highlight the fact that as the Cyprus Football

Association had refused to take responsibility for implementing the *Fan ID Card'* system it had fallen to the Cyprus Sports Association, and as such the ministry was no longer responsible for the procedure.

After several delays and appeals relating to the tendering process this long-awaited measure was now being closely monitored by the Auditor General.

***

On Wednesday 7 June 2017, in the early hours of the morning, the vehicle that was allegedly involved in the incident during disturbances in Limassol between AEL and Apollon fans was the subject of an arson attack.

At about 1.35am the vehicle was doused in a flammable liquid and set fire to in Limassol

On the same day Limassol District Court finalised a case involving fourteen AEL fans who had tried to force their way into Tsirion Stadium in Limassol before a match between AEL and Aris in 2015.

Eleven of them were made the subject of six-month

community service orders and fined 300 euros after being found guilty of rioting.

Three others were fined 300 euros and banned from attending matches for six months.

***

Whilst there were some clear indications that the previous season had seen a number of positive actions, with more arrests by police, as well as in some cases speedier court action, and a degree of progress with the 'fan-card' issue, the reality is that for the time being **'the hooligans are still among us'** in Cyprus.

***

Michael Layton QPM (2017)

Acknowledgements/References

Stephen Burrows – **'Bostin Books'** and author.andry Christou-
Layton – former SBA Police Officer.Michael Hadjidemetriou –
Retired Chief Inspector (Republic of Cyprus Police). Sakis Savvides
Press/Sports Photographer – a special thanks for allowing use of his
photographs for cover pictures.the **Cyprus Mail** Archives, and also
with special thanks to reporters George Psyllides, and Constantinos
Psyllides for their help and support, and Editor Jean Christou

***

University of Cyprus PollPancyprian Football Association (PFA)
SurveyCouncil of European Report EU (2002/2003)Cyprus
Sociological Association (2002 Project)Antonis Raftis (2007)
Psychologist and SociologistDr Dino Domic (2009) Assistant
Professor – European University of Cyprus SBA Control of
Violence in Sports Ground Ordinance 2009Report 'Racist Violence
in Cyprus' (March 2011)Centre of Research and Development in
Sports Leisure and Tourism (2012) Cyprus Footballers Association
Survey (2015)Footballers Association (PASP) Survey (2015)

Personal Biography of Author

Michael Layton QPM joined the British Transport Police as a

Cadet on the 1 September 1968 and, after three years, was appointed

as a Police Constable in 1971, serving at Birmingham New Street

Station. In 1972 he transferred to Birmingham City Police, which

amalgamated in 1974 to become the West Midlands Police, where he

eventually reached the rank of Chief Superintendent in 1997. On

retirement from that Force in 2003 he went on to see service with the

Sovereign Bases Police in Cyprus, and then returned to the British

Transport Police in 2004, initially as a Detective Superintendent

(Director of Intelligence), and then in his last two years as the

Operations Superintendent at Birmingham, where he continued with

his passion for combating football violence, until finally retiring

again in 2011. In the January 2003 New Year's Honours List he was

awarded the Queens Police Medal for distinguished police service.

He is the author/co-author of other books entitled:*'Hunting

the Hooligans – the true story of Operation Red Card'* which was

published in July 2015 by Milo Books, co-written with Robert

Endeacott. *'Tracking the Hooligans – A history of football violence on the UK rail network'* Amberley Publishers – co-written with Alan

Pacey. *'Police Dog Heroes – the history of the British Transport*

Police Dog Section' Amberley Publishers – co-written with Bill

Rogerson. *'Birmingham's Front Line – True Police Stories'*

Amberley Publishers. *'Black Over Bill's Mothers – A Storm Is*

Coming' – co-written with Stephen Burrows. *'Keep Right On'* - co-

written with Stephen Burrows. *'The Noble Cause'* – co-written with

Stephen Burrows. *'Walsall's Front Line – Volume One'* – co-written

with Stephen Burrows. *'The Hooligans Are Still Among Us'*

Amberley Publishers – co-written with Bill Rogerson. *'The Night The*

Owl Cried- A Taste of Cyprus' – co-written with Andry Christou

Layton

Michael is a self-employed consultant engaged

predominantly with crime and community safety issues.

Printed in Great Britain
by Amazon